NES English Language Arts
301
Teacher Certification Exam

Sharon A. Wynne, M.S.

XAMonline, INC.
Boston

Copyright © 2017 XAMonline, Inc.
All rights reserved. No part of the material protected by this copyright notice may be reproduced or utilized in any form or by any means, electronic or mechanical, including photocopying, recording or by any information storage and retrievable system, without written permission from the copyright holder.

To obtain permission(s) to use the material from this work for any purpose including workshops or seminars, please submit a written request to:

XAMonline, Inc.
21 Orient Avenue
Melrose, MA 02176
Toll Free 1-800-509-4128
Email: info@xamonline.com
Web www.xamonline.com
Fax: 1-617-583-5552

Library of Congress Cataloging-in-Publication Data
Wynne, Sharon A.

NES English Language Arts 301: Teacher Certification / Sharon A. Wynne.
ISBN 978-1-60787-615-1

1. English Language Arts   2. Study Guides   3. NES
4. Teachers' Certification & Licensure.   5. Careers

Disclaimer:
The opinions expressed in this publication are the sole works of XAMonline and were created independently from the National Education Association, Educational Testing Service, or any State Department of Education, National Evaluation Systems or other testing affiliates. Between the time of publication and printing, state specific standards as well as testing formats and website information may change that is not included in part or in whole within this product. Sample test questions are developed by XAMonline and reflect similar content as on real tests; however, they are not former tests. XAMonline assembles content that aligns with state standards but makes no claims nor guarantees teacher candidates a passing score. Numerical scores are determined by testing companies such as NES or ETS and then are compared with individual state standards. A passing score varies from state to state.

Printed in the United States of America   œ-1
NES English Language Arts 301
ISBN: 978-1-60787-615-1

TEACHER CERTIFICATION STUDY GUIDE

TABLE OF CONTENTS

DOMAIN I   VOCABULARY, READING COMPREHENSION, AND TEXT TYPES 1

OBJECTIVE 1   VOCABULARY AND READING COMPREHENSION STRATEGIES 1

Skill 1.1   Identify word meanings through syntax, word structure, and context 1

Skill 1.2   Understand word and phrase meanings (denotative and connotative) 3

Skill 1.3   Connect English language words and phrases to their derivations from other languages 5

Skill 1.4   Identify multiple influences on the English language (historical, social, cultural, regional, and technological) 5

Skill 1.5   Use prior knowledge of words, phrases, concepts, and experiences to understand new words and phrases 9

Skill 1.6   Demonstrate knowledge of key reading strategies to use for different texts and purposes 9

Skill 1.7   Demonstrate knowledge of effective pre-, post-, and during reading comprehension strategies 13

OBJECTIVE 2   STRATEGIES FOR READING INFORMATIONAL TEXTS 16

Skill 2.1   Identify key characteristics of different informational texts 16

Skill 2.2   Demonstrate understanding of how knowledge of text features and structures facilitates comprehension of informational texts 17

Skill 2.3   Evaluate an informational text to identify the main idea, purpose, and intended audience 17

Skill 2.4   Identify key concepts and supporting details in informational texts 19

Skill 2.5   Evaluate the evidence and examples in informational texts to determine relevance 20

Skill 2.6   Evaluate sources in informational texts for credibility and reliability 21

English Language Arts

TEACHER CERTIFICATION STUDY GUIDE

Skill 2.7	Determine the accuracy of a summary of an informational text	22
Skill 2.8	Analyze information from texts containing tables, charts, graphs, maps, and illustrations	22

OBJECTIVE 3   **STRATEGIES FOR READING PERSUASIVE TEXTS** 25

Skill 3.1	Identify key characteristics of different persuasive texts, including advertisements, editorials, persuasive essays, and propaganda	25
Skill 3.2	Demonstrate understanding of how knowledge of text features and structures facilitate comprehension of persuasive texts	26
Skill 3.3	Evaluate a persuasive text to identify the main idea, purpose, and intended audience	27
Skill 3.4	Identify facts and opinions in persuasive texts	27
Skill 3.5	Evaluate reasoning, evidence, and examples in persuasive texts	28
Skill 3.6	Evaluate sources in persuasive texts for credibility and reliability	31
Skill 3.7	Evaluate persuasive techniques and rhetorical devices in persuasive texts	31
Skill 3.8	Analyze information from persuasive texts containing photographs and illustrations	32

OBJECTIVE 4   **READING TECHNICAL AND FUNCTIONAL TEXTS** 34

Skill 4.1	Identify key characteristics of different functional and technical texts	34
Skill 4.2	Apply information from technical texts to develop knowledge and skills	35
Skill 4.3	Apply information from procedural/functional texts to perform tasks and verify facts	36
Skill 4.4	Analyze information from technical/functional texts containing tables, flowcharts, graphs, map keys and legends, schematics, and diagrams	36

DOMAIN II   **ANALYZING AND INTERPRETING LITERATURE** 38

English Language Arts

TEACHER CERTIFICATION STUDY GUIDE

OBJECTIVE 5	**ANALYZE AND INTERPRET LITERARY NONFICTION, FICTION, AND DRAMA**	**38**
Skill 5.1	Evaluate the characteristics of various literary genres (e.g., drama, biography, fiction)	38
Skill 5.2	Analyze various literary and rhetorical devices (e.g., symbolism, style, allusion, irony, foreshadowing, tone, figurative language, syntax)	40
Skill 5.3	Demonstrate knowledge of point of view, tone, voice, and mood in literary prose	43
Skill 5.4	Identify and interpret structural elements in literary prose (denouement and flashback)	46
Skill 5.5	Evaluate the effect of words and word combinations in literary prose	47
Skill 5.6	Analyzing elements of fiction (plot, character, setting) in a literary text	47
Skill 5.7	Identify and analyze central ideas or themes in literary prose	49
OBJECTIVE 6	**ANALYZING AND INTERPRETING POETRY**	**51**
Skill 6.1	Evaluate the characteristics of various forms of poetry (e.g., epic, sonnet, haiku)	51
Skill 6.2	Demonstrate knowledge of how poetic devices are used in a poem	57
Skill 6.3	Demonstrate knowledge of how figures of speech are used in a poem	59
Skill 6.4	Demonstrate knowledge of point of view, tone, voice, and mood in a poem	60
Skill 6.5	Identify and interpret how stanzaic and metrical structures and verse forms are used in a poem	61
Skill 6.6	Identify and interpret formal rhyme schemes and sound devices in a poem	65
Skill 6.7	Identify and interpret central ideas or themes in a poetic text	68
OBJECTIVE 7	**UNDERSTANDING WORLD LITERATURE (MAJOR CHARACTERISTICS)**	**69**
Skill 7.1	Identify major literary genres, styles, and trends in world literatures	69

English Language Arts

Skill 7.2	Identify characteristics of major works and writers in world literature	70
Skill 7.3	Identify characteristics of major movements and periods in world literatures	74
Skill 7.4	Identify characteristics of major literary genres and works in the oral tradition	79

OBJECTIVE 8 — HISTORICAL, SOCIAL, CULTURAL, AND POLITICAL ASPECTS OF LITERATURE FROM AROUND THE WORLD 81

Skill 8.1	Understand the ways in which historical, social, cultural, and political events and movements influenced the development of world literatures	81
Skill 8.2	Recognize the ways in which diverse values, attitudes, and ideas are expressed in world literatures	83
Skill 8.3	Recognize the ways in which writers from diverse backgrounds have commented on major events and issues and influence public understanding of these events through literature	85
Skill 8.4	Analyze the ways in which major sociocultural and sociopolitical issues are addressed in contemporary and classical literature	87

DOMAIN III — ENGLISH LANGUAGE CONVENTIONS, COMPOSITION, WRITING PROCESS, AND RESEARCH 88

OBJECTIVE 9 — STANDARD AMERICAN ENGLISH AND ELEMENTS OF EFFECTIVE COMPOSITION 88

Skill 9.1	Understand spelling and capitalization conventions when composing a text	88
Skill 9.2	Understand capitalization conventions when composing a text	89
Skill 9.3	Understand punctuation conventions when composing a text	90
Skill 9.4	Understand and apply appropriate word usage and grammar when composing a text	93
Skill 9.5	Demonstrate knowledge of developing an effective introduction for a written text (interest, topic, thesis)	97

Skill 9.6	Demonstrate knowledge of how to develop the body of a written text (clearly presents, contrasts, and links ideas) 98
Skill 9.7	Demonstrates knowledge of how to develop a conclusion (summary, course of action, or personal commentary)... 99

OBJECTIVE 10   THE WRITING PROCESS 100

Skill 10.1	Understand and apply methods for matching forms of writing to audience and purpose... 100
Skill 10.2	Understand and apply methods for generating and organizing ideas for writing 100
Skill 10.3	Understand and apply methods for writing an effective draft of a text ... 101
Skill 10.4	Understand and apply methods of revising and editing text................... 102
Skill 10.5	Understand and apply methods for proofreading and preparing a text for publication.. 103

OBJECTIVE 11   RESEARCH 104

Skill 11.1	Demonstrate knowledge of how to select and refine a research topic ... 104
Skill 11.2	Demonstrate knowledge of how to compose effective research questions 104
Skill 11.3	Demonstrate knowledge of how to identify and locate resources for research 105
Skill 11.4	Demonstrate knowledge of how to assess the credibility and reliability of sources 107
Skill 11.5	Demonstrate knowledge of how to gather and organize information for research 107
Skill 11.6	Demonstrate knowledge of how to paraphrase, summarize, and quote sources and how to integrate these summaries into a written text 108
Skill 11.7	Demonstrate knowledge of how to cite sources in a written text............ 110

DOMAIN IV   MODES OF WRITING 112

OBJECTIVE 12   NARRATIVE WRITING 112

Skill 12.1	Apply and understand various purposes and forms of narrative writing	112
Skill 12.2	Demonstrate knowledge of how to choose and narrow down a subject for narrative writing	112
Skill 12.3	Apply and understand various organizational structures used in narrative writing	113
Skill 12.4	Demonstrate knowledge of how to use language to evoke sensory details in narrative writing	114
Skill 12.5	Identify ways to choose a style, voice, and tone for a narrative writing purpose and audience	114

OBJECTIVE 13   EXPOSITORY WRITING 116

Skill 13.1	Apply and understand various purposes and forms of expository writing	116
Skill 13.2	Demonstrate knowledge of how to choose and narrow down a subject for expository writing	117
Skill 13.3	Demonstrate knowledge of how to formulate good essay questions and theses in writing expository texts	117
Skill 13.4	Apply and understand various organizational structures used in expository writing	118
Skill 13.5	Demonstrate knowledge of how to use effective and appropriate supporting details in expository texts	120
Skill 13.6	Identify ways to make expository writing clear, direct, and succinct	120

OBJECTIVE 14   PERSUASIVE WRITING 122

Skill 14.1	Apply and understand various purposes and forms of persuasive writing	122
Skill 14.2	Demonstrate knowledge of how to choose a position or idea for a subject for persuasive writing	122
Skill 14.3	Apply and understand various organizational structures used in persuasive writing, including using supporting details	123

TEACHER CERTIFICATION STUDY GUIDE

Skill 14.4 Demonstrate knowledge of how to anticipate counterarguments and incorporate responses in a persuasive writing text 124

Skill 14.5 Identify ways to choose a style, voice, and diction for a persuasive writing purpose and audience 125

OBJECTIVE 15 CRITICAL/ANALYTICAL WRITING **127**

Skill 15.1 Apply and understand various purposes and forms of critical or analytical writing 127

Skill 15.2 Demonstrate knowledge of how to formulate specific critical or analytical questions and an effective thesis statement 127

Skill 15.3 Apply and understand various organizational structures used in critical or analytical writing 128

Skill 15.4 Demonstrate knowledge of how to develop a solid literary analysis in critical or analytical writing 128

Skill 15.5 Identify ways to relate or connect characters, themes, and points of view in various literary works 129

DOMAIN V ORAL AND VISUAL COMMUNICATION **130**

OBJECTIVE 16 EFFECTIVE LISTENING AND SPEAKING STRATEGIES (INCLUDING GROUP DISCUSSION) **130**

Skill 16.1 Understand purposes of listening, listening strategies, and challenges to effective listening 130

Skill 16.2 Understand the ways in which interpersonal communication is influenced by social norms/conventions, individual and cultural factors 131

Skill 16.3 Understand strategies for effective participation in group discussions ... 132

Skill 16.4 Understand how to craft and present effective oral presentations including language, style, rhetorical devices, and vocal techniques 133

OBJECTIVE 17 EFFECTIVE MEDIA VIEWING, ANALYZING, AND PRESENTING STRATEGIES **136**

Skill 17.1 Interpret and evaluate visual images in various forms of media (messages, themes, bias, meanings) 136

Skill 17.2   Understand the ways in which visual images can be used as persuasive texts in various forms of media 136

Skill 17.3   Understand the role of the viewer's/reader's background, prior knowledge, and point of view in interpreting visual images in various forms of media 138

Skill 17.4   Demonstrate knowledge of how to craft a presentation for a particular purpose and audience 138

Skill 17.5   Demonstrate knowledge of how to incorporate images and effective use of technology into presentations 139

Skill 17.6   Understand the importance of ethical issues relating to using viewing and presenting media (copyright, citation, and so on) 140

Additional Works Cited 141

Sample Test 142

Answer Key 186

Rationales 187

TEACHER CERTIFICATION STUDY GUIDE

About This Test

The NES: English Language Arts for Educator Licensure exam consists of approximately 150 multiple-choice questions. The NES: English Language Arts exam is a three-hour, computer-based exam designed to measure your knowledge of subject matter, teaching practices, and issues essential for teaching English Language Arts.

The test is comprised of five areas. See the table below for descriptions of their content, number of questions, and weight in determining the final test score. The National Benchmark passing score on the NES: English Language Arts exam is 220, but for New Mexico, a passing score is 231 and for Oregon, a passing score is 236.

Subarea	Approximate number of test questions	Approximate test weighting
I. Vocabulary, Reading Comprehension, and Reading Various Text Forms	35	23%
II. Analyzing and Interpreting Literature	34	23%
III. English Language Conventions, Composition, Writing Process, and Research	29	19%
IV. Modes of Writing	34	23%
V. Oral and Visual Communication	18	12%

Details of the content covered in areas I–V are contained within this testing guide.

TEACHER CERTIFICATION STUDY GUIDE

Great Study and Testing Tips!

What to study in order to prepare for the subject assessments is the focus of this study guide but equally important is *how* you study.

You can increase your chances of truly mastering the information by taking some simple, but effective steps.

Study Tips:

1. Some foods aid the learning process. Foods such as milk, nuts, seeds, rice, and oats help your study efforts by releasing natural memory enhancers called CCKs (*cholecystokinin*) composed of *tryptophan*, *choline*, and *phenylalanine*. All of these chemicals enhance the neurotransmitters associated with memory. Before studying, try a light, protein-rich meal of eggs, turkey, and fish. All of these foods release the memory enhancing chemicals. The better the connections, the more you comprehend.

Likewise, before you take a test, stick to a light snack of energy boosting and relaxing foods. A glass of milk, a piece of fruit, or some peanuts all release various memory-boosting chemicals and help you to relax and focus on the subject at hand.

2. Learn to take great notes. A by-product of our modern culture is that we have grown accustomed to getting our information in short doses (i.e., TV news sound bites or *USA Today*-style newspaper articles.)

Consequently, we've subconsciously trained ourselves to assimilate information better in *neat little packages*. If your notes are scrawled all over the paper, it fragments the flow of the information. Strive for clarity. Newspapers use a standard format to achieve clarity. Your notes can be much clearer through use of proper formatting. A very effective format is called the *"Cornell Method."*

> Take a sheet of loose-leaf lined notebook paper and draw a line all the way down the paper about 1–2" from the left-hand edge.
>
> Draw another line across the width of the paper about 1–2" up from the bottom. Repeat this process on the reverse side of the page.

Now look at the result. You have ample room for notes, a left margin for special emphasis items or inserting supplementary data from the textbook, a large area at the bottom for a brief summary, and a little rectangular space for just about anything you want. This should make your note-taking much more effective.

3. Get the concept then the details. Too often we focus on the details and don't gather an understanding of the concept. However, if you simply memorize only dates, places, or names, you may well miss the whole point of the subject.

English Language Arts

TEACHER CERTIFICATION STUDY GUIDE

A key way to understand things is to put them in your own words. If you are working from a textbook, automatically summarize each paragraph in your mind. If you are outlining text, don't simply copy the author's words.
Rephrase them in your own words. You'll remember your own thoughts and words much better than someone else's, and subconsciously tend to associate the important details to the core concepts.

4. Ask Why? Pull apart written material paragraph by paragraph and don't forget the captions under the illustrations.

Example: If the heading is "Stream Erosion," flip it around to read "Why do streams erode?" Then answer the questions.

If you train your mind to think in a series of questions and answers, not only will you learn more, but it also helps to lessen the test anxiety because you are used to answering questions.

5. Read for reinforcement and future needs. Even if you only have 10 minutes, put your notes or a book in your hand. Your mind is similar to a computer; you have to input data in order to have it processed. *By reading, you are creating the neural connections for future retrieval.* The more times you read something, the more you reinforce the learning of ideas.

Even if you don't fully understand something on the first pass, *your mind stores much of the material for later recall.*

6. Relax to learn so go into exile. Our bodies respond to an inner clock called biorhythms. Burning the midnight oil works well for some people, but not everyone.

If possible, set aside a particular place to study that is free of distractions. Shut off the television, cell phone, and pager, and exile your friends and family during your study period.

If silence bothers you, try background music. Light classical music at a low volume has been shown to aid in concentration over other types of music. Music that evokes pleasant emotions without lyrics is highly suggested. Try just about anything by Mozart. It relaxes you.

7. Use arrows not highlighters. At best, it's difficult to read a page full of yellow, pink, blue, and green streaks. Try staring at a neon sign for a while and you'll soon see that the horde of colors obscure the message.

A quick note, a brief dash of color, an underline, and/or an arrow pointing to a particular passage is much clearer than a horde of highlighted words.

English Language Arts

TEACHER CERTIFICATION STUDY GUIDE

8. Budget your study time. Although you shouldn't ignore any of the material, *allocate your available study time in the same ratio that topics may appear on the test.*

Testing Tips:

1. Get smart, play dumb. Don't read anything into the question. Don't make an assumption that the test writer is looking for something else than what is asked. Stick to the question as written and don't read extra things into it.

2. Read the question and all the choices *twice* before answering the question. You may miss something by not carefully reading, and then re-reading both the question and the answers.

If you really don't have a clue as to the right answer, leave it blank on the first time through. Go on to the other questions, as they may provide a clue as to how to answer the skipped questions. If later on, you still can't answer the skipped ones . . . ***Guess.*** The only penalty for guessing is that you *might* get it wrong. Only one thing is certain; if you don't put anything down, you will get it wrong!

3. Turn the question into a statement. Look at the way the questions are worded. The syntax of the question usually provides a clue. Does it seem more familiar as a statement rather than as a question? Does it sound strange?

By turning a question into a statement, you may be able to spot if an answer sounds right, and it may also trigger memories of material you have read.

4. Look for hidden clues. It's actually very difficult to compose multiple-foil (choice) questions without giving away part of the answer in the options presented. In most multiple-choice questions, you can often readily eliminate one or two of the potential answers. This leaves you with only two real possibilities and automatically your odds go to fifty-fifty for very little work.

5. Trust your instincts. For every fact that you have read, you subconsciously retain something of that knowledge. On questions that you aren't really certain about, go with your instincts. **Your first impression on how to answer a question is usually correct.**

6. Mark your answers directly on the test booklet. Don't bother trying to fill in the optical scan sheet on the first pass through the test.

Just be very careful not to miss-mark your answers when you eventually transcribe them to the scan sheet.

7. Watch the clock! You have a set amount of time to answer the questions. Don't get bogged down trying to answer a single question at the expense of 10 questions you can more readily answer.

English Language Arts

Current Teaching Trends

Digital pedagogy and the use of 21st century teaching methods have shifted the landscape of teaching to create a bigger focus on student engagement. Student-centered classrooms now utilize technology to create efficiencies and increase digital literacy. Classrooms that once relied on memorization and the regurgitation of facts now push students to *create* and *analyze* material. The Bloom's Taxonomy chart below gives a great visual of the higher order thinking skills that current teachers are implementing in their learning objectives. There are also examples of the verbs that you might use when creating learning objectives at the assignment, course, or program level.

21st Century Bloom's Taxonomy

Lower- order			Higher- order		
Remember	Understand	Apply	Analyze	Evaluate	Create
• Define • Describe • Recall	• Classify • Explain • Summarize	• Determine • Organize • Use	• Deduct • Estimate • Outline	• Argue • Justify • Support	• Construct • Adapt • Modify

Most importantly, you'll notice that each of these verbs will allow teachers to align a specific assessment to assess the mastery of the skill that's being taught. Instead of saying "Students will learn about parts of speech," teachers will insert a measurable verb into the learning objective. The 21st century model uses S.M.A.R.T. (Specific, Measurable, Attainable, Realistic, Time-bound) assessment methods to ensure teachers can track progress and zero in on areas that students need to revisit before they have fully grasped the concept.

When reading the first objective below, you might ask yourself the following questions:

Students will:
1. Learn about parts of speech

How will they learn? How will you assess their learning? What does "learn" mean to different teachers? What does "learn" look like to different learning styles?

In this second example, the 21st century model shows specific ways students will use parts of speech.

Students will be able to:
1. Define parts of speech (lower)
2. Classify parts of speech (lower)
3. Construct a visual representation of each part of speech (higher)

Technology in the 21st Century Classroom

Student-centered classrooms now also rely heavily on technology for content delivery (PowerPoint, LMS) assessment (online quizzes) and collaborative learning (GoogleDrive). Particular to ESL classrooms, teachers can now record themselves speaking using lecture capture software. Students can then watch the video multiple times to ensure they've understood concepts. They have the ability to pause/rewind/replay any sections they are confused about, and they can focus on taking better notes while having the ability to watch the video a second or third time.

Online assessments also give students and teachers a better idea for comprehension level. These quick, often self-grading assessments give teachers more time to spend with students instead of grading. They eliminate human error and give teachers data needed to zero in on concepts that need to be revisited. For example, if 12 of 15 students got number 5 wrong, the teacher will know to discuss this concept in class. Online assessments may include listening, speaking, reading, and/or writing practice. This reinforces the content that was taught in the classroom and gives opportunity for practice at students' leisure. In addition, adaptable learning will help teachers by tracking user data to demonstrate learning gains. This can be completed in pre-posttest form, with conditionals within an assessment, or through small, formative assessments.

SMART Technologies, Inc. is a very popular company that creates software and hardware for educational environments. You may have heard of a "SmartBoard" before. These are promethean boards (interactive whiteboards) and are most commonly gained using grant money. They can be used as a projector for PowerPoints, their speakers can be used for audio practice, and their video options can allow you to "bring" a guest speaker into your classroom using videoconferencing, such as Skype. They record notes made on the whiteboard and record audio from lectures, which can then be saved and sent to students that were absent, or used to review for tests on varying concepts.

Google has created ample opportunity for secondary teachers in creating efficiencies for document sharing, assessment tools, and collaborative learning environments. Their drive feature can allow for easy transfer of assignment instructions, essays, and group projects. Slides can be used to create and post PowerPoints for students to have ongoing access. Forms is a great way to create quizzes, and the data can be sorted and manipulated in a number of ways. They can also be used for self-assessment, peer evaluation, and for pre-post analyses.

As technology continues to evolve, it's critical for teachers to continue to implement tools that make their classrooms more effective and efficient while also preparing students to successfully function in a technology-driven society. Through simple lessons and technology demonstrations, students will have a great start at applying technology skills in the outside world. The classroom is a great starting place for ESL students to learn how to use technology and how to practice their own reading, writing, listening, and speaking.

TEACHER CERTIFICATION STUDY GUIDE

DOMAIN I   **VOCABULARY, READING COMPREHENSION, AND TEXT TYPES**

OBJECTIVE 1   **VOCABULARY AND READING COMPREHENSION STRATEGIES**

Skill 1.1   Identify word meanings through syntax, word structure, and context

Root, Base, and Compound Words
Structural elements within words can be used independently to determine meaning. Often including a historical element, root words commonly stem from Latin or Greek origins. Base words are considered language in the simplest form. Compound words create meaning through the combination of two words that are able to stand alone.

Root words: A root word is a word from which another word is developed. The second word can be said to have its "root" in the first. This structural component lends itself to an illustration of a tree and its roots, which can concretize the meaning for readers. Typically, root words cannot stand alone.

Aquatic (aqua = water)
Submerge (sub = under)
Junction (junct = connect)

Base words: Unlike root words, base words are stand-alone linguistic units that cannot be deconstructed or broken down into smaller words. Prefixes and suffixes are connected to base words to create meaning.

Retell (base = tell)
Instructor (base = instruct)
Sampled (base = sample)

Compound words: Compound words occur when two or more base words are connected to form a new word. The meaning of the new word is in some way connected to the meanings of the base words.

Everything (every + thing)
Backpack (back + pack)
Notebook (note + book)

Prefixes and Suffixes
Prefixes are beginning units of meaning that can be added (affixed) to the beginning of a base word or root word. They are also known as bound morphemes, meaning that they cannot stand alone as words.

Prefix	Meaning	Example
Re-	To do again	Reread
Anti-	Against	Anticlimactic
Uni-	One	Unibrow
Mis-	Incorrect	Misunderstood

Suffixes are ending units of meaning that can be affixed to the end of a base word or root word. Suffixes transform the original meanings of base and root words. Like prefixes, they are also known as bound morphemes because they cannot stand alone as words.

Suffix	Meaning	Example
-able	Ability	Likeable
-er	One who	Teacher
-less	Without	Careless
-est	Comparative	Smartest

Inflectional endings: Inflectional endings are types of suffixes that impart a new meaning to the base word or root word. These endings change the gender, number, tense, or form of the base or root word. Just like other suffixes, these are bound morphemes.

Ending	Original word	New word
-s	Road	Roads
-es	Mix	Mixes
-ing	Write	Writing
-ed	Sample	Sampled

Aside from using roots and affixes to identify word meanings, other context clues can be used, such as contrast, logic, definition, and examples or illustrations.

Context clue	Example
Contrast	Odysseus is **adroit**, whereas the Cyclops was clumsy.
Logic	She needed to **debunk** his lies so that her friends would trust her again.
Definition	They were **zealots**, fanatics.
Example	He was **adamant**; he would not yield to the opposition.

English Language Arts

By looking at new words using context clues combined with a knowledge of syntactical rules and word structure, readers have the tools to identify a word's meaning. Take, for example, the following sentence: "The Supreme Court decision effectively **nullified** previous state laws."

A syntactic analysis shows that "nullified" is a verb. A root word analysis shows that "null" means "zero" and that "-ed" is a past-tense ending. Using the context of the sentence, it is clear that nullified must mean something like "eliminated or canceled previous state laws."

(See Skill 1.6 for more explanations and examples of context clues.)

Skill 1.2 Understand word and phrase meanings (denotative and connotative)

Connotation and Denotation

Denotation refers to the literal meaning of a word, as opposed to its connotative meaning.

Connotation refers to the implications and associations of a given word, distinct from the denotative or literal meaning. Connotation is used when a subtle tone is preferred. It may stir up a more effective emotional response than if the author had used blunt, denotative diction. For example, "Good night, sweet prince, and flights of angels sing thee to thy rest," a line from Shakespeare's *Hamlet*, literally refers to death; connotatively, it renders the harsh reality of death in gentle terms such as those used in putting a child to sleep.

Informative connotations are definitions agreed upon by the society in which the learner operates. A skunk is "a black and white mammal of the weasel family with a pair of pineal glands that secrete a pungent odor." The *Merriam-Webster Collegiate Dictionary* adds ". . . and offensive" odor. The color, species, and glandular characteristics are informative. The interpretation of the odor as offensive is affective.

Affective connotations are the personal feelings a word arouses. A child who has no personal experience with a skunk and its odor will feel differently about the word "skunk" than a child who has smelled the spray or been conditioned vicariously to associate offensiveness with the animal-denoted "skunk." The fact that our society views a skunk as an animal to avoid will affect the child's interpretation of the word.

In fact, it is not necessary for one to have actually seen a skunk (that is, have a denotative understanding) to use the word in a connotative expression. For example, calling someone a skunk implies that they are "an obnoxious or disliked person" (*Merriam-Webster*).

Synonyms and Antonyms

A synonym is an equivalent of another word and can substitute for it in certain contexts. Diversifying vocabulary in your writing by incorporating synonyms will improve your writing, giving you the best chance for a high score on the written sections of AP exams.

Original word	Synonyms
Required	Necessary, mandatory, needed, essential
Many	Numerous, several
Smart	Intelligent, bright, intellectual

An antonym represents the opposite meaning for a word.

Original word	Antonym
Before	After
Optional	Required
Complex	Simple

A homonym is a word that looks and/or sounds like another word with a different meaning. Some common examples of homophones are:

Sounds like another word: principle/principal, site/sight/cite

Sounds and looks like another word: bark (wood) and bark (utter a command aggressively); row (neat line) and row (paddle a boat)

Homonyms are important to consider when contemplating the meanings of words (denotative and connotative), particularly when reading works of literature that incorporate puns and wordplay.

Wordplay on the word "son/sun":

But swear by thyself, that at my death thy Son
Shall shine as he shines now, and heretofore;
And, having done that, thou hast done;
I fear no more.

—John Donne, in "A Hymn to God the Father"

Homonyms and homophones can also pose a bit of a comprehension challenge because they create ambiguity, as in this headline:

Kids Make Nutritious Snacks

The ambiguity here is easy to decode, but note that that ambiguity is greatly reduced when readers have a thorough knowledge of homonyms and homophones and when they can use context clues to help determine the meaning of specific words and phrases.

Skill 1.3 Connect English language words and phrases to their derivations from other languages

Many English language words and phrases are derived from other languages either as English spread across different countries and cultures or as people who speak different languages immigrated to predominantly English-speaking countries. Typically these words are seen as borrowed or loaned words, although the process was not actually borrowing or loaning.

Some common examples of these words are:

chandelier, ballet, faux pas (French)
armada, canyon, mosquito (Spanish)
bazaar, giraffe, caravan (Arabic)
avocado, hurricane, potato, skunk (Amerindian)

Being able to identify words and phrases that originated in languages other than English can be a tool for reading comprehension. These words will be harder to interpret using word structures or roots but can be learned and then understood. Also, understanding the origins of the words helps increase readers' understanding and appreciation of other countries, cultures, and languages.

Skill 1.4 Identify multiple influences on the English language (historical, social, cultural, regional, and technological)

History and Development of the English Language
English is an Indo-European language that evolved through several periods. The origin of English dates to the settlement of the British Isles in the fifth and sixth centuries by Germanic tribes called the Angles, the Saxons, and the Jutes. The original Britons spoke a Celtic tongue, while the Angles spoke a Germanic dialect.

Modern English derives from the speech of the Anglo-Saxons, who imposed not only their language but also their social customs and laws on their new land. From the fifth to the tenth century, Britain's language was the tongue we now refer to as Old English. During the next four centuries, the many French attempts at English conquest introduced many French words to English. The grammar and syntax of the language, however, remained Germanic.

English Language Arts

Middle English, most evident in the writings of Geoffrey Chaucer, dates loosely from 1066 to 1509. William Caxton brought the printing press to England in 1474 and increased literacy. Old English words required numerous inflections to indicate noun cases and plurals as well as verb conjugations. Middle English treated these inflections as separately pronounced syllables. "English" in 1300 would have been written "Olde Anglishe," with the *e*'s at the ends of the words pronounced as our "short a" vowel. Even adjectives had plural inflections: "long dai" became "longe daies," pronounced "long-a day-as." Spelling was phonetic, and thus every vowel had multiple pronunciations, a fact that continues to affect the English language.

Modern English dates from the introduction of the Great Vowel Shift because it created guidelines for spelling and pronunciation. Before the printing press, books were copied laboriously by hand; language was subject to the individual interpretations of the scribes. Printers and subsequently lexicographers, such as Samuel Johnson and Noah Webster, influenced the guidelines. As reading matter became mass produced, the reading public was forced to adopt the speech and writing habits of those who wrote and printed the books.

Despite many readers' insistence to the contrary, Shakespeare's writings are in Modern English. Language, like social conventions and other factors, is constantly subject to change. Immigration, inventions, and cataclysmic events change language just as any other facet of life is affected by these changes.

American English today is somewhat different in pronunciation and sometimes vocabulary from British English. The British call a truck a "lorry," a baby carriage a "pram"—short for "perambulator"—and an elevator a "lift." The two languages have few syntactical differences, and even the tonal qualities that were once so clearly different are converging.

Though Modern English is less complex than Middle English, having lost many unnecessary inflections, it is still considered difficult to learn because of its many exceptions to the rules. It has, however, become the world's dominant language by reason of the political, military, and social power of England from the fifteenth to the nineteenth century and of America in the twentieth century.

Modern inventions, such as the telephone, radio, TV, film, video, and the Internet, have especially affected English pronunciation. Regional dialects, once a hindrance to clear understanding, have fewer distinct characteristics. Speakers from different parts of the United States can be identified by their accents, but as educators and media personalities stress uniform pronunciations and proper grammar, the differences are diminishing.

The English language has a more extensive vocabulary than any other language; it is a language of synonyms, words borrowed from other languages, and coined words—many of them introduced by the rapid expansion of technology.

Language is in constant flux. We can see this in action when we view or listen to media and/or talk to people of different ages, cultures, and parts of the country. We can practice this when use language for specific purposes and audiences.

How Language Changes

Language changes in all its manifestations. At the phonetic level, the sounds of a language will change, as will its orthography (spelling). The vocabulary level will probably manifest the greatest changes. Changes in syntax are slower and less likely to occur. For example, English has changed in response to the influences of many other languages and cultures as well as internal cultural changes such as the development of the railroad and the computer. English syntax still relies on language and linguistics on word order, however. The English language has not shifted to an inflected system, even though many of the cultures that have impacted it do, in fact, have an inflected language—for example, Spanish.

Blending of Cultures

The most significant influence on a language is the blending of cultures. The Norman Conquest, which brought the English speakers in the British Isles under the rule of French speakers, changed the language, but the fact that English speakers did not adopt the language of the ruling class is significant. English speakers did not become speakers of French. Even so, many vocabulary items entered the language during that period. The Great Vowel Shift that occurred between the fourteenth and sixteenth centuries is somewhat of a mystery, although it is generally attributed to the migration to Southeast England following the plague. The Great Vowel Shift largely accounts for the discrepancy between orthography and speech in modern English.

Colonization

Beginning with the colonization of the New World by England and Spain, English and Spanish became dominant languages in the Western Hemisphere. Colonization also brought new vocabulary into the language and contributed to the development of the varieties of English overseas. Indian English has its own easily recognizable attributes, as do Australian and North American English. The fact that English is the most widely spoken and understood language in the world in the twenty-first century implies that it is constantly in flux.

Modern Inventions

Other influences, of course, impact language. The introduction of television and its domination by the United States has had a great influence on the English that is spoken and understood all over the world. The same is true of the computerization of the world. (Tom Friedman called it "flattening" in his book *The World Is Flat: A Brief History of the Twenty-First Century*.) New terms have been added ("blog"), old terms have changed meaning ("mouse"), and nouns have been verb-ized ("prioritize").

Origins of English Words

Just as countries and families have histories, so do words. Knowing and understanding the origin of a word—where and how it has been used through the years—and the history of its meaning as it has changed are important components of the writing and language teacher's tool kit.

Never before in the history of the English language, or any other language for that matter, have the forms and meanings of words changed so rapidly. When America was settled originally, immigration from many countries made it a "melting pot." Immigration accelerated rapidly within the first hundred years, resulting in pockets of language throughout the country.

When trains began to make transportation available and affordable, individuals from those various pockets came in contact with one another, shared vocabularies, and attempted to converse. From that time forward, every generation brought the introduction of a technology that made language interchange not only more possible but also more necessary.

The trend to standardize dialects began with radio. A Bostonian might not be understood by a Houstonian, who therefore might hesitate in turning the dial to hear the advertisements of vendors that had a vested interest in being heard and understood. Soap and soup producers knew a gold mine when they saw it and created a market for radio announcers and actors who spoke without a pronounced dialect. In return, listeners began to hear the English language in a dialect different from the one they spoke, and as it settled into their thinking processes, it eventually made its way to their tongues; consequently, spoken English began to lose some of its local peculiarities.

This change has been a slow process, but most Americans can easily understand other Americans and English speakers no matter where they come from. The introduction of television carried the evolution further, as did the proliferation of electronic communications devices.

An excellent example of the changes that have occurred in English is a comparison of Shakespeare's original works with modern translations. Without help, twenty-first-century Americans would be unable to read the *First Folio*.

Teachers can learn from the vocabularies and etymologies of their readers, who are on the receiving end of the escalation brought about by technology and increased global influence. In the past, the *Oxford English Dictionary* has been one of the most reliable sources for etymologies. Some of the collegiate dictionaries are also useful.

In addition to etymologies, knowing how and when to label a word usage "jargon" or "colloquial" is important. Teachers must be aware of the possibility that a word that was previously considered "jargon" is now accepted as standard. To be on top of this, teachers must continually keep up with the etymological aids that are available, particularly online.

Skill 1.5 Use prior knowledge of words, phrases, concepts, and experiences to understand new words and phrases

Prior knowledge can be defined as all of one's prior experiences, learning, and development. Prior knowledge is what one brings to the table when entering a specific learning situation or attempting to comprehend a specific text. Sometimes prior knowledge can be erroneous or incomplete.

Obviously, if there are misconceptions in a reader's prior knowledge, these must be corrected so that the reader's overall comprehension skills can continue to progress. Prior knowledge includes the accumulated positive and negative experiences that the reader has acquired, both in and out of educational settings.

Prior knowledge might come from:

- Travel
- Life experiences (family, friends, education)
- Various forms of media (TV, films, print, video, music)
- Visits to museums, libraries, art galleries, and other arts and science institutions
- Community service

Whatever prior knowledge you or your readers bring to a reading experience can help increase understanding of new words and phrases, thus improving comprehension. The more reading you do and the more independent reading and writing readers do, the better. Reading expands our knowledge base, which then adds to the prior knowledge we bring to new reading experiences.

When preparing to read a challenging text or to begin reading any text with your readers, you must consider the following concerning the readers' prior knowledge:

1. What prior knowledge can be activated to help with reading comprehension?

2. How independent are the readers in using strategies to activate their prior knowledge?

The answers to these questions should help guide instruction so that readers, with practice, are able to use these strategies on their own. This will result in an increased development of their reading comprehension skills.

Skill 1.6 Demonstrate knowledge of key reading strategies to use for different texts and purposes

All text contains a message. Even when a child cannot read the words and instead "play reads" text using pictures and memory, the child demonstrates an understanding of this concept. Comprehension is important to literacy because it is the reason and purpose behind reading (i.e., we learn to read, so we can read to learn).

The concept that print carries meaning is demonstrated every day in the elementary classroom as the teacher holds up a selected book to read it aloud to the class. The teacher explicitly and deliberately thinks out loud about how to hold the book, how to focus the class on looking at its cover, where to start reading, and in what direction to begin. Even in writing the morning message on the board, the teacher provides a lesson on print concepts. The children see that the message is placed at the top of the board and is then followed by additional activities and a schedule for the rest of the day.

Children become curious about printed symbols once they recognize that print, like talk, conveys meaningful messages that direct, inform, or entertain people. By school age, many children are eager to continue their exploration of print. As readers progress through grades six to 12, the goal is to develop fluent and proficient readers who are also knowledgeable about the reading process.

Effective reading instruction should enable readers to become self-directed readers who can:

- Construct meaning from various types of texts
- Recognize that there are different kinds of reading materials and different purposes for reading
- Select strategies appropriate for different reading activities
- Develop a lifelong interest and enjoyment in reading a variety of material for different purposes

As readers develop in age, grade level, and proficiency, they learn from reading and interpreting a wide variety of fiction and nonfiction resources, including:

- Signs and labels
- Poetry and songs
- Picture books, chapter books, short stories, articles, novels
- Plays, screenplays, scripts
- Maps, charts, diagrams, infographics
- Print resources from all subject areas
- Notes, messages, letters, emails, texts, blog posts
- Folktales, myths and legends, fables, origin stories
- Writing by readers and teachers, including mentor texts
- Newspapers, magazines, pamphlets, brochures, forms, manuals, instructions

Classroom resources should stimulate readers' imaginations and kindle their curiosity. Familiarization with narrative and expository materials and frequent opportunities to write in all subject areas facilitate the reading process. By becoming authors themselves, readers increase their awareness of the organization and structure of printed language.

Readers also need to know that these different text types have different features and that different text types and different purposes require specific strategies.

For example, when looking at informational texts, readers might use the strategies of looking at headings and subheadings, illustrations and visual elements, and overviews to enhance reading comprehension. Even within the genre of informational texts, we might read for different purposes. Sometimes we are looking for specific information, and sometimes we might be reading an entire article or book.

When looking for specific information, readers might use the strategy of looking at a table of contents or using an index to find exactly what they want. When reading an entire article or book, readers might take notes on key concepts and supporting details so that they remember what is important or so that they can summarize later (depending on the purpose of the reading).

Similarly, when reading literary texts, readers might be reading for enjoyment or they might be reading for a book club or class assignment. If reading for a group or class assignment, they might want to use strategies like predicting, forming opinions, or making mental images to help with understanding and remembering. Readers will want to focus on the characteristics of specific literary texts such as plot, character, setting, and theme.

Graphic texts also contain specific features and reading purposes that will also require shared reading strategies with informational and literary and some different. Within each general type of text, there are more specific text types and different purposes for reading. Providing students with a general set of strategies and understandings of textual features and purposes prepares them to effectively and efficiently comprehend what they are reading.

Cues: Cues are pieces of information used to direct or monitor reading comprehension literature and understanding text. As they self-monitor their reading comprehension, readers have to integrate various sources of information, or cues, to help them construct meaning from the text and graphic illustrations.

Comprehension occurs when readers correctly interpret the text and construct meaning from it.

Context clues: Context clues help readers determine the meanings of words they are not familiar with. The context of a word is the sentence or sentences that surround the word. Sometimes the writer offers synonyms, or words that have nearly the same meaning. Context clues can appear within the sentence itself, within the preceding and/or following sentence(s), or within the passage as a whole.

Read the following sentences and attempt to determine the meanings of the words in bold print.

*The **luminosity** of the room was so incredible that there was no need for lights.*

If there was no need for lights, then one must assume that the word "luminosity" has something to do with giving off light. The definition of luminosity, therefore, is "the emission of light."

*Jamie could not understand Joe's feelings. His mood swings made understanding him somewhat of an **enigma**.*

The fact that Joe could not be understood made him somewhat of a puzzle. The definition of enigma is "a mystery or puzzle."

Word forms: Sometimes a familiar word can appear as a different part of speech. You may have heard that fraud involves a criminal misrepresentation, so when the word appears in the adjective form fraudulent ("He was suspected of fraudulent activities"), you can make an educated guess as to its meaning.

You probably know that something out-of-date is obsolete; therefore, when you read about "built-in obsolescence," you can guess the meaning of the unfamiliar word.

Sentence clues: Often, a writer will actually define a difficult or particularly important word for you the first time it appears in a passage. Phrases like "that is," "such as," "which is," or "is called" might announce the writer's intention to give just the definition you need. Occasionally, a writer will simply use a synonym or near synonym joined by the word "or."

Look at the following examples:

*The **credibility**—that is to say, the believability—of the witness was called into question by evidence of previous perjury.*

*Nothing would **assuage**, or lessen, the child's grief.*

Punctuation: At the sentence level, punctuation is often a clue to the meaning of a word. Commas, parentheses, quotation marks, and dashes tell readers that a definition is being offered by the writer.

*A tendency toward **hyperbole**, extravagant exaggeration, is a common flaw among persuasive writers.*

*Political **apathy**—lack of interest—can lead to the death of the state.*

Explanation: A writer might simply give an explanation in other words that readers can understand in the same sentence:

*The **xenophobic** townspeople were suspicious of every foreigner.*

English Language Arts

Writers also explain a word in terms of its opposite at the sentence level:

His **incarceration** was ended, and he was elated to be **out of jail**.

Adjacent sentence clues: The context for a word goes beyond the sentence in which it appears. At times, the writer uses adjacent (adjoining) sentences to present an explanation or definition:

The two hundred dollars for the car repair would have to come out of the contingency fund. Fortunately, Angela's father had taught her to keep some money set aside for just such emergencies.

Analysis: The second sentence offers a clue to the definition of the word "contingency" as used in this sentence: "emergencies." Therefore, a fund for contingencies would be money tucked away for unforeseen and/or urgent events.

Entire passage clues: On occasion, you must look at an entire paragraph or passage to figure out the definition of a word or term. In the following paragraph, notice how the word "nostalgia" undergoes a form of extended definition throughout the selection rather than in just one sentence.

> *The word "nostalgia" links the Greek words for "away from home" and "pain." If you're feeling nostalgic, then you are probably in some physical distress or discomfort, suffering from a feeling of alienation and separation from loved ones or loved places. Nostalgia is that awful feeling you remember from the first time you went away to camp or spent the weekend with a friend's family—homesickness, or some condition even more painful than that. But in common use, nostalgia has come to have more sentimental associations. A few years back, for example, a nostalgia craze had to do with the 1950s. We resurrected poodle skirts and saddle shoes, built new restaurants to look like old ones, and tried to make chicken à la king just as Mother probably never made it. In TV situation comedies, we re-created a pleasant world that probably never existed and relished our nostalgia, longing for a homey, comfortable lost time.*

Using context cues is a research-based, effective strategy for developing reading comprehension and reading independence.

Skill 1.7 Demonstrate knowledge of effective pre-, post-, and during reading comprehension strategies

Reading comprehension strategies are not just about what readers do while they are reading. Effective reading comprehension instruction incorporates activities readers can do before, during, and after they read. This way they are more likely to understand and remember what they have read and to be able to increasingly use tools and strategies independently to help them understand increasingly complex literary, informational, and graphic texts. Educators should have a set of strategies to teach readers at various grade and proficiency levels.

Examples include:

Prereading activities: These can be a great way to motivate and enhance readers' comprehension because they become actively involved. The following guidelines will help generate meaningful questions that will trigger constructive reading of expository texts.

- Read the title and think about what might be the main idea in the story (literary) *or* read the title, headings, and subheadings to identify what the main idea in the text might be (informational).
- Think about other books you have read by the same author (literary).
- Identify why you are reading this particular text (informational).
- Think about what you know about the topic and what questions you might have about the topic (all text types).

During reading activities: As they read, students often realize that what they are reading is not making sense. They then need a plan for making sense out of the excerpt—a "stop and think" strategy. If they conclude that the material is not making sense, they can reread the text, read ahead in the text, look up unknown words, or ask for help. Some readers will try these approaches without ever being explicitly taught to use them in school by a teacher:

- Make predictions (literary).
- Make notes or keep a journal about what you think of plot, characters, and so on (literary).
- Make connections to experiences, people, or events you know (all text types).
- Organize your reading by reading smaller passages or sections and taking notes as you finish each section (all text types).
- Read complex materials twice; skim the first time to get the main idea and then read slowly for elaboration, arguments, and evidence (informational).
- Write down questions you may have relating to understanding or elaboration or ideas (all text types).

Postreading activities: These ask the readers to pull into a cohesive whole the essential bits of information within a longer passage or excerpt of text:

- Do something with your favorite quotations, passages, or ideas from the text; share them in some way (writing, video, audio, discussion, arts) (all text types).
- Check back on your predictions and/or your questions about the book/topic. Did your predictions come true? Were your questions answered? Did you change your opinions (all text types)?
- Retell/summarize the content in your own words, using multiple media.

Summarizing: After a first read of a text, readers can learn how to summarize informational or text by following these guidelines:

1. Look at the topic sentence of the paragraph or the text and ignore the details.
2. Search for information that has been mentioned more than once and make sure it is included only once in the summary.
3. Find related ideas or items and group them under a unifying heading.
4. Search for and identify a main idea sentence.
5. Write (or use media to create) a summary.

Additional Comprehension Strategies
Determining the author's context entails examining the author's feelings, beliefs, past experiences, goals, needs, and physical environment as suggested by the prose. Readers' experiences will be enriched if they can appreciate and understand how these elements may have affected the writing.

Understanding symbols can help unearth a meaning the author might have intended but not expressed or even never intended at all. Often referred to as a sign, a symbol designates something that stands for something else. In most cases, a symbol stands for something that has a deeper meaning than its literal denotation. Symbols can have personal, cultural, or universal associations.

Different text types and different purposes for reading will determine some of the pre-, post-, and during reading comprehension activities you encourage your readers to use, but many of the strategies are general enough to be easily adapted to all purposes and text types.

OBJECTIVE 2   STRATEGIES FOR READING INFORMATIONAL TEXTS

Skill 2.1   Identify key characteristics of different informational texts

Informational books and articles make up much of the reading of modern Americans. Magazines began to be popular in the nineteenth century in this country, and, while many of the contributors to those publications intended to influence the political/social/religious convictions of their readers, many also simply intended to pass on information.

A book or article whose purpose is simply to be informative—that is, not to persuade—is called exposition. An example of an expository book is the *MLA Style Manual*. The writers do not intend to persuade their readers to use the recommended stylistic features in their writing; they are simply making them available in case a reader needs such a guide.

(See Skills 2.3 and 2.4 for Persuasive and procedural/technical texts.)

Informational texts can express information about social studies, science, the arts, or any subject. Text types include zines, textbooks, reference materials, newspapers, and online texts including encyclopedias, journals, and blogs. Each of these text types uses a combination of text features. Common informational text features include:

Category	Features
Navigational features	Table of contents, indexes, appendices, glossaries, citations/references, prefaces, clickable links (of different types) for online informational texts
Graphic features	Photos, drawings, diagrams, infographics, maps, charts, cross-sections, timelines
Organizational/design features	Font choices: bold, colors, sizes, fonts Lists: bullets, numbers Headings: titles, headings, subheadings, captions, labels, sidebars

Authors of informational text use a combination of these features to effectively and efficiently communicate with readers. For example, a zine or blog would not use indexes or appendices, but a zine would use a table of contents and a blog would use clickable links. Both online and print encyclopedias and reference materials would include a list of citations/sources/references at the end of the text.

The print version of the *MLA Style Manual* would use traditional navigational features and probably steer free of stylistic designs that distracted from the information they want to communicate. The online version, however, might use design features to draw readers' attention to the most common elements of the manual that they know people are looking for.

Being able to identify the type of text by its characteristics can help students develop independent reading comprehension and facilitate the competent writing of different types of texts as well.

Informational texts may include specific organizational structures, such as cause and effect, problem and solution, temporal sequence, and compare and contrast, in order to communicate information.

(See Skill 2.2 for how to use text structures and features to enhance reading comprehension of texts.)

Skill 2.2 Demonstrate understanding of how knowledge of text features and structures facilitates comprehension of informational texts

Just as students can learn to identify informational text types by their characteristics, they can increase comprehension by using those features and structures to draw their attention to what is essential in the text.

Titles, headings, and subheadings draw readers' attention to the way information is organized. This helps readers select the parts of the text that they want to read. Indexes and appendices can help readers locate information even more specifically if they do not want to read the text from cover to cover and/or they want to start with a specific aspect of the topic they are learning about.

Links to sources, more information, and/or definitions that are features of online informational texts can help students more fully understand what they are reading, as can graphic features. Students who know how to use graphic information to supplement written information are more likely to understand both the big ideas and the supporting details in the informational text they are reading.

In addition, if students can determine whether the organizational structure of the text they are reading is cause and effect or a temporal sequence, they will have an organized way to think about and take notes on the key concepts they are learning.

Even younger children can use these strategies to enhance comprehension and read informational texts.

Skill 2.3 Evaluate an informational text to identify the main idea, purpose, and intended audience

A quick look at a text's characteristics and organizational features can help readers quickly identify a text's purpose and intended audience. Taking a closer look at features and structures can help readers quickly identify a text's central idea.

Being able to evaluate an informational text quickly to determine purpose, audience, and main idea can save readers time in two ways. One, they may learn that they need to choose a different text that is better suited to their task or their age; and two, they will have a basic understanding of the main idea of a text before they start a more concentrated reading. Learning how to read an informational text provides students with some scaffolding for comprehending increasingly complex texts and helps lay a foundation for students to learn how to write informational texts.

Looking at the Wikipedia entry below, readers can see that the purpose of this text is to explain what a concept means and that the audience is probably older than age 15 or 16. The links in the body of the text provide more information to the readers, and the links in the sidebar show categories under which this topic is linked conceptually. A skim of the first few paragraphs of the text indicates that the main idea is that "freedom of the press" is something many countries believe to be crucial enough to legislate.

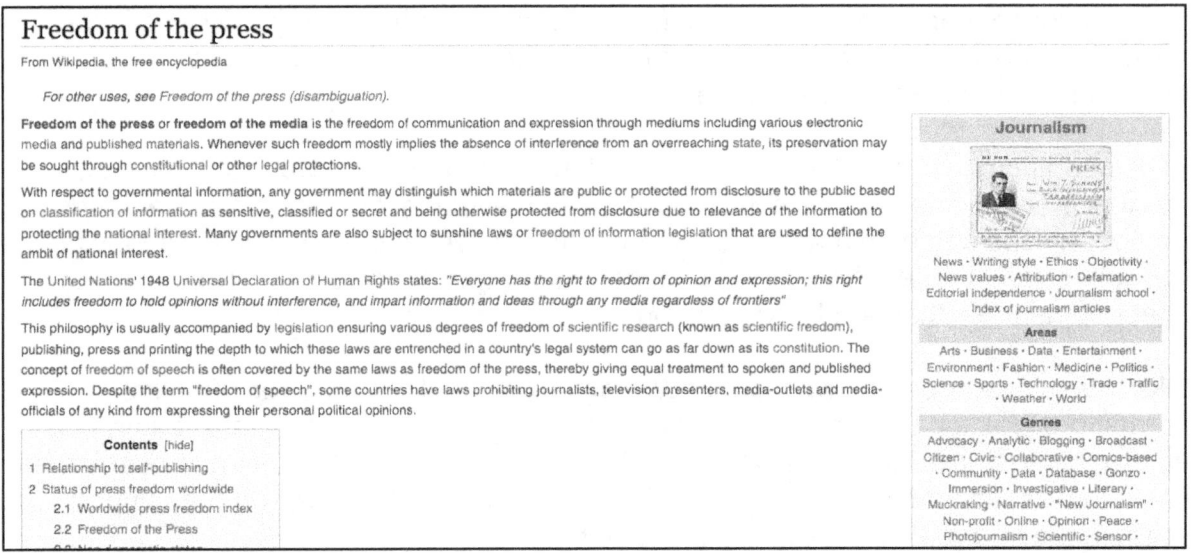

In the image from How Stuff Works below, the heading, illustration, and caption indicate that the main idea of the text is to explain what a double pulsar is and how it works. A quick skim of the first paragraph indicates to readers that the audience is an adult (references to 1995, rave and weekend parties) who does not have a scientific understanding of space.

Each informational text type will have its own features that help readers identify purpose, audience, and main idea.

Skill 2.4   Identify key concepts and supporting details in informational texts

A written document can be expected to have a thesis—either expressed or derived. To discover the thesis, readers need to ask what point the writer intended to make. The writing can also be expected to be organized in some logical way and to have subpoints that support or establish that the thesis is valid. It is also reasonable to expect that there will be details or examples that will support the subpoints. Knowing this, readers can make a decision about reading techniques required to achieve the objective that has already been established.

If readers need to know only the gist of a written document, speed-reading skimming techniques may be sufficient: using the forefinger, moving the eyes down the page, picking up the important statements in each paragraph, and deducing the basic content and message of the document. If readers need a better grasp of how the writer has achieved his or her purpose in the document, a quick and cursory glance—a skimming—of each paragraph will yield the subpoints, the topic sentences of the paragraphs, and how the thesis is developed, resulting in a greater understanding of the author's purpose and method of development. These techniques can help readers stay focused on the main points rather than getting sidetracked by elaborative details.

A more in-depth type of reading requires readers to scrutinize each phrase and sentence, looking first for the thesis and then for the topic sentences in the paragraphs that develop the thesis, and, at the same time, looking for connections such as transitional devices that provide clues to the direction the reasoning is taking. This type of reading also requires readers to identify the differences between main ideas and specific details within paragraphs.

Structurally oriented graphic organizers can help students identify and remember main ideas. For example, graphic organizers can help students identify cause and effect, compare and contrast, and question and answer, and understand general and temporal descriptions of information or events. Organizing notes in this way helps readers identify both the main points in the piece and the relevance of specific details used to elaborate on those points.

In addition, readers should identify a purpose for reading a particular text. The purpose for reading informational texts varies with the kind of information the text contains or conveys. If the text is information about culture and/or history, the purpose in reading it is to gain information and learning through understanding culture and/or history. If the text is persuasive in nature, readers will be presented with an opinion backed by some research and will need to employ the strategies of sifting through the strengths of the sources and arguments and possibly assessing them in relationship to works of a different opinion or conclusion. If the purpose of the nonliterary text is procedural, students are to learn a process or set of applicable skills. There may be other purposes behind nonliterary texts as well.

Skill 2.5 Evaluate the evidence and examples in informational texts to determine relevance

After identifying the main ideas in informational texts and paragraphs, readers need to analyze the reasoning and arguments. Readers must be able to connect the topics in paragraphs to the main idea and be able to trace the reasoning of the argument or thesis. In addition, readers should look for evidence or examples to support these points.

Using textual features and structures to identify the central idea can help readers closely trace the evolution of that idea or thesis through arguments and evidence. Readers can then use comprehension strategies, including graphic organizers and/or mind maps (outlines), to record what they are learning so that they can evaluate the arguments and evidence to form their own opinions.

It is essential that readers are able to analyze the relevance and importance of evidence and examples and to determine if there is enough of each to convincingly support the main idea of the informational text. Students should do this before checking evidence or examples for credibility, which may save them some time.

Read through the informational text in detail and ask yourself the following questions: Does the main idea make sense? Do the reasons or arguments follow the main idea? Does the evidence or examples support the reasons?

Graphic organizers and discussions with teachers and/or in small groups can greatly facilitate these types of skills so that students are able to do this more and more independently and with increasingly challenging informational texts.

Skill 2.6   Evaluate sources in informational texts for credibility and reliability

As readers, researchers, and writers, students need to know how to evaluate sources in informational texts for credibility and reliability, particularly now, when students do most of their reading and research on sites that have not been curated by librarians and educators.

When students read and/or download digital informational texts, they need to learn essential strategies for evaluating the sources of these articles.

Even in print texts selected by librarians and educators, once students have determined whether the evidence and examples support the reasoning and central idea in the text, they need to assess the evidence itself to make sure that it is reliable.

The first step in doing this is to look at the sources. In the case of a printed text, readers can use textual features to identify sources, footnotes, and bibliographies. With these parts of the text, students need to apply some strategies for assessing the credibility and reliability of both digital and print evidence and examples.

Some examples of common strategies include asking the following questions about the source(s):

- Who is the author of the source? What else has he or she written? Is the author affiliated with specific institutions? If so, which ones? Has the author been cited in other texts or by other scholars?
- Where was the source published? What are the credentials of the place where it is published? Is it a credible source of news? Is it a Website affiliated with a particular point of view? Was the text subjected to a peer review?
- When was the text written? Sometimes if a source used in an informational text is too old, new information has been discovered on the topic that may nullify some of the arguments or evidence in the text.
- Who is the intended audience of the source? If it is for researchers, academics, or scholars, there might be a bibliography for the source that readers can also use in their research.

A great way to begin to help students learn these skills is to have them practice by investigating Websites that look credible at first glance in order to fool viewers/readers. A popular example of this is the Pacific Northwest Tree Octopus site.

These kinds of evaluative strategies become increasingly necessary as readers begin to read more informational texts independently rather than choosing texts from a curated list presented by teachers.

Skill 2.7 Determine the accuracy of a summary of an informational text

Just as evaluating source credibility is an essential tool for reading and researching comprehension, so is the skill of being able to identify credibility in summaries of these texts. Students may want to use these skills when reading other students' interpretations of the same texts that they have read.

Readers will also want to use these strategies when reading secondary sources; they will want to make sure that those texts accurately summarize primary sources. If they don't, students may need to find a new secondary source or even change their opinion or topic because their purpose or objective is not as clear.

Readers will also want to employ this skill when reading news so that if something doesn't make sense to them, they can do more research to find a credible source.

Readers can use many strategies to determine the accuracy of a summary, including comparing their notes (from a graphic organizer) to the summary in question. Readers can also summarize a text after they read it and compare and contrast that with the summary provided. They can also go backward and read the summary first and then the article or primary source, using the same tools. Remember: These reading strategies should focus solely on the texts and not on other factors.

Skill 2.8 Analyze information from texts containing tables, charts, graphs, maps, and illustrations

Visuals are an effective and dynamic way to add meaning to a text. They can clarify meaning, emphasize important data, summarize points, and add visual appeal. More often, they supplement the written text rather than stand independent. Learning how to interpret the data in various graphics is a useful skill for students.

Graphics
When children learn to read, they are also learning to interpret graphics. In a recent study of visual literacy development in young children, researchers concluded that children develop basic graphic concepts along with print concepts. Some of these concepts are summarized below.

Graphics can be used to identify or show:

- **Action:** Show flow or interactions.
- **Relevance:** Support ideas in written text.

- **Extensions:** Provide additional information to readers.
- **Importance:** Highlight the most important information in a text.
- **Intention:** Illustration with a communicative purpose within a text (political cartoon).
- **Partiality:** Not everything written in the text is illustrated.

Common Forms of Graphics

Tables
Tables depict exact numbers and other data in rows and columns. Those that simply store descriptive information in a form available for general use are called repository tables. They usually contain primary data, which simply summarize raw data. They are not intended to analyze the data, so any analysis is left to the readers. A good example of a repository table would be a report of birth statistics by the federal Health and Human Services Department. An analytical table, on the other hand, is constructed from some sort of analysis of primary or secondary data, possibly from a repository table or from the raw data itself. An example of an analytical table would be one that compares birth statistics in 1980 to birth statistics in 2005 for the country at large. It might also break the data down into comparisons by state.

Graphs
Graphs depict trends, movements, distributions, and cycles more readily than tables. While graphs can present statistics in a more interesting and comprehensible form than tables, they are less accurate. For this reason, the two will often be shown together.

Maps
While the most obvious use for maps is to locate places geographically, they can also show specific geographic features such as roads, mountains, and rivers. They can also show information according to geographic distribution such as population, housing, or manufacturing centers.

Illustrations
A wide range of illustrations, such as pictures, drawings, and diagrams, may illuminate the text in a document. They may also be part of a graphic layout designed to make the page more attractive.

Some functions of graphics include:

- Qualitative descriptions: Would drawing conclusions about the quality of a particular treatment or course of action be revealed by the illustration?
- Quantitative descriptions: How much do the results of one particular treatment or course of action differ from another one, and is that variation significant?
- Classification: Is worthwhile information derived from breaking the information down into classifications?
- Estimations: Is it possible to estimate future performance on the basis of the information in the illustration?

- Comparisons: Is it useful to make comparisons based on the data?
- Relationships: Are relationships between components revealed by the scrutiny of the data?
- Cause-and-effect relationships: Does the data suggest that there were cause-and-effect relationships that were not previously apparent?
- Mapping and modeling: If the data were mapped and a model drawn up, would the point of the document be demonstrated or refuted?

To begin analyzing information from graphics, readers can ask (and answer) the questions below:

1. Why is it in this document?
2. What was the writer's purpose in putting it in the document and why at this particular place?
3. Does it make a point clearer?
4. What implications are inherent in the particular table, graph, chart, or infographic that you are looking at?
5. What does the graphic/illustration have to do with the point and purpose of this piece of writing?
6. Is there adequate preparation in the text for the inclusion of the illustration?
7. Does the illustration underscore or clarify any of the points made in the text?
8. Is there a clear connection between the illustration and the subject matter of the text?

TEACHER CERTIFICATION STUDY GUIDE

OBJECTIVE 3 — STRATEGIES FOR READING PERSUASIVE TEXTS

Skill 3.1 Identify key characteristics of different persuasive texts, including advertisements, editorials, persuasive essays, and propaganda

Persuasive texts attempt to influence readers or viewers to do, think, want, or feel something. This can be accomplished through three main appeals, which can be used individually or in a combination:

Ethos: The credibility of the writer/speaker might lead the listeners/readers to a change of mind or a recommended action.

Logos: Reasoning is important in persuasive discourse. No one wants to accept a new viewpoint or take action just because he or she likes and trusts the person who recommended it. Logic comes into play in reasoning that is persuasive.

Pathos: Emotional appeal can convince people to behave differently in a way that logic does not. Sometimes we know what we should do, but we don't do it. Pathos can give us the final push to change our behaviors.

The most common types of persuasive texts are essays, editorials, letters to the editor, opinion pieces, speeches and debates, and advertisements and propaganda. Each type of persuasive text shares the key characteristics of persuasion but can easily be identified as a separate text form.

Just as with informational texts, persuasive texts have specific features that differentiate them from one another.

Category	Features
Navigational features	Headings, titles, subheads, introductions, prefaces, conclusions/call to action, statistics, clickable links (of different types) for online informational texts
Graphic/interactive features (used as evidence as well as to explain)	Drawings, diagrams, maps, charts, cross-sections, timelines Images (photos and illustrations) may feature more prominently. Surveys, polls, statistics, infographics
Organizational/design features	Font choices: bold, colors, sizes, fonts Lists: bullets, numbers Headings: titles, headings, subheadings, captions, labels, sidebars Use of borders, backgrounds, layout

Advertisements and propaganda, for example, often include colorful headings, images, and text with fewer words and the use of visual symbols or triggers.

Editorials, opinion pieces, and persuasive essays are often longer pieces of writing with few illustrations or graphics to support the argument; they leave language to do the persuading but may use statistics or numbers as evidence.

Debates and speeches are meant to be performed, and spoken text contains different features than other forms of persuasion. Almost all forms of persuasion include a call to action, repetition, simplicity, and legitimacy to try to persuade readers.

(See Objectives 14 for persuasive writing and Objective 17 for effective media viewing, analyzing, and presenting strategies.)

Skill 3.2   Demonstrate understanding of how knowledge of text features and structures facilitate comprehension of persuasive texts

A basic knowledge of text features and structures of a persuasive text can help readers determine whether something is an ad or an illustration, an editorial or a news report, an accurate infographic or a piece of propaganda. This is especially helpful for students when researching topics and/or learning about news events. They need to be able to identify whether they are reading sponsored content or a new report.

Looking at the text below, a modern reader may find it challenging to understand. The first task is to identify it as a persuasive text. To do this, readers may note that there is only one line of written text and that it reads as sort of a warning. They would also see that the text is a poster. Combining the two observations, the text looks like it is designed to persuade someone to think, feel, and/or do something.

After a closer look at the text features and the content, readers might observe the colors (this poster was originally in color), the image (of a sinking ship with smoke billowing out of it), and the words in the text and their relationship to each other. After identifying the text as a propaganda poster, the ship as older, and the expression as something they have not necessarily heard of, readers might interpret correctly that this is a war propaganda poster from World War II. At this point, even if the written expression was meaningless to readers when they first looked at it, they are now well on their way to interpreting its meaning.

Knowing text features and structures can help readers identify main ideas because they will know where to find them in the text. In a persuasive editorial or essay, readers know that the claims are made in the first part of the text, supported in the middle of the text, and emphasized at the end of the text. Readers can skim each section to glean claims and support.

TEACHER CERTIFICATION STUDY GUIDE

Skill 3.3 Evaluate a persuasive text to identify the main idea, purpose, and intended audience

In a recent study by Stanford University, researchers found that 80 percent of the middle school students they surveyed believed that sponsored content (an advertisement) was a real news story. Readers need to learn to use text features and structures, in combination with careful reading, when they are evaluating persuasive texts. Students and all readers need to make sure that they are reading the kind of text they are looking for (i.e., a news story and not an ad). In addition, they need to use these skills and strategies to help them distinguish between facts and opinions presented in a persuasive text. *(See Skill 3.4.)*

Using the text type characteristics can help readers quickly identify the purpose of a persuasive text and its intended audience(s). Taking a closer look at features and structures can help readers quickly identify that text's central idea. The strategies readers use to identify the central idea, purpose, and intended audience in persuasive texts is the same as they would use in informational texts. *(See Skill 2.3.)*

An additional strategy students can use is the SQ3R (Survey, Question, Read, Recite, and Review) method. The SQ3R method can help readers comprehend more complex and lengthy persuasive and informational written texts. After surveying or scanning the text as a whole to catch the title, major headings, subheadings, and graphics, students may then formulate questions, including the question of purpose, and read the texts to discern it. Reciting the answer, reviewing the main ideas and significant information, and further reflecting upon it will help students ascertain purpose, main idea, and audience.

Skill 3.4 Identify facts and opinions in persuasive texts

Facts are statements that are verifiable. Opinions are statements that must be supported in order to be accepted. Facts are used to support opinions.
For example, "Jane is a bad girl" is an opinion. But "Jane hit her sister with a baseball bat" is a *fact* upon which the opinion is based.

Facts report what has happened and come from observation, measurement, or calculation. Judgments are opinions, decisions, or declarations based on observation or reasoning that express approval or disapproval. Facts can be tested and verified, whereas opinions and judgments cannot. They can only be supported with facts.

Some statements cannot be so clearly distinguished. For example, "I believe that Jane is a bad girl" is a fact. The speaker believes that Jane is a bad girl. It obviously, however, includes a judgment that another person who might believe otherwise could dispute. The "fact," then, is about the speaker, rather than about Jane. Whether Jane is a bad person or not is still a matter of opinion or judgment. In many persuasive texts, judgments are not usually stated so firmly. They are, rather, plausible opinions that provoke thought or lead to factual development.

When reading persuasive informational texts, readers can use a postreading comprehension strategy to summarize the text's claims, support, and evidence. Readers should be able to identify whether opinions and claims made in persuasive texts are supported or unsupported.

Readers should also be able to evaluate the main ideas and supporting details in several texts representing different viewpoints on the same topic and be able to point to the texts for support. One of the skills involved in doing this well involves discerning evidence given in support of an argument and whether it is credible, relevant, and of high quality.

When analyzing speeches, posters, media, and other forms of persuasive texts, students should recognize rhetorical devices used to persuade and convince.

Skill 3.5 Evaluate reasoning, evidence, and examples in persuasive texts

The two forms of reasoning used to support an argument are inductive and deductive.

Inductive reasoning goes from particular observations to a general conclusion. For example:

I first observe that all the green apples I have ever tasted have been sour.

- I have tasted some from my grandfather's orchard.
- I have tasted the Granny Smiths that my mother buys in the grocery store.
- I have tasted the green apples in my friend's kitchen.
- All have been sour.

Then I can generalize that all green apples are sour. This is the conclusion. Inductive reasoning is a prevalent aspect of the way we think and deal with one another and is essential to persuasive discourse.

Deductive reasoning, on the other hand, reverses the order by going from general to particular. For example, the generalization drawn in the previous illustration, "All green apples are sour," can be used to make a statement about a particular apple.

Suppose a new variety of green apples has appeared in the grocery store. Arguing from the generalization that all green apples are sour, I may reject this new variety because I am sure that it is going to be sour. I am applying my general experience to a specific one (that I haven't even experienced yet).

Deductive reasoning is based on the following syllogism:

All green apples are sour.
This apple is green.
Therefore, this apple is sour.

A court trial is a good example of how inductive reasoning is used. When a prosecutor presents a case in a courtroom, he or she typically first puts forth a statement of fact:

On November 2, in an alley between Smith and Jones Street at the 400 block, Donald Cartwright was brutally murdered. The coroner has concluded that he was bludgeoned with a blunt instrument at or around midnight, and his body was found by a shopkeeper the next morning.

Following the outline of the facts of the case, the prosecutor will use inductive reasoning to accuse the person on trial of the crime by providing a list of facts that seem to connect the accused to the crime:

1. Terry Large, the accused, was seen in the neighborhood at 11:30 p.m. on November 2.
2. He was carrying a carpenter's tool kit, which was later recovered,
3. A hammer with evidence of blood on it was found in that tool kit.
4. The blood was tested, and it matched the victim's DNA.

Ultimately, the prosecutor will use the above facts to reach the generalization that Terry Large murdered Donald Cartwright.

Persuasive texts use deductive and inductive reasoning to persuade readers.

Another type of reasoning that persuasive texts use is to try to convince readers that a certain thing is good or bad, moral or immoral, valuable or worthless. It focuses less on knowledge and more on beliefs and values.

Finally, some persuasive texts are explicit calls for action, arguing that something should be done, improved, or changed. Its goal is action from readers, but it also seeks passive agreement with the proposition proposed. It appeals to both reason and emotion and tells readers what they can do and how to do it.

A fallacy is, essentially, an error in reasoning. In persuasive texts, **logical fallacies** are flaws in reasoning that make an argument invalid.

For example, a **premature generalization** occurs when one forms a general rule based on only one or a few specific cases.

An illustration of this is the argument "Bob Marley was a Rastafarian singer. Therefore, all Rastafarians sing." A common fallacy in reasoning is the post hoc, ergo propter hoc ("after this, therefore because of this") or the false-cause fallacy. This type of fallacy occurs in cause-and-effect reasoning, which may go either from cause to effect or from effect to cause.

The following is an example of a post hoc fallacy:

Our sales shot up 35 percent after we ran that television campaign; therefore, the campaign caused the increase in sales.

The television campaign might have caused the increase in sales, of course, but more evidence is needed to prove so. Sales may have increased for other reasons.

A **post hoc fallacy** happens when an inadequate cause is offered for a particular effect, when the possibility of more than one cause is ignored, and when an invalid connection is made between a particular cause and a particular effect. The following is an example of an inadequate cause for a particular effect:

An Iraqi truck driver reported that Iraq had nuclear weapons; therefore, Iraq is a threat to world security.

In this case, more causes are needed to prove the conclusion.

The following is an example of ignoring the possibility of more than one possible cause:

John Brown was caught in a thunderstorm, and his clothes got wet before he was rescued. Therefore, he developed influenza the next day because he got wet.

Being chilled may have played a role in the illness, but Brown would have had to contract the influenza virus before he could have come down with influenza, whether or not he had gotten wet.

The following is an example of failing to make a valid connection between a particular cause and a particular effect:

Anna fell into a putrid pond on Saturday; on Monday she came down with polio. Therefore, the pond caused the polio.

This, of course, is not an acceptable argument unless the poliovirus is found in a sample of water from the pond. The connection must be proven.

Being able to identify rhetorical devices and logical fallacies can help readers evaluate reasoning, evidence, and examples in persuasive texts.

TEACHER CERTIFICATION STUDY GUIDE

Skill 3.6   Evaluate sources in persuasive texts for credibility and reliability

Evaluating sources is the same skill in persuasive and informational reading.

(See Skill 2.5 for strategies to use when evaluating sources for credibility and reliability.)

Skill 3.7   Evaluate persuasive techniques and rhetorical devices in persuasive texts

The art of rhetoric was first developed in ancient Greece. Its pioneer was Socrates, who recognized the crucial role that rhetoric played in education, politics, and storytelling. Socrates established three types of appeals used in persuasive speech. These appeals have been identified in Skill 3.1, but we will list them again here because they relate to other appeals and rhetorical devices.

Types of Appeals
Ethos establishes the speaker as a reliable and trustworthy authority by focusing on the speaker's credentials.

Pathos emphasizes the fact that an audience responds to ideas with emotion.

Logos uses the idea that facts, statistics, and other forms of evidence can convince an audience to accept a speaker's argument.

Today, the structures of many governments and judicial systems reflect rhetorical tactics established by the Greeks long ago. The media has taken rhetoric to a whole new level and has refined it to a skilled art. Every word, as well as the method of presentation, is carefully planned. The audience is taken into account and speech tailored to its needs and motivations.

Some additional rhetorical devices that are used in persuasive texts are:

Allusion: References an event, literary work, or person.
             Example: "She's as fast as the Flash."

Antanagoge: Places a criticism and compliment together.

Euphemism: Replaces a harsh plain phrase with a less offensive one.
             Example: referring to "collateral damage" rather than dead civilians

Hyperbole: Exaggerates a statement.

Irony: Says something contrary to make a point.

Metaphor: Compares two things, usually used conceptually in persuasive text, rather than as a figure of speech.

Metonymy: Uses a similar word as a substitute for the actual word, usually used in persuasive text for connotative value.

Simile: Compares one object to another with "like" or "as."
Example: "With this shampoo, your hair will shine like the sun."

Synecdoche: Uses parts of the whole to name a whole.
Example: "Our men's cologne isn't just for suits."

It is helpful to be able to identify these techniques so that readers can help identify purpose and differentiate between fact and opinion.

A knowledge of advertising techniques can also help readers evaluate evidence and claims in all types of persuasive texts.

(See Skills 17.1 and 17.2 for details and explanations.)

Skill 3.8 Analyze information from persuasive texts containing photographs and illustrations

(See Skill 2.8 for how to analyze graphics in informational skills. See Skills 17.1 and 17.2 for how to analyze visual images used in various media.)

When a persuasive text includes images, readers would benefit from applying critical reading skills to analyze the information from those images and the intended effect that the images have on the readers/viewers.

For example, there is a whole industry dedicated to the art of arranging and photographing food for restaurants, food companies, and advertisements. Companies and advertisers want people to buy the food in the pictures, so the food in the pictures has to look good. Photographers and food stylists spend hours arranging and photographing food to make your mouth water. This is true for travel sites, any consumer product, home sales, and even dating Websites. Images play a powerful role in convincing readers and viewers to think, do, or buy something.

When readers understand this, they are less likely to be manipulated by the power of the image. A reader can view a photograph and know that the real product might not look like that at all.

Sometimes a persuasive text uses an image (photo or illustration) to tell a story. For example, in a text written to encourage student bystanders to intervene in a bullying situation, there might be an illustration or photo of a child sitting curled up, head down, in shadow. The story here is that this child has just been bullied and is hurt (physically and/or emotionally). The image tells the story in a way that a text-based description could not. It appeals to the empathy (and guilt) of the readers.

When persuasive texts use photographs or illustrations of attractive people having fun, the intention is that the readers/viewers will identify with the people and want to think, do, or buy what is being "sold" in the text. Sometimes authors use cute pictures of animals, nature, and/or everyday objects to do make readers feel good and associate that feeling with what is being "sold."

In a series of experiments conducted in 2012, researchers found that photographs used alongside textual claims made people more likely to believe the claims. For example, participants in the study were shown a statement about a specific type of nut being in the same family as the peach. Participants were more likely to believe the claim when a photograph of that nut was used alongside the text. Even though the photo showed no correlation to the "fact," it added credibility to the claim. This isn't a case of using a reader's emotions to persuade him or her to do something; it's using an image to persuade a reader to think or believe something that is not true.

It is essential that readers critically analyze and interpret images and illustrations in persuasive texts. This skill will help them improve textual comprehension and make them more empowered readers/viewers.

OBJECTIVE 4 READING TECHNICAL AND FUNCTIONAL TEXTS

Skill 4.1 Identify key characteristics of different functional and technical texts

Functional and technical texts are related in that both types of texts are informational and both provide information for readers that relates to how to do something, how something works, and/or documents that readers may need in the workplace, as citizens, or as students. Examples of technical and functional texts include contracts, application forms, how-to-manuals and articles, instructions, recipes, consumer documents, brochures and fliers, and directions and maps.

Some common characteristics of these text types include use of bold or italic print; maps, diagrams, and charts; and captions and labels. The heading of the text will usually help readers determine whether something is intended for them to follow a procedure or whether something is a document that needs to be filled out. In addition, readers can look for other distinguishing text features including:

Type of text	Purpose	Some key characteristics
Forms	Applications (job, driver's license, government services)	Blank spaces or boxes for filling out information Labels for types of info required Lines for signatures Checkboxes Questions with answers to be circled
Instructions	Recipes, assembling or building things	Numbered lists of materials and/or short procedures with spaces between the numbers Supporting Illustrations
Functional information: shorter texts	Directions, timetables, and schedules	Maps, legends, keys Tables organized by date, time, or task Numbered lists
Functional information: longer texts	Employee rights, contracts, and warranties	Numbered lists of longer information (paragraphs or longer sentences than instructions and directions) Footnotes Formal language Reference to dates, serial numbers, and so on

TEACHER CERTIFICATION STUDY GUIDE

Skill 4.2   Apply information from technical texts to develop knowledge and skills

Using reading comprehension techniques and knowledge of text features and characteristics, readers should be able to use information presented in technical texts to develop knowledge and skills in the text-subject area. For example, readers should be able to read a workplace safety document and be able to understand and apply the knowledge in the text as well as practice the procedures for what to do if they feel workplace safety may be at risk from a particular event or person.

To help students apply information from technical texts to develop knowledge and skills in different subjects and/or topics, teachers can explicitly teach:

- Reading comprehension strategies
- How to identify textual features, structures, and characteristics
- How to recognize central ideas and details
- The difference between understanding, knowing, and doing

To facilitate the transition from comprehending a technical text to applying it, readers should skim the paper first to ensure that the knowledge and skills are what they wanted to learn and that the language is at the right level for them to learn it.

Use a *during reading* comprehension strategy of taking notes while reading. This will help readers remember significant facts and supporting details. Using a graphic organizer that follows the structure of the text, i.e., problem/solution, will help facilitate efficient note-taking.

Depending on the type of text and the purpose for learning from it, readers may want to paraphrase, make drawings, use mind maps to connect ideas, write any questions for further research or explanation, and/or come up with examples of how the new skill would work or how the knowledge would explain something.

For some, reading technical and functional texts is challenging. In this case, the reading environment (time and space) becomes important. Readers should ensure that they have a distraction-free environment and a comfortable space for staying alert while studying. In addition, some readers may need to take quick breaks between chunks of text in order to process what they have learned and prepare for the next section of information.

In addition, when teaching these skills to students, teachers should provide plenty of opportunities to read and practice these strategies with real-world texts for authentic purposes.

Skill 4.3 Apply information from procedural/functional texts to perform tasks and verify facts

Using reading comprehension techniques and knowledge of text features and characteristics, readers should be able to use information presented in functional texts to perform tasks, such as planning an event, applying for a job, or baking a cake.
To help students apply information from functional texts to perform tasks and confirm facts in different subjects and/or topics, teachers can explicitly teach:

- Reading comprehension strategies
- How to identify textual features, structures, and characteristics
- How to recognize central ideas and details

In addition, when reading and applying information from procedural texts, readers must understand the importance of following steps in a sequence and not skipping any of the steps.

Questions to focus on while reading and/or note-taking are:

1. What is the task you are learning about?
2. How do you know what steps to take and in what order to take them?
3. Why is the step order important for this particular task?
4. What materials might you need before you begin the task?
5. Are there any graphics that might help you understand what you need to do?
6. How will you know that you have completed the task?
7. What do you do if you make a mistake somewhere along the way?

The text might not have all of these features or answers, but thinking about these questions will go a long way toward helping readers perform tasks and verify facts when reading procedural/functional texts.

In addition, teachers should provide students with plenty of opportunities to read and practice these strategies individually and in groups, using real-world texts for authentic purposes.

Skill 4.4 Analyze information from technical/functional texts containing tables, flowcharts, graphs, map keys and legends, schematics, and diagrams

Strategies for analyzing graphic information in general informational texts can be applied to analyzing functional/technical texts for the most part. *(See Skill 2.8.)*

Readers need to also have a more thorough understanding of how to "read" flowcharts and schematics, for example, which are more common in functional and technical texts. These texts will come up in real-world settings as well as different content areas in school, so learning how to interpret a variety of graphic features can help students in many ways.

In looking at the graphic below, readers should be able to determine the type of graphic (diagram) and the object represented (human body). The next step in analyzing the information provided in the graphic is to look at the labels. The labels indicate the names of the internal parts of the body they point to.

Analyzing this graphic also involves noticing what isn't there. The diagram is mostly of the top of the human body. Also, it involves noticing what the labeled parts have in common: What is the relationship between the parts of the body that are labeled? They all seem to be related to the digestive system.

With more information (accompanying text and additional diagrams), readers can use this diagram to help them comprehend and analyze technical information.

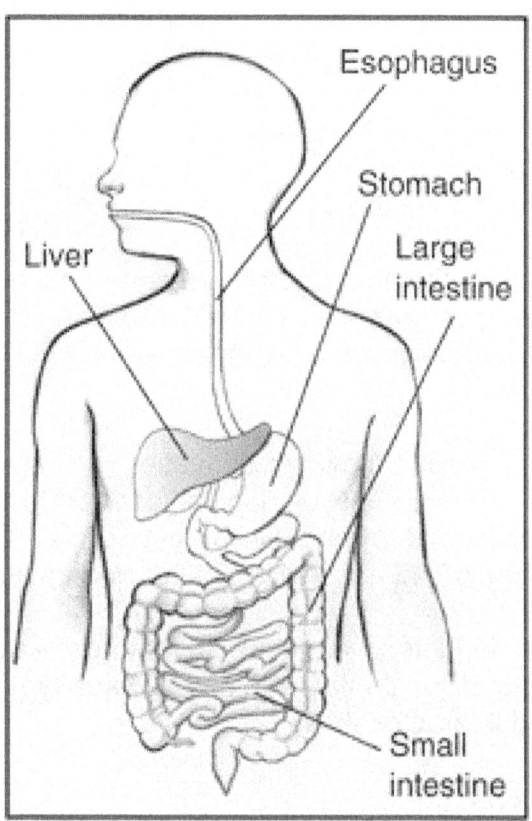

The article "Diagrams, Timelines, and Tables," by Kathryn Roberts, Rebecca Norman, Nell Duke, Paul Morsink, and Nicole Martin, outlines additional strategies teachers and students can use to distinguish between graphic forms and to improve reading comprehension of graphical devices.

TEACHER CERTIFICATION STUDY GUIDE

DOMAIN II	ANALYZING AND INTERPRETING LITERATURE
OBJECTIVE 5	ANALYZE AND INTERPRET LITERARY NONFICTION, FICTION, AND DRAMA

Skill 5.1 Evaluate the characteristics of various literary genres (e.g., drama, biography, fiction)

Fiction
A work of fiction typically has a central character, called the protagonist, and a character who stands in opposition, called the antagonist. The antagonist might be something other than a person. In Stephen Crane's short story, "The Open Boat," for example, the antagonist is a hostile environment, a stormy sea.

Conflicts between the protagonist and antagonist are typical of a work of fiction, and the climax is the turning point at which those conflicts are resolved. The plot is the sequence of events during which the conflicts occur as the characters and plot move toward a resolution.

A fiction writer artistically uses devices labeled characterization to reveal character. Characterization can depend on dialogue, description, or the attitude or attitudes of one or more characters toward one another.

Enjoying fiction depends upon the ability of the readers to suspend disbelief. Readers make a deal with the writer that, for the time the readers take to read the story, they will replace their own beliefs with the convictions expressed by the writer and will accept the reality created by the writer.

A *Bildungsroman* (German) means "novel of education" or "novel of formation" and is a novel that traces the spiritual, moral, psychological, or social development and growth of the main character from childhood to maturity. Charles Dickens's *David Copperfield* represents this genre, as does Thomas Wolfe's *Look Homeward Angel*.

Types of fiction include crime, detective, action adventures, fantasy, horror, mystery, romance, science fiction, western, thriller, and so on. Each type of fiction has distinct characteristics and shared characteristics.

Short Story
Typically a terse narrative with less developmental background about characters, a short story may include description, the author's point of view, and tone. Edgar Allan Poe emphasized that a successful short story should create one focused impact. Some other great short story writers are Ernest Hemingway, William Faulkner, Mark Twain, James Joyce, Shirley Jackson, Flannery O'Connor, Guy de Maupassant, Saki (H. H. Munro), and Alexander Pushkin.

Nonfiction

Literary nonfiction informational texts include essays, opinion pieces, editorials, and personal accounts of scientific, historic, economic, and other events. Autobiographies and biographies also fit within this category, as do information picture books for younger children. Literary nonfiction texts are usually narratively organized with a beginning, middle, and end.

In nonfiction the writer must stick to verifiable facts. Thus, a writer of nonfiction is not free to create a character from imagination, no matter how realistic the author makes that character seem. All nonfiction characters have actually lived. The writer of nonfiction declares in the choice of that genre that the work is reliably based upon reality.

Biography

This is a portrait of the life of an individual other than oneself. Biographical prose is a subcategory of nonfiction. The earliest biographical writings were probably funeral speeches and inscriptions, usually praising the life and example of the deceased. Early biographies evolved from this and were almost invariably uncritical, even distorted, and always laudatory.

Autobiography

This is a form of the biography written by the subject himself or herself. Autobiographies can range from formal works to intimate journals and diaries over the course of a life, without a conscious eye toward publication.

Drama

In its most general sense, a drama is any work that is designed to be performed by actors onstage. It can also refer to a literary genre broadly divided into comedy and tragedy. Contemporary usage, however, denotes drama as a work that treats serious subjects and themes but does not aim for the same grandeur as tragedy. Drama usually deals with characters of a less stately nature than tragedy. A classic example is Sophocles's tragedy *Oedipus Rex,* while a modern example is Eugene O'Neill's *Iceman Cometh.*

Comedy

The comedic form of dramatic literature is meant to amuse and often ends happily. It uses techniques such as satire or parody, and can take many forms, from farce to burlesque. Examples include Dante Alighieri's *Divine Comedy,* Noel Coward's *Private Lives,* some of Geoffrey Chaucer's *Canterbury Tales,* and some of William Shakespeare's plays, such as *A Midsummer's Night Dream.*

Tragedy

Tragedy is comedy's other half. It is defined as a work of drama written in either prose or poetry, telling the story of a brave, noble hero who, because of some tragic character flaw (*hamartia*), brings ruin upon himself. It is characterized by serious, poetic language that evokes pity and fear.

English Language Arts

In modern times, dramatists have tried to update drama's image by drawing its main characters from the middle class and showing their nobility through their nature instead of their standing. Sophocles's *Oedipus Rex* is the classic example of tragedy, while the plays of Henrik Ibsen (*Hedda Gabler*) and Arthur Miller (*Death of a Salesman*) epitomize modern tragedy.

Dramatic Monologue
A dramatic monologue is a speech given by an actor as if talking to himself or herself, but is actually intended for the audience. It reveals key aspects of the character's psyche and sheds insight on the situation at hand. The audience takes the part of the silent listener, passing judgment and giving sympathy at the same time. This form was invented and used predominantly by Victorian poet Robert Browning.

Tempo
Interpretation of dialogue must be connected to motivation and detail. During this time, the director is also concerned with pace and seeks a variation of tempo. If the overall pace is too slow, then the action becomes dull and dragging. If the overall pace is too fast, then the audience will not be able to understand what is going on, for they are being hit with too much information to process.

Dramatic Arc
Good drama is built on conflict of some kind—an opposition of forces or desires that must be resolved by the end of the story. The conflict can be internal, involving emotional and psychological pressures, or it can be external, drawing the characters into tumultuous events. These themes are presented to the audience in a narrative arc.

Although any performance may have a series of rising and falling levels of intensity, in general the opening should set in motion the events that will generate an emotional high toward the middle or end of the story. Then, regardless of whether the ending is happy, sad, bittersweet, or despairing, the resolution eases the audience down from those heights and establishes some sense of closure. Reaching the climax too soon undermines the dramatic impact of the remaining portion of the performance, whereas reaching it too late rushes the ending and creates a jarringly abrupt end to events.

Skill 5.2   **Analyze various literary and rhetorical devices (e.g., symbolism, style, allusion, irony, foreshadowing, tone, figurative language, syntax)**

Figurative Language
Figurative language allows for the statement of truths that more literal language cannot. Skillfully used, a figure of speech will help readers see more clearly and focus upon particulars. Figures of speech add many dimensions of richness to our reading and understanding of a literary text and of a poem; they also provide many opportunities for worthwhile analysis.

Allusion: An allusion is much like a symbol, and the two sometimes tend to run together. An allusion is defined by Merriam-Webster's *Encyclopedia of Literature* as "an implied reference to a person, event, thing, or a part of another text." Allusions are based on the assumption that there is a common body of knowledge shared by poet and reader and that a reference to that body of knowledge will be immediately understood. Allusions to the Bible and classical mythology are common in Western literature on the assumption that they will be immediately understood. This is not always the case, of course. T. S. Eliot's *Waste Land* requires research and annotation for understanding. He assumed more background on the part of the average reader than actually exists.

The use of allusion is a sort of shortcut for poets. They can use an economy of words and count on meaning to come from the reader's own experience.

Analogy: An analogy illustrates an idea by means of a more familiar idea that is similar or parallel to it.

Climax: A number of phrases or sentences are arranged in ascending order of rhetorical forcefulness. Example from Herman Melville's *Moby Dick*:

> *All that most maddens and torments; all that stirs up the lees of things; all truth with malice in it; all that cracks the sinews and cakes the brain; all the subtle demonisms of life and thought; all evil, to crazy Ahab, were visibly personified and made practically assailable in Moby Dick.*

Denotation: What a word literally means, as opposed to its connotative meaning.

Diction: The right word in the right place for the right purpose. The hallmark of a great writer is precise, unusual, and memorable diction.

Epiphany: The moment when the something is realized and comprehension sets in. James Joyce used this device in his short story collection *The Dubliners*.

Euphemism: The substitution of an agreeable or inoffensive term for one that might offend or suggest something unpleasant. Many euphemisms are used to refer to death to avoid using the real word, such as "passed away," "crossed over," or nowadays "passed."

Exposition: Fill-in or background information about characters meant to clarify and add to the narrative; the initial plot element that precedes the buildup of conflict.

Foreshadowing: An author gives a clue or hint about what is going to happen in the story. This can be revealed through a chapter title, through dialogue, or through an event in the story.

Hyperbole: Exaggeration for a specific effect. An example from Shakespeare's *Merchant of Venice*:

> Why, if two gods should play some heavenly match
> And on the wager play two earthly women,
> And Portia one, there must be something else
> Pawned with the other, for the poor rude world
> Hath not her fellow.

Irony: An unexpected disparity between what is written or stated and what is really meant or implied by the author. Verbal, dramatic, and situational are the three literary ironies. Verbal irony is when an author says one thing and means something else. Dramatic irony is when an audience perceives something that a character in the literature does not know. Irony of situation is a discrepancy between the expected result and actual results. Shakespeare's plays contain numerous and highly effective use of irony. O. Henry's short stories have ironic endings.

Metaphor: Indirect comparison between two things. It is the use of a word or phrase denoting one kind of object or action in place of another to suggest a comparison between them. While poets use them extensively, they are also integral to everyday speech. For example, chairs are said to have "legs" and "arms" although we know that humans and other animals have these appendages.

Motif: A key, oft-repeated phrase, name, or idea in a literary work. Dorset and Wessex in Thomas Hardy's novels and the moors and the harsh weather in the Brontë sisters' novels are effective use of motifs. Shakespeare's *Romeo and Juliet* represents the ill-fated "young lovers" motif.

Personification: Human characteristics are attributed to an inanimate object, abstract quality, or animal. For example, John Bunyan wrote characters named Death, Knowledge, Giant Despair, Sloth, and Piety in *The Pilgrim's Progress.* The metaphor of an arm of a chair is a form of personification. Carl Sandburg, in his poem "Fog," writes: "The fog comes / on little cat feet. // It sits looking / over harbor and city / on silent haunches / and then moves on."

Simile: Direct comparison between two things using "like," "as," or "such as." For example: "My love is like a red, red rose."

Soliloquy: A highlighted speech, in drama, usually delivered by a major character expounding on the author's philosophy or expressing, at times, universal truths. This is done with the character alone on the stage, as in Hamlet's famous "To be or not to be" soliloquy.

Stream of consciousness: A style of writing that reflects the mental processes of the characters expressing, at times, jumbled memories, feelings, and dreams. James

Joyce, Virginia Woolf, and William Faulkner use stream of consciousness in their writings.

Symbolism: A symbol is an object or action that can be observed with the senses in addition to suggesting many other things. The lion is a symbol of courage; the cross a symbol of Christianity; the color green a symbol of envy.

These can almost be defined as metaphors because society agrees on the one-to-one meaning of them. Symbols used in literature are usually of a different sort. They tend to be private and personal; their significance is evident only in the context of the work where they are used. A good example of a symbol in poetry is the mending wall in Robert Frost's poem "Mending Wall."

A symbol can certainly have more than one meaning, and the meaning may be as personal as the memories and experiences of the particular reader. In analyzing a poem or story, students should identify the symbols and their possible meanings.

Look for a character with the name of a prophet who does little but utter prophecy or a trio of women who resemble the Three Fates. A symbol may be a part of a person's body, such as the eye of the murder victim in Edgar Allan Poe's story "The Tell-Tale Heart" or a look, voice, or mannerism.

Some things a symbol is not: an abstraction such as truth, death, and love; in narrative, a well-developed character who is not at all mysterious; or the second term in a metaphor. In Emily Dickinson's "The Lightning Is a Yellow Fork," the symbol is the lightning, not the fork.

Synecdoche: A synecdoche is a figure of speech in which the word for part of something is used to mean the whole; for example, "sail" for "boat," or vice versa.

Skill 5.3   Demonstrate knowledge of point of view, tone, voice, and mood in literary prose

Style, Mood, and Tone
Writers often have an emotional stake in their subject. Their purpose is to convey those feelings, either explicitly or implicitly, to the readers. In such cases, the writing is generally subjective—that is, it stems from opinions, judgments, values, ideas, and feelings.

In literature, style refers to a distinctive manner of expression and applies to all levels of language, beginning at the phonemic level with word choices, alliteration, assonance, and so on; and moving to the syntactic level, characterized by length of sentences, choice of structure and phraseology (diction), and patterns; and even extending beyond the sentence to paragraphs and chapters.

Critical readers can determine what is distinctive about the writer's use of these elements. All of the author's style choices are instrumental in creating tone. The tone of a written passage is the author's attitude toward the subject matter. The tone (mood, feeling) is revealed through the qualities of the writing and is a direct product of such stylistic elements as language and sentence structure.

The tone of a written passage is much like a speaker's voice; instead of being spoken, however, it is the product of words on a page. Tone may be thought of as the author's attitude toward the subject matter of a written passage, revealed through word choice and sentence structure. Below is a statement about snakes that demonstrates tone:

Many species of snakes live in Florida. Some of those species, both poisonous and nonpoisonous, have habitats that coincide with those of human residents of the state.

The voice of the writer in this statement is neutral. The sentences are declarative (not exclamations or fragments or questions). The adjectives are few and nondescript—many, some, poisonous (balanced with nonpoisonous). Nothing much in this brief paragraph would alert readers to the feelings of the writer about snakes. The paragraph has a neutral, objective, detached, and impartial tone.

If the writer's attitude toward snakes involved admiration, or even affection, the tone would generally be positive:

Florida's snakes are a tenacious bunch. When they find their habitats invaded by humans, they cling to their home territories as long as they can, as if vainly attempting to fight off the onslaught of the human hordes.

The writer uses adjectives like tenacious to describe feelings about snakes. The writer also humanizes the reptiles, making them brave, beleaguered creatures.

If the writer's attitude toward snakes involved active dislike and fear, then the tone would reflect that attitude:

Countless species of snakes, some more dangerous than others, still lurk on the urban fringes of Florida's towns and cities. They will often invade domestic spaces, terrorizing people and their pets.

Here, obviously, the snakes are the villains. They lurk, they invade, and they terrorize. In the same manner, a writer can use language to portray characters as good or bad. A writer uses positive and negative adjectives, as seen above, to convey the manner of a character.

Voice
A verb is in the active voice when its subject is the doer of the action. A verb is in the passive voice when its subject is the receiver of the action.

TEACHER CERTIFICATION STUDY GUIDE

Active voice	Passive voice
The director adjourned the meeting. *The subject (the director) performs the action (adjourning the meeting).*	The meeting was adjourned by the director. *The subject (the meeting) is not performing the action; instead, it is receiving the action (was adjourned).*
"You know, at one time, I <u>used to break</u> into pet shops to liberate the canaries. But I <u>decided</u> that was an idea way before its time. Zoos are full, prisons are overflowing. Oh my, how the world still dearly <u>loves</u> a cage."	America <u>was discovered</u> accidentally by a great seaman who was looking for something else... America <u>was named</u> after a man who discovered no part of the New World. History is like that, very chancy."

"In the beginning the Universe <u>was created</u>. This has made a lot of people angry and <u>has been widely regarded</u> as a bad move."

How do you recognize passive voice? Look at the verb. A passive-voice verb has at least two parts:

1. A form of the verb to be (am, is, are, was, were, be, been)
2. A past participle form of the main verb (thrown, driven, planted, talked)

In addition, you can check for the following features of the passive voice:

- Sometimes the subject is in an object position in the sentence.
- Watch for a "by" statement between the verb phrase and the object.
- Sometimes the doer is not even present.

Point of View
Point of view seems simple on the surface, but it rarely is in a story. In fact, Edmund Wallace Hildick wrote *Thirteen Types of Narrative* to explain point of view. In literature, a story told in the first person is told from the point of view of the narrator. In this point of view, the only clues as to what the characters are like come from the narrator. The attitude of the narrator toward the theme or the characters will be an important part of the story and should be dealt with in an analysis. Sometimes, it's apparent that the narrator's view does not square with reality. In this case, the narrator becomes unreliable and readers must determine what is real and what is not. If a writer uses this device, it's essential that the analyst point it out and analyze what it does for the story.

The first-person narrator may know what one or more of the characters are thinking, and that will be important to the analysis of the story. If the narrator knows this, how did he or she acquire the knowledge? The most logical way is that that character or those characters told the story to the narrator in the first place.

Third-person objective is another common form of development. In this point of view, there is no narrator. An unseen observer tells the story. Readers do not know what anyone is thinking, only what is being said and described.

Third-person omniscient is also fairly common. In this point of view, the story is being told by an unseen observer, but the observer is able to know what at least one person is thinking, which is sometimes called limited omniscient point of view. Readers may also know what most or all of the characters are thinking, and this point of view is called third-person omniscient.

In more modern works, works told in the third person usually concentrate on the point of view of one character or the changes in point of view are clearly delineated, as in *Cold Mountain*, by Charles Frazier, who names each chapter after the person whose point of view is being shown.

Point of view is extremely powerful in the way a story is perceived and must be dealt with in a written analysis.

Skill 5.4   Identify and interpret structural elements in literary prose (denouement and flashback)

Structural elements in literary texts form a significant part of how we read and interpret literature and have influenced narration in other forms of media such as film. These elements may allow an author to tell a story without having to tell it in a solely linear fashion (flashback), or they may be what allows a story to end (denouement).

The flashback allows authors to begin a story in the middle of the action and then "flash back" to the past so that readers can discover how events in the story have unfolded. Flashbacks can be used several times in the narrative throughout the text. They can be used to create suspense, provide more depth for characters, and elaborate on the inner conflict of a character. Here is an example of a flashback from Howard Norman's novel *The Bird Artist*:

My name is Fabian Vas. I live in Witless Bay, Newfoundland. You would not have heard of me. Obscurity is not necessarily failure, though; I am a bird artist, and have more or less made a living at it. Yet I murdered the lighthouse keeper, Botho August, and that is an equal part of how I think of myself.

I discovered my gift for drawing and painting birds early on.

With this new paragraph, readers' attention is drawn to the structure that the narrator is about to flash back in time to narrate something from his past.

Denouement

The denouement of a story is something that all readers expect when they are reading a story, thus it is a structural element of literary prose. The denouement ties loose ends together after the climax; it is the true end of the story. If readers read literature that ended right after the climax finished, it would throw them off because it is not what we are used to reading.

Sometimes an author deliberately leaves out the denouement in order to keep readers in suspense until another book in a series is published. Readers know that another book is coming, so they are not confused by the ending of the book they are currently reading.

Structural elements like flashbacks are so rooted in our reading experiences that they allow authors the freedom to step out of space and time in the telling of the story. Structural elements like denouement can sometimes limit an author from doing something radically different with the narrative of a particular work of literary prose.

Skill 5.5   Evaluate the effect of words and word combinations in literary prose

Language as a medium of communication is often open to interpretation because it is imprecise. This is true in literature, though the degree to which language plays a role in analyzing a work varies based on the writer's style, the particular work, and/or the genre of writing. Shakespeare is perhaps the classic example of an English language writer whose use of language is absolutely essential to the understanding of a work.

Every work of literary prose consists of building blocks of words. The ways in which authors string these words together to form meaningful passages, paragraphs, and pages is a craft that is worthy of study and analysis.

(To analyze the effect of words and word combinations in literary prose, see Skill 5.2 on figurative language and literary devices and Skill 5.3 on voice, tone, mood, and point of view.)

Skill 5.6   Analyzing elements of fiction (plot, character, setting) in a literary text

The analysis of prose, similar to the analysis of poetry, also calls for attention to structural elements so as to discern meaning, purpose, and themes. The author's intentions are gleaned through the elements he or she uses and how they are used. Because your written response questions will most likely include either poetry or prose within the prompt, it's critical to deeply analyze all structural elements (plot, characters, setting, and point of view). This will help you support your own claims and give you the best opportunity for a high score on the writing portion.

Plot

The plot is the sequence of events (it may or may not be chronological) that the author chooses to include in the story—both the underlying story and the externals of the occurrences the author relates. An author may use flashbacks to tell the backstory (or what happened before the current events begin). Often, authors begin their stories in medias res (in the middle of things) and, over time, supply the details of what has gone before to provide a clearer picture to readers of all the relevant events.

Sometimes an author tells parallel stories to make his or her point. For example, in Leo Tolstoy's classic *Anna Karenina*, the unhappy extramarital affair of Anna Karenina and Count Vronsky is contrasted with the happy marriage of Lev and Kitty through the use of alternating chapters devoted to each couple. The plot consists of the progress of each couple: Anna and Count Vronsky into deeper neurosis, obsession, and emotional pain, and Lev and Kitty into deeper and more meaningful partnership through growing emotional intimacy, parenthood, and caring for members of their extended family.

In well-written novels, each part of the plot is necessary and has a purpose. For example, in *Anna Karenina*, a chapter is devoted to a horse race Count Vronsky participates in. This might seem like mere entertainment, but, in fact, Vronsky is riding his favorite mare and, in a moment of carelessness in taking a jump, puts the whole weight of his body on the mare's back, breaking it. The horse must be shot. Vronsky loved and admired the mare, but being overcome by a desire to win, he kills the very thing he loves. Similarly, Anna descends into obsession and jealousy as their affair isolates her from society and separates her from her child, and she ultimately kills herself. The chapter symbolizes the destructive effect that Vronsky's love, coupled with inordinate desire, has upon what and whom he loves.

Other authors use repetitious plotlines to reveal the larger story over time. For example, in Joseph Heller's tragicomedy *Catch-22*, the novel repeatedly returns to a horrific incident in an airplane during a combat mission. Each time the protagonist, Yossarian, recalls the incident, more detail is revealed. Readers know from the beginning that this incident is key to why Yossarian wants to be discharged from the army, but it is not until the full details of the gruesome incidents are revealed late in the book that they discover why the incident has driven Yossarian almost mad. Interspersed with comedic and ironic episodes, the book's climax (the full revealing of the incident) remains powerfully with the readers, showing the absurdity, insanity, and inhumanity of war. The comic device of *Catch-22*, a fictitious army rule from which the title is derived, makes this point in a funny way: The book states that a soldier cannot be discharged from the army unless he is crazy; yet, if he wants to be discharged from the army, he is not crazy. This rule seems to embody the insanity, absurdity, and inhumanity of war.

Characters

Characters usually represent or embody an idea or ideal acting in the world. For example, in the Harry Potter series, Harry Potter's goodness, courage, and unselfishness, as well as his capacity for friendship and love, make him a powerful opponent to Lord Voldemort, whose selfishness, cruelty, and isolation make him the leader of the evil forces in the epic battle of good versus evil. Memorable characters are many-sided: Harry is not only brave, strong, and true, he is also vulnerable and sympathetic; orphaned as a child, bespectacled, and often misunderstood by his peers, Harry is not a stereotypical hero.

Charles Dickens's *Oliver Twist* is the principle of goodness, oppressed and unrecognized, unleashed in a troubled world. Oliver encounters a great deal of evil, which he refuses to cooperate with, and also a great deal of good in people who have sympathy for his plight. In contrast to the gentle, kindly, and selfless Maylie, who take Oliver in, recognizing his goodness, are the evil Bill Sykes and Fagin—thieves and murderers—who are willing to sell and hurt others for their own gain. When Nancy, a thief in league with Sykes and Fagin, essentially "sells" herself to help Oliver, she represents redemption from evil through sacrifice.

Setting
The setting of a work of fiction adds a great deal to the story. Historical fiction relies firmly on an established time and place: Esther Forbes's *Johnny Tremain* takes place in revolutionary Boston; the story could not take place anywhere else or at any other time. Ray Bradbury's *Most Dangerous Game* requires an isolated, uninhabited island for its plot. Settings are sometimes changed in a work to represent different periods of a person's life or to compare and contrast life in the city or life in the country.

Skill 5.7   Identify and analyze central ideas or themes in literary prose

"*If there were only one truth, you couldn't paint a hundred canvases on the same theme.* " —Pablo Picasso

Theme in a work of fiction is similar to a thesis in an essay. It's the point the story makes. In a story, it may possibly be spoken by one of the characters, but more often, it is left to the writer to determine. This requires careful reading and should take into account the other aspects of the story before a firm decision is made with regard to the point of the story. Different analysts will come to different conclusions about what a story means. Often the thesis of an analytical essay will be the writer's declaration of the theme according to an individual well-reasoned opinion.

Why did the author write this story? This question will lead to the theme—the underlying main idea. Whether a story is escapist or interpretive, it will have a controlling idea that is integral to its development. This idea is more than a topic (love, anger, guilt, jealousy); it is the author's view of the moral.

Sometimes the title of a story will help reveal the theme. For example, in "The Tell-Tale Heart," Edgar Allan Poe tells us a story about guilt and the effect it has on one's conscience. The title foreshadows the outcome and helps readers understand how all these elements contribute to an effective story.

The theme can be said to be the meaning of a story, the glue that holds the story together, and often the big idea that resonates with diverse readers and reading interactions. It is crucial for readers to be able to identify the theme or themes of a work of literary prose so that they can understand the big picture and both the way in which the text is situated in time and space and in the almost timeless way in which the text is part of a series of works addressing the human condition.

OBJECTIVE 6   ANALYZING AND INTERPRETING POETRY

Skill 6.1   Evaluate the characteristics of various forms of poetry (e.g., epic, sonnet, haiku)

Poetry is the use of words to convey image and emotion. Poetry is often less explicit than prose, relying on implication and suggestion rather than overt statement of fact. Poetry is not always concerned with realism, often shirking basic tenets of grammar and syntax for better artistic effect. There are few true "answers" in poetry, as poems are often interpreted in a variety of ways, but certain conclusions can be drawn from a close reading of the text.

Below are some characteristics of different forms of poetry. This list is not complete but rather a sample to help you learn to identify characteristics that differentiate various forms.

Narrative Poetry
The greatest difficulty in analyzing narrative poetry is that it partakes of many genres. It can have all the features of poetry—meter, rhyme, verses, and stanzas—but it can also have all the features of prose, not only fictional prose but also nonfictional. It can have a protagonist, characters, conflicts, action, plot, climax, theme, and tone. It can also be a persuasive discourse and have a thesis (real or derived) and supporting points. The arrangement of an analysis will depend to a great extent on the peculiarities of the poem itself. In drama that follows a narrative arc, reaching the climax too soon undermines the dramatic impact of the remaining portion of the performance, whereas reaching it too late rushes the ending and creates a jarringly abrupt end to events. Narrative poetry has been very much a part of the output of modern American writers, totally apart from epics. Many of Emily Dickinson's poems are narrative in form and retain the features we look for in the finest of American poetry. The first two verses of "A Narrow Fellow in the Grass" illustrate the use of narrative in a poem:

A narrow fellow in the grass
Occasionally rides;
You may have met him—did you not?
His notice instant is.
The grass divides as with a comb,
A spotted shaft is seen;
And then it closes at your feet
And opens further on. . . .

This is certainly narrative in nature and has many of the aspects of prose narrative. At the same time, it is a poem with rhyme, meter, verses, and stanzas and can be analyzed as such.

Epic Poetry

In an epic, the conflicts take place in the social sphere rather than the personal sphere. An epic has a historical basis or one that is accepted as historical. The conflict is between opposing nations or races and involves diverging views of civilization that are the foundation of the conflict.

Often an epic poem will involve the pitting of a group that conceives of itself as a "higher" civilization against a "lower" civilization and, more often than not, divine will determines that the "higher" civilization wins, exerting its force over the lower, barbarous, and profane enemy. Examples are the conflict of Greece with Troy, the fates of Rome with the Carthaginian and the Italian, the Crusaders with the Saracen, or even of Milton's Omnipotent versus Satan.

In analyzing these works, the protagonist and antagonist need to be clearly identified, the conflicts clearly established, and the climax and final outcome (that presumably sets the world right) clearly shown. At the same time, the form of the epic as a poem must be considered. What meter, rhyme scheme, verse form, and stanza form has the author chosen to tell the story? Is the form consistent? If it varies, where does it vary and what does the variation do for the poem/story? What about figures of speech? Does the author use alliteration or onomatopoeia? The epic is a major literary form historically, although it began to fall out of favor by the end of the seventeenth century.

At that time the short story and the novel began to take over the genre. There have been notable efforts to produce an American epic, but these efforts always seem to slide into prose. Even so, some would say that *Moby Dick* is an American epic.

Lyric Poetry

The Greek poets used to sing their poetry and accompany their songs by playing a lyre. Thus a musical quality characterizes the many types of lyric poetry.

Ballad

A ballad is also a genre of music or song and shares with its poetic counterpart a strong theme usually relating to love, religion, or tragedy. The ballad, as with lyric poetry, began as a song and then in the nineteenth century transformed more into a written genre with the help of poets like Samuel Taylor Coleridge and William Wordsworth.

Here is an excerpt from William Butler Yeats's "The Ballad of Father Gilligan":

The old priest, Peter Gilligan,
Was weary night and day;
For half his flock were in their beds,
Or under green sods lay.

Once, while he nodded on a chair,
At the moth-hour of eve,
Another poor man sent for him,
And he began to grieve.

Blank Verse

Poetry that is written in iambic pentameter but unrhymed is blank verse. Works by Williams Shakespeare and John Milton are epitomes of blank verse. Milton's *Paradise Lost* states:

Illumine, what is low raise and support,
That to the height of this great argument
I may assert Eternal Providence
And justify the ways of God to men.

Cinquain

A cinquain is a poem with a five-line stanza. American poet Adelaide Crapsey called a five-line verse form a cinquain and invented a particular meter for it. Similar to the haiku, there are two syllables in the first and last lines, and four, six, and eight syllables in the middle three lines. It has a mostly iambic cadence. Her poem, "November Night," is an example:

Listen…
With faint dry sound
Like steps of passing ghosts,
the leaves, frost-crisp'd, break from the trees
And fall.

Haiku

Haiku is a popular unrhymed form that is limited to 17 syllables arranged in three lines with five, seven, and five syllables. This verse form originated in Japan in the seventeenth century where it is accepted as serious poetry and is Japan's most popular form. Originally, a haiku was to deal with the season, time of day, and landscape. Although as it has come into more common use, the subjects have become less restricted. The imagist poets and other English writers used the form or imitated it. It's a form much used in classrooms to introduce students to the writing of poetry.

Here's an example by Japanese poet Kobayashi Issa, translated by American poet Robert Hass:

New Year's morning—
everything is in blossom!
I feel about average.

Analysis of a cinquain and a haiku poem should focus on form first. Does the haiku poem conform to the 17-syllable requirement, and is it arranged in a five-, seven-, and five-syllable pattern? For a cinquain, does it have only five lines? Does the poem distill the words so that as much meaning as possible can be conveyed? Does it treat a serious subject? Is the theme discernable? Short forms like these seem simple to dash off; however, they are not effective unless the words are chosen and pared down so that the meaning intended is conveyed. The impact should be forceful, and that often takes more effort, skill, and creativity than longer forms. Students should consider all of this in their analyses.

Metaphysical Poetry
This type of verse is characterized by ingenious wit, unparalleled imagery, and clever conceits. The greatest metaphysical poet is John Donne. Henry Vaughn and other seventeenth-century British poets contributed to this movement as in Vaughn's "World": "I saw eternity the other night, like a great ring of pure and endless light."

Ode
The Greek poets used to sing their poetry and accompany their songs with a lyre. This musical quality characterizes the many types of lyric poetry. An ode is an example of this type of poetry. An ode is a poem that expresses a strong feeling about a person, event, or thing.

Here is an excerpt from William Wordsworth's "Ode on Intimations of Immortality from Recollections of Early Childhood":

There was a time when meadow, grove, and stream,
The earth, and every common sight
To me did seem
Apparelled in celestial light,
The glory and the freshness of a dream.
It is not now as it hath been of yore;—
Turn wheresoe'er I may,
By night or day,
The things which I have seen I now can see no more.

And another example from Pablo Neruda's playful "Ode to a Large Tuna in the Market":

Here,
among the market vegetables,
this torpedo
from the ocean
depths,
a missile
that swam,
now
lying in front of me
dead.

Sonnet

A poetic form that originated in Italy, a sonnet consists of 14 lines that follow a clear alternating rhyme scheme. Conventions of sonnets have shifted through the centuries, and the form has proved popular in England, Italy, and France. Here is an example from Mary Elizabeth Frye's "Do Not Stand at My Grave and Weep":

Do not stand at my grave and weep:
I am not there; I do not sleep.
I am a thousand winds that blow,
I am the diamond glints on snow,
I am the sun on ripened grain,
I am the gentle autumn rain.
When you awaken in the morning's hush
I am the swift uplifting rush
Of quiet birds in circling flight.
I am the soft starshine at night.
Do not stand at my grave and cry:
I am not there; I did not die.

This sonnet showcases much of what is attractive about the form to poets. The simple rhyme scheme is unpretentious and readable, and the poem's format lends itself well to repetition. The repeated "I am's" create a soothing rhythm, sort of a lullaby quality. The subject matter is bittersweet, as with many sonnets that have explored romance, mortality, or spirituality. The first and last two lines mirror each other, suggesting change and finality. The poem's subject matter insists we not fear the end, and this is reflected in the sonnet's form.

Tanka

Like the haiku, a tanka is a type of Japanese poetry. It consists of 31 syllables organized by five lines in the following syllabic pattern: 5/7/5/7/7. Like the sonnet, the tanka is framed around a central subject with a split between a focus on the subject and a focus on the narrator's response to that subject. Here is an example from Tada Chimako's "A Spray of Water":

*the round spoon
with the curvature
of a concave mirror
scoops out my eye
and swallows it*

Villanelle

A villanelle is a 19-line poem consisting of two choruses or refrains and two repeating rhymes. The structure is formal in terms of rhyme scheme. One of the most famous examples of a villanelle is Dylan Thomas's "Do Not Go Gentle into That Good Night":

*Do not go gentle into that good night,
Old age should burn and rave at close of day;
Rage, rage against the dying of the light.*

*Though wise men at their end know dark is right,
Because their words had forked no lightning they
Do not go gentle into that good night.*

*Good men, the last wave by, crying how bright
Their frail deeds might have danced in a green bay,
Rage, rage against the dying of the light.*

*Wild men who caught and sang the sun in flight,
And learn, too late, they grieved it on its way,
Do not go gentle into that good night.
Grave men, near death, who see with blinding sight
Blind eyes could blaze like meteors and be gay,
Rage, rage against the dying of the light.*

*And you, my father, there on the sad height,
Curse, bless, me now with your fierce tears, I pray.
Do not go gentle into that good night.
Rage, rage against the dying of the light.*

To distinguish the characteristics of different forms of poetry, readers should evaluate a poem by looking at:

- The pattern of the sound and rhythm
- The visible shape it takes
- The type of rhyme or verse
- The theme or subject

Skill 6.2   Demonstrate knowledge of how poetic devices are used in a poem

Poetry, one of the densest forms of communications, is embedded with meaning. For readers to appreciate all that a poem can communicate, they should be able to peel away the layers to find the depth of meaning. One way they can do this is by understanding some of the poetic or literary devices that poets use to craft their work:

Allusion
The use of allusion is a sort of shortcut for poets. They can use an economy of words and count on meaning to come from the reader's own experience.

Apostrophe
This literary device addresses an absent or dead person, an abstract idea, or an inanimate object. Sonneteers such as Sir Thomas Wyatt, John Keats, and William Wordsworth address the moon, stars, and the dead Milton. For example, in William Shakespeare's *Julius Caesar*, Mark Antony addresses the corpse of Caesar in the speech that begins: "O, pardon me, thou bleeding piece of earth / That I am meek and gentle with these butchers! / Thou art the ruins of the noblest man / That ever lived in the tide of times. / Woe to the hand that shed this costly blood!"

Conceit
Conceit is a comparison, usually in verse, between seemingly disparate objects or concepts. John Donne's metaphysical poetry contains many clever conceits. For instance, "The Flea" compares a flea bite to the act of love, and in "A Valediction: Forbidding Mourning," separated lovers are likened to the legs of a compass, the leg drawing the circle, eventually returning home to "the fixed foot."

Connotation
This is the ripple effect surrounding the implications and associations of a given word, distinct from the denotative or literal meaning. For example, the word "rest" in Hamlet's words "Good night, sweet prince, and flights of angels sing thee to thy rest" refers to a burial.

Imagery
Imagery can be described as a word or sequence of words that refers to any sensory experience—that is, anything that can be seen, tasted, smelled, heard, or felt on the skin or fingers. While prose writers may also use these images, they are most distinctive of poetry. The poet intends to make an experience available to the readers. To do that, the poet must appeal to one of the senses. The one most often used is, of course, the visual sense. The poet will deliberately paint a scene in such a way that the readers can see it. The purpose is not simply to stir the visceral feeling, however, but also to stir the emotions.

A good example is "The Piercing Chill I Feel," by Taniguchi Buson:

The piercing chill I feel:
My dead wife's comb, in our bedroom,
Under my heel . . .

In only a few short words, the readers can feel many things: the shock that might come from touching the corpse, a literal sense of death, the contrast between her death and the memories he has of her when she was alive. Imagery might be defined as speaking of the abstract in concrete terms, a powerful device in the hands of a skillful poet.

Inversion
Inversion is an atypical sentence order to create a given effect or interest. Francis Bacon's and John Milton's work use inversion successfully. Emily Dickinson was fond of arranging words outside of their familiar order. For example in "Chartless," she writes: "Yet know I how the heather looks" and "Yet certain am I of the spot." Instead of saying "Yet I know" and "Yet I am certain," she reverses the usual order and shifts the emphasis to the more significant words.

Irony
Irony is expressing something other than, and often the opposite of, the literal meaning, such as words of praise when blame is intended. In poetry, it is often used as a sophisticated or resigned awareness of contrast between what is and what ought to be and expresses a controlled pathos without sentimentality. It is a form of indirection that avoids overt praise or censure. An early example is the Greek comic character Eiron, a clever underdog who by his wit repeatedly triumphs over the boastful character Alazon.

Paradox
A paradox is a seemingly untrue statement that, when examined, more closely proves to be true. John Donne's sonnet "Death, Be Not Proud" postulates that death shall die and humans will triumph over death, at first thought not true but ultimately explained and proven in this sonnet.

Symbolism
A symbol is an object or action that can be observed with the senses in addition to its suggesting many other things.

Looking for symbols is often challenging, especially for novice poetry readers. These suggestions may be useful, however: First, pick out all the references to concrete objects, such as a newspaper, black cats, or other nouns. Note any that the poet emphasizes by describing in detail, repeating, or placing at the beginning or ending of a poem. Ask yourself, What is the poem about? What does it add up to? Paraphrase the poem and determine whether the meaning depends on certain concrete objects. Then ponder what the concrete object symbolizes in this particular poem.

TEACHER CERTIFICATION STUDY GUIDE

Skill 6.3   Demonstrate knowledge of how figures of speech are used in a poem

Poets use figures of speech to sharpen the effect and meaning of their poems and to help readers see things in ways they have never seen them before. Marianne Moore observed that a fir tree has "an emerald turkey-foot at the top." Her poem makes us aware of something we probably had never noticed before. The sudden recognition of the likeness yields pleasure in the reading. The approach to take in analyzing a poem on the basis of its figures of speech is to ask the questions: What does it do for the poem? Does it underscore meaning? Does it intensify understanding? Does it increase the intensity of our response?

Hyperbole

Hyperbole is deliberate exaggeration for dramatic or comic effect. Here is an example from Shakespeare's *Merchant of Venice*:

> *Why, if two gods should play some heavenly match*
> *And on the wager play two earthly women,*
> *And Portia one, there must be something else*
> *Pawned with the other, for the poor rude world*
> *Hath not her fellow.*

Metaphor

A metaphor is an indirect comparison between two things, denoting one object or action in place of another to suggest a comparison between them. This is distinct from a simile, which directly compares two things using words such as "like" or "as." Here is an example from Sylvia Plath's poem, "Metaphors":

> *I'm a riddle in nine syllables*
> *An elephant, a ponderous house.*
> *A melon strolling on two tendrils.*
> *O red fruit, ivory, fine timbers!*

Appropriately enough, this poem contains several playful metaphors used to describe her pregnancy. Plath uses herself as a subject, comparing her pregnant state to an elephant, a melon, and in several ways to a shelter for the life growing inside her. At first the metaphors seem self-deprecating and humorous, but later in the poem, where she calls herself a "means, a stage" and mentions how she's "boarded the train there's no getting off", the metaphors take on darker connotation as they reflect her dehumanization and resigned acceptance that she's become merely an incubator for the child she now carries.

Metonymy

Metonymy is when you replace the name of something with something else that it's associated with. One example of this is that when you ask someone to give you a hand, you are asking them to help you. Here is a poetic example from Robert Frost's "Out, Out":

*As he swung toward them holding up the hand
Half in appeal, but half as if to keep
The life from spilling*

In this case, the word "life" has replaced the word "blood." Blood is something we associate with life.

Personification
Personification is when human qualities are applied to a nonhuman entity, such as an animal, emotion, object, or something more esoteric. Here is an example from Langston Hughes's "April Rain Song":

*Let the rain kiss you
Let the rain beat upon your head with silver liquid drops
Let the rain sing you a lullaby*

In this poem, Hughes suggests that the rain has the human ability to kiss and sing. Rather than merely describing pleasant, "realistic" aspects of rain, he personifies it as a friendly, motherly figure to better describe his feelings toward rain.

Simile
A simile is a direct comparison between two things using the words "like," "as," and "such as." For example: "My love is like a red-red rose."

Poets use figures of speech to sharpen the effect and meaning of their poems and to help readers see things in ways they have never seen them before.

Figurative language allows for the statement of truths that more literal language cannot. Skillfully used, a figure of speech will help readers see more clearly and focus upon particulars. Figures of speech add many dimensions of richness to our reading and understanding of a poem; they also allow many opportunities for worthwhile analysis.

The approach to take in analyzing a poem on the basis of its figures of speech is to ask the following questions:

- What does it do for the poem?
- Does it underscore meaning?
- Does it intensify understanding?
- Does it increase the intensity of our response?

Skill 6.4   Demonstrate knowledge of point of view, tone, voice, and mood in a poem

(See Skill 5.3 to read about how to analyze point of view, tone, voice, and mood in a literary work.)

In general, you can use the same strategies to analyze these features in a poem, especially point of view. You can look for words that refer to the speaker and whom the speaker is addressing to quickly determine these features.

One important aspect of point of view is to not just focus on the voice being used to tell the poem but also focus on the perspective from which the poem is being told. In a poem that alludes to the story of *The Three Little Pigs*, for example, even if the poem is using the third-person omniscient point of view, the author may write the poem from the perspective of the wolf. Thus, the point of view would help the readers understand the wolf more than the pigs. Analyzing poetry and literature means going beyond a first read to carefully interpret the ways in which meaning is produced.

Poems are generally shorter than literary works, so mood, point of view, and tone have to be established quickly. Word choice, or diction, become even more important.

Haiku writers know that they have only 22 syllables in which to establish a mood and that the writer of a novel can take a few chapters to do the same thing. Poets choose each word carefully, following the form of the poem and working within its restraints.

When analyzing poetry, it is helpful to try to distinguish between tone and mood if possible. A good way to understand the difference is to see the tone as representing the feelings of the subject or narrator of the poem and the mood as the atmosphere or feeling that the author wants to evoke in the readers. Sometimes there is an interplay between tone and mood when they are different. The author of the poem may want to create tension by, for example, creating a romantic or happy tone but a gloomy or mournful mood. The tension is created because the readers know what the subject of the poem does not, and, with this example, the subject of the poem is unaware that he or she is about to lose his or her happiness or romance.

Skill 6.5 Identify and interpret how stanzaic and metrical structures and verse forms are used in a poem

Poets use literary techniques to enhance the relationship between form and meaning.

Rhythm
In poetry, rhythm refers to the recurrence of stresses at equal intervals. A stress (accent) is a greater amount of force given to one syllable in speaking than is given to another. For example, we put the stress on the first syllable of such words as "father," "mother," "daughter," and "children". The unstressed or unaccented syllable is sometimes called a slack syllable. All English words carry at least one stress except articles and some prepositions such as "by," "from," or "at." Indicating where stresses occur is to scan; doing this is called scansion.

Little is gained in understanding a poem or making a statement about it by merely scanning it. The pattern of the rhythm—the meter—should be analyzed in terms of its overall relationship to the message and impression of the poem.

Slack syllables recur in pairs and cause rhythmic trippings and bouncings; on the other hand, recurrent pairs of stresses create a heavier rocking effect. The rhythm is dependent on the words to convey meaning. Alone, they communicate nothing. When examining the rhythm and meaning of a poem, a good question to ask is whether the rhythm is appropriate to the theme. A bouncing rhythm, for example, might be dissonant in a solemn elegy.

Stops are those places in a poem where the punctuation requires a pause. An end-stopped line is one that ends in a pause. A line that has no punctuation at its end is read with only a slight pause. Called a run-on, the running on of its thought into the next line is called enjambment. Poets use these to underscore, intensify, and communicate meaning.

Rhythm, then, is a pattern of recurrence and in poetry is made up of stressed and relatively unstressed syllables. The poet can manipulate the rhythm by making the intervals between stresses regular or varied, by making lines short or long, by end-stopping lines or running them over, by choosing words that are easier or less easy to say, or by choosing polysyllabic words or monosyllables. What's important to remember about rhythm is that it conveys meaning.

The basic unit of rhythm is called a **foot** and is usually one stressed syllable with one or two unstressed ones or two stressed syllables with one unstressed one. A foot made up of one unstressed syllable and one stressed one is called an **iamb**. If a line is made of five iambs, it is **iambic pentameter**. A rhymed poem typically establishes a pattern such as iambic pentameter, and even though there will be syllables that don't fit the pattern, the poem will nevertheless be said to be in iambic pentameter. In fact, a poem may be considered weak if the rhythm is too monotonous.

Some typical patterns of English poetry:

- Alexandrine: a line of iambic hexameter
- Ballad stanza: four iambic feet in lines 1 and 3, three in lines 2 and 4; rhyming is abcb
- Blank verse: unrhymed iambic pentameter
- Couplet: two-line stanza, usually rhymed and typically not separated by white space
- Free verse: no conventional patterns of rhyme, stanza, or meter
- Heroic couplet or closed couplet: two rhymed lines of iambic pentameter, the first ending in a light pause, the second more heavily end-stopped
- Quatrain: four-line stanza, the most popular in English
- Refrain: a line or lines repeated in a ballad as a chorus
- Tercet: a three-line stanza that, if rhymed, usually keeps to one rhyme sound

English Language Arts

- Five-line stanza: does not frequently occur
- Six-line stanza: occurs more frequently than five-line ones
- Rime royal: seven-line stanza in iambic pentameter with rhyme ababbcc
- Octava rima: eight-line stanza of iambic pentameter with rhyme abababcc
- Spenserian stanza: nine lines, with rhyme ababbcbcc for eight lines, then concludes with an Alexandrine
- Terza rima: the middle line of the tercet rhymes with the first and third lines of the next tercet

Meter

Meter is the basic rhythmic structure of a poem, the "music" of it. Some poetic forms prescribe their own metrical structure, but other poets invent or modify their own.

Shall I compare thee to a summer's day?
Thou art more lovely and more temperate
Rough winds do shake the darling buds of May,
And summer's lease hath all too short a date.
—William Shakespeare, "Sonnet 18"

Almost any poem could be said to have some form of meter, but Shakespeare's "iambic pentameter" is among the most famous styles. This metrical style is divided into five iambs per line, each containing a stressed and unstressed syllable. The pattern could be described as "ba-BUM, ba-BUM, ba-BUM," not unlike the beating of a heart. This metrical rhythm permeates Shakespeare's work, proving attractive to actors who appreciate the clear, emphatic delivery.

Stanza

A stanza is a group of lines, offset by punctuation or spacing, forming a metrical unit or verse in a poem.

Do not go gentle into that good night,
Old age should burn and rave at close of day;
Rage, rage against the dying of the light.
Though wise men at their end know dark is right,
Because their words had forked no lightning they
Do not go gentle into that good night.
—Dylan Thomas, "Do Not Go Gentle into That Good Night"

Each short stanza contains three lines and ends with either "do not go gentle into that good night" or "rage, rage against the dying of the light." This ending rhyme repeats throughout the entire poem, ensuring that each stanza delivers the essential message in a profound and affecting way.

Meters in Poetry

- Monometer: a line of one foot

- Dimeter: a line of two feet
- Trimeter: a line of three feet
- Tetrameter: a line of four feet
- Pentameter: a line of five feet
- Hexameter: a line of six feet
- Heptameter: a line of seven feet
- Octameter: a line of eight feet

Longer lines are possible, but readers tend to break them up into shorter lengths.

Caesura

A caesura is a pause, usually signaled by punctuation, in a line of poetry. The earliest usage occurs in *Beowulf*, an epic dating from the Anglo-Saxon era. Here is a more modern example from Alexander Pope.

To err is human, / to forgive, divine

Couplet

A couplet is a pair of rhyming lines with the same meter. A "heroic couplet" is a couplet in iambic pentameter that is "self-contained" and not enjambed. Shakespeare often ended his sonnets with a heroic couplet, allowing the piece to build toward a climactic, self-contained final rhyme that delivered the sonnet's chief message. Here is an example from Alexander Pope's "Rape of the Lock":

Sol thro' white Curtains shot a tim'rous Ray,
And op'd those Eyes that must eclipse the Day;
Now Lapdogs give themselves the rowzing Shake,
And sleepless Lovers, just at Twelve, awake

This poem is a satirical narrative poem written entirely in heroic couplets. The subject matter of the piece, regarding a baron's attempts to gain a lock of a woman's hair, is silly and banal. Thus, the constant use of triumphant, heroic couplets renders the whole thing a bizarre parody.

Enjambment

An enjambed line flows into the next without a break. No punctuation divides one line from the next; it simply continues. Here is an example from T. S. Eliot's "Waste Land":

April is the cruellest month, breeding
Lilacs out of the dead land, mixing
Memory and desire, stirring
Dull roots with spring rain.

Eliot's use of enjambment in this poem creates a sense of suspense. The action of breeding, mixing, and stirring are lent equal or superior importance to the actual subjects these actions are done to. The enjambment also creates a slant rhyme as well, with each line ending on an "-ing" until we arrive at "rain."

Free Verse
This kind of poetry avoids an identifiable meter or rhyme scheme and could be said to be "free." The style became more popular among the avant-garde, modern, and postmodern poets. It was comparatively rare in classical poetry. Here is an example from e. e. cummings's "i carry your heart with me":

> i carry your heart with me(i carry it in
> my heart)i am never without it(anywhere
> i go you go,my dear;and whatever is done
> by only me is your doing,my darling)

cummings's style shirked literary conventions, creating poems that challenged traditional assumptions about form and aesthetic appeal through his use of strange capitalization, heavy enjambment, and free verse. His poems defy clear explanation, but some critics suggest he wrote in this manner to evoke a childish, earnest state of mind.

Quatrain
A quatrain is a poetic stanza composed of four lines. A Shakespearean or Elizabethan sonnet is made up of three quatrains and ends with a heroic couplet.

To appreciate the craft and meaning in poetry, readers should learn how poetic meter and stanza structures relate to the poem's overall effect.

Skill 6.6 Identify and interpret formal rhyme schemes and sound devices in a poem

Sound devices and rhyme schemes help give a poem life, as poetry is often meant to be spoken, read, or performed in some way. Although not all poems follow rhyme schemes, many do and these schemes influence the meaning and effect of the poem as well as helping readers identify the form of poetry.

Alliteration
Alliteration occurs when the initial sounds of a word, beginning with either a consonant or a vowel, are repeated in close succession. Examples include "Athena and Apollo," "Nate never knows," and "people who pen poetry."

Note that the words only have to be close to one another: Alliteration that repeats and attempts to connect a number of words is little more than a tongue twister.

The function of alliteration, like rhyme, might be to accentuate the beauty of language in a given context or to unite words or concepts through a kind of repetition. Alliteration, like rhyme, can follow specific patterns. Sometimes the consonants aren't always the initial ones, but they are generally the stressed syllables. Alliteration is less common than rhyme, but because it is less common, it can call our attention to a word or line in a poem that might not have the same emphasis otherwise.

In its simplest form, it reinforces one or two consonant sounds. Here is an example from Shakespeare's "Sonnet 12":

When I do count the clock that tells the time.

Some poets have used more complex patterns of alliteration by creating consonants both at the beginning of words and at the beginning of stressed syllables within words.

Here is an example from Percy Bysshe Shelley's "Stanzas Written in Dejection Near Naples":

The City's voice itself is soft like Solitude's

Assonance
If alliteration occurs at the beginning of a word and rhymes at the end, assonance takes the middle territory. Assonance occurs when the vowel sound within a word matches the same sound in a nearby word, but the surrounding consonant sounds are different. Here is an example from Robert Frost's "Stopping by Woods on a Snowy Evening":

And miles to go before I sleep,
And miles to go before I sleep.

The repeated *o* sounds create a sense of speed and urgency. The sound carries us through the line, creating contrast with the *e* sound in "sleep," where both the narrator and reader finally rest. Assonance might be especially effective when rhyme is absent: It gives the poet more flexibility, and it is not typically used as part of a predetermined pattern. Like alliteration, it does not so much determine the structure or form of a poem, but rather it is more ornamental.

Onomatopoeia
These are words used to evoke the sound in its meaning. The early Batman series used "pow," "zap," "whop," "zonk," and "eek" in an onomatopoetic way. It names a thing or action by a vocal imitation of the sound associated with it, such as buzz or hiss or the use of words whose sound suggests the sense. Here is an example from "The Brook," by Alfred Lord Tennyson:

I chatter over stony ways,
In little sharps and trebles,
I bubble into eddying bays,
I babble on the pebbles.

English Language Arts

Rhyme

Rhyme indicates a repeated end sound of lines or words within a poem. Rhymes usually occur at the ends of lines, though they can also be internal. Here is an example from Emily Dickinson's "Because I Could Not Stop for Death":

Because I could not stop for Death
He kindly stopped for me
The Carriage held but just Ourselves
And Immortality.

"Me" and "Immortality" rhyme in this poem, lending a sense of finality to the last line and giving it a pleasing rhythm.

Rhyme Scheme

A rhyme scheme is the pattern of rhymes in each line of a poem. Rhyme schemes are usually indicated with letters. Some poets follow strict rhyme schemes, some shirk them entirely, but most employ repetitive rhyme schemes when aesthetically appropriate and then subvert them for stronger effect. Here is a poem from Dixon Lanier Merritt:

A wonderful bird is the pelican;
His beak can hold more than his belly-can.
He can hold in his beak
Enough food for a week,
Though I'm damned if I know how the hell-he-can!

This is an example of a limerick, a short, humorous poem employing a five-line rhyme scheme. Limericks always follow an aabba rhyme scheme—the first two lines rhyme, the next two shorter lines have a different rhyme, and the fifth line calls back to the original rhyme. Limerick structure is intentionally simplistic, highlighting the absurdity of the subject matter and allowing the poet to focus more on wordplay. The B rhymes of the third and fourth lines build anticipation for the final reveal on the fifth line, where the author can reveal a witty subversion.

Slant Rhyme

A slant rhyme is also known as a "near rhyme," "half rhyme," or "lazy rhyme." Slant rhymes sometimes have the same vowel sounds but different consonants, or the reverse. Slant rhymes are sometimes considered childish or uncreative, but many poets have used them to avoid clichés, create disharmony in a piece, or draw unusual connections between words. Here is an example from William Butler Yeats's "Lines Written in Dejection":

WHEN have I last looked on
The round green eyes and the long wavering bodies
Of the dark leopards of the moon?
All the wild witches, those most noble ladies

"On" and "moon" are slant rhymes, as are "bodies" and "ladies." This could be said to suggest the author's discordant, dejected state of mind. Perhaps in a happier poem these rhymes would be clearer and more musical. But not here.

Skill 6.7   Identify and interpret central ideas or themes in a poetic text

The first step in identifying the central idea or theme in a poetic text is to think about how the structures, language, meter, and sound devices in the poem work together to create an image or feeling.

The next skills required are the same as identifying theme in a literary text. *(See Skill 5.7.)* In a poem, pay close attention to diction. When authors have fewer words to use and when they write within the constraints of a poetic form, words are carefully selected and arranged.

OBJECTIVE 7 UNDERSTANDING WORLD LITERATURE (MAJOR CHARACTERISTICS)

Skill 7.1 Identify major literary genres, styles, and trends in world literatures

A complete understanding of the long history of literature is impossible. Some major influences on modern writing stand out, however.

World Folk Epics
These poems (or sometimes prose works) are an integral part of the worldview of a people. In many cases, they were originally oral texts that were eventually written by a single author or several. Some examples of world folk epics include:

- *Sundiata*, an African epic
- *Tunkashila*, a Native American epic
- *Gilgamesh*, the oldest known epic, from Mesopotamia
- *Aeneid*, a Roman epic

National Myths
A national myth is an inspiring narrative or anecdote about a nation's past. These often overdramatize true events, omit significant historical details, or add details for which there is no evidence. It can be a fictional story that no one takes to be true, such as Paul Bunyan, which was created by French Canadians during the Lower Canada Rebellion of 1837 (also known as the Patriots War), when they revolted against the young English queen. In older nations, national myths may be spiritual and refer to the nation's founding by God or gods or other supernatural beings.

Some national myths in English literature:

- The legend of King Arthur
- Sir Francis Drake
- The Pilgrims and the *Mayflower*
- The legendary ride of Paul Revere
- The last words of Nathan Hale
- George Washington and apocryphal tales about him, such as his cutting down a cherry tree with a hatchet and then facing up to the truth and saying "I cannot tell a lie"

Some Genres and Styles of World Literatures

Genre/style/trend	Characteristics	Part of the world
Magical realism	Incorporation of fantastical elements in realistic fiction	Latin America
Cosmogenic epics (epics that work with mythical narratives)	Combines the epic genre with the cosmogenic myth. Epic: long poem narrating the deeds of a hero Cosmogenic myth: origin of the world or natural phenomena	Middle East, Greece
Bildungsromans	Coming-of-age stories	Northern Europe
Travel narratives	Documented journeys that illuminates places and cultures (those of the writer as much as of the places the writer visits)	Southern Europe
Ghost narratives	Stories of omnipresent ghosts	East Asia, Middle East, Greece
Ghazal poems	Poems about love and loss and beauty with rhyming couplets and a refrain	Anatolia, Middle East, South Asia
Picaresque novels	Adventures of a roguish hero	Spain
Epistolary novels	Stories told through documents or letters	Spain, France, England

(See Skill 7.2 for influential authors and works of world literature, 7.3 for significant movements in world literature, and 7.4 for influential works and genres of oral tradition in world literature.)

Skill 7.2 Identify characteristics of major works and writers in world literature

Different regions of the world have had powerful impacts on literature around the world at different times. Writers from different literary traditions have, at different times, been at the vanguard of innovation in writing. Their ideas and styles have spread to different countries and regions regardless of language. While each of these may continue to have a powerful literary culture, their wider influence may wax and wane over time.

Ancient Greece

Greece will always be foremost in literary assessments for Homer's epics: *The Iliad* and *The Odyssey*. No one except Shakespeare is more often cited. Add to these the works of Plato and Aristotle for philosophy; the dramatists Aeschylus, Euripides, and Sophocles for tragedy; and Aristophanes for comedy. Greece is the cradle not only of democracy but of literature as well.

Africa

African literary greats include South Africans Nadine Gordimer (Nobel Prize for literature) and Peter Abrahams (*Tell Freedom: Memories of Africa*, an autobiography of life in Johannesburg). Chinua Achebe (*Things Fall Apart*) and the poet Wole Soyinka hail from Nigeria. Mark Mathabane wrote an autobiography, *Kaffir Boy,* about growing up in South Africa. Egyptian writer Naguib Mahfouz(*The Cairo Trilogy, The Children of Gebelawi*) and Doris Lessing (The Golden Notebook) from Zimbabwe write about race relations in their respective countries. Because of her radical politics, Lessing was banned from her homeland and the Union of South Africa, as was Alan Paton, whose seemingly simple story, *Cry, the Beloved Country*, helped highlight the injustice of apartheid to the rest of the world.

Central American/Caribbean Literature

The Caribbean and Central America encompass a vast area and cultures that reflect oppression and colonialism by England, Spain, Portugal, France, and the Netherlands. The Caribbean writers include Samuel Selvon (*The Lonely Londoners*) from Trinidad and the poet Armando Valladares of Cuba. Central American authors include dramatist Carlos Solórzano from Guatemala, whose plays include *Doña Beatriz*, *The Hapless*, *The Magician*, and *The Hands of God*.

East Asia

The classical age of Japanese literary achievement includes father and son Kiyotsugu Kan'ami and Motokiyo Zeami, who developed the theatrical experience known as Noh drama to its highest aesthetic degree. The son is said to have authored more than 200 plays, of which 100 are still extant.

Katai Tayama (*The Quilt and Other Stories*) is touted as the father of the genre known as the Japanese confessional novel. He also wrote in the "ism" of naturalism. His works are definitely not for the squeamish.

The "slice of life" psychological writings of Ryunosuke Akutagawa gained him acclaim in the Western world. His short stories, especially "Rashamon" and "In a Grove," are greatly praised for style as well as content.

China, too, has a long, rich literary tradition. Li Po, the T'ang dynasty poet from the Chinese golden age, revealed his interest in folklore by preserving the folk songs and mythology of China. Po further enables his readers to enter into the Chinese philosophy of Taoism and to know this feeling against expansionism during the T'ang dynastic rule. During the T'ang dynasty, which was one of great diversity in the arts, the Chinese version of a short story was created with the help of the monk Jiang Fang. His themes often express love between a man and a woman.

Revered as Japan's most famous female author, Fumiko Hayashi (*Drifting Clouds*) had written more than 270 literary works by the time of her death.

In 1968 the Nobel Prize for literature was awarded to Yasunari Kawabata (*The Sound of the Mountain, The Snow Country*), considered to be his masterpieces. His *Palm-of-the-Hand Stories* takes the essentials of haiku poetry and transforms them into the short story genre.

Modern feminist and political concerns are written eloquently by Ting Ling, who used the pseudonym Chiang Ping-Chih. Her stories reflect her concerns about social injustice and her commitment to the women's movement.

France
France has a multifaceted canon of great literature that is universal in scope, almost always championing a social cause from the poignant short stories of Guy de Maupassant to the poetry of Charles Baudelaire (*Fleurs du Mal*) and the groundbreaking lyrical poetry of Arthur Rimbaud and Paul-Marie Verlaine. Drama in France is best represented by Edmond Rostand's *Cyrano de Bergerac* and the neoclassical dramas of Jean Racine *(Andromaque)* and Pierre Corneille (*El Cid*). The great French novelists include André Gide (*The Immoralist*),, Honoré de Balzac (*Cousin Bette*), Stendhal (*The Red and the Black*), and Alexandre Dumas (*The Three Musketeers* and *The Man in the Iron Mask*).

Additional influential French authors include Victor Hugo, who penned *The Hunchback of Notre-Dame* and *Les Misérables*. Marcel Proust's stream of consciousness (*Remembrance of Things Past*) and Eugène Ionesco (*The Rhinoceros*) contributed to the impressive body of literature written in France.

Finally, modernist French literature is defined by the existentialism of Jean-Paul Sartre (*No Exit*, *The Flies*, *Nausea*); André Malraux (*The Fall*); and Albert Camus (*The Stranger*, *The Plague*), the recipient of the 1957 Nobel Prize for literature; and by the feminist writings of Sidonie-Gabrielle Colette *(Cheri)* and Simone de Beauvoir (*The Second Sex*).

Germany
German poet and playwright Friedrich von Schiller is best known for his historical plays, *William Tell* and *The Maid of Orleans*. He is a leading literary figure in Germany's golden age of literature. Also from Germany, Rainer Maria Rilke, the great lyric poet, is one of the poets of the unconscious, or stream of consciousness. Germany has also

given the world Herman Hesse (*Siddhartha*), Günter Grass (*The Tin Drum*), and Johann Wolfgang von Goethe (*Faust*).

Great Britain
Great Britain has had a large influence on American literary traditions. With a common language and its role as colonial "parent" to the United States, Great Britain influenced early American writers in terms of both style and theme. Later, as the country sought to establish itself as an independent country, the fight for freedom from Great Britain inspired some of America's great early thinkers and writers. Later, as close allies, the two countries shared many of the same experiences (wars, industrialization, an increasingly diverse society) that affected both countries' writers. *(See Skill 7.3)*

Italy
Italy's great writers include Virgil, who wrote the great epic *The Aeneid*; Giovanni Boccaccio (*The Decameron*); and Dante Alighieri (*The Divine Comedy*).

North American Literature
North American literature is divided between the United States, Canada, and Mexico. Canadian writers of note include Margaret Atwood (*The Handmaid's Tale*); Alice Munro, a remarkable short story writer; and Rohinton Mistry (A Fine Balance).Mexican writers include 1990 Nobel Prize–winning poet Octavio Paz (*The Labyrinth of Solitude*), feminist Rosario Castellanos (*The Nine Guardians*), and Carlos Fuentes (*Christopher Unborn, The Death of Artemio Cruz*). *(See Skill 7.3)*

Russia
Russian literature is vast and monumental. Fyodor Dostoyevsky's *Crime and Punishment* and *The Brothers Karamazov* and Leo Tolstoy's *War and Peace* are famous examples of psychological realism. Dostoyevsky's influence on modern writers cannot be overly stressed. Tolstoy's *War and Peace* is the sweeping account of the invasion of Russia and Napoleon's taking of Moscow, abandoned by the Russians. Alexander Pushkin is famous for short stories; Anton Chekhov for drama (*Uncle Vanya, The Three Sisters, The Cherry Orchard*); and Yevgeny Yevtushenko for poetry (*Babi Yar*).

Additional influential Russian authors include Boris Pasternak, who won the Nobel Prize (*Dr. Zhivago*), Aleksandr Solzhenitsyn (*The Gulag Archipelago*), and Ilya Varshavsky, who creates fictional societies that are dystopias.

Scandinavia
Hans Christian Andersen of Denmark contributed to the fairy tale genre with tales such as "The Little Mermaid" and "Thumbelina" as well as stories like "The Ugly Duckling" that have become literary allusions. The social commentary of Henrik Ibsen of Norway startled the world of drama with such issues as feminism (*The Doll's House, Hedda Gabler, The Wild Duck, Ghosts*). Sweden's Selma Lagerlöf is the first woman to ever win the Nobel Prize for literature. Her novels include *Gösta Berling's Saga* and the world-renowned *The Wonderful Adventures of Nils*, a children's work.

Slavic Nations

Austrian writer Franz Kafka (*The Metamorphosis, The Trial, The Castle*) is considered by many to be the literary voice of the first half of the twentieth century. Representing the Czech Republic is the poet Václav Havel. Slovakia has dramatist Karel Capek (*R.U.R.*). Romania is represented by Nobel Prize winner Elie Wiesel (*Night*).

South American Literature

Chilean Gabriela Mistral was the first Latin American writer to win the Nobel Prize for literature. She is best known for her collections of poetry, *Desolation and Feeling*.

Chile was also home to Pablo Neruda, who, in 1971, also won the Nobel Prize for literature for his poetry. His 29 volumes of poetry have been translated into more than 60 languages, attesting to his universal appeal. *Twenty Love Poems and a Song of Despair* is justly famous. Isabel Allende is carrying on the Chilean literary standards with her acclaimed novel, *House of Spirits*. Argentine Jorge Luis Borges is considered by many literary critics to be the most important writer of his century from South America. His collections of short stories, *Ficciones*, brought him universal recognition. Also from Argentina, Silvina Ocampo, a collaborator with Borges on a collection of poetry, is famed for her poetry and short story collections, which include *The Fury* and *The Days of the Night*. In the works of Gabriel García Márquez, the world became familiar with magic realism, and his work went on to influence generations of writers in Latin America and beyond.

Spain

Spain's great writers include Miguel de Cervantes (*Don Quixote*) and the poet Juan Ramón Jiménez *(Almas de violeta)*. The anonymous national epic *El Cid* has been translated into many languages.

South Asia

Asia has many modern writers who are being translated for the western reading public. India's Krishan Chandar has authored more than 300 stories. Rabindranath Tagore won the Nobel Prize for literature in 1913 (*Song Offerings*). R. K. Narayan, India's most famous writer (*The Guide*), is interested in mythology and legends of India. Santha Rama Rau's autobiography *Gifts of Passage* is a true story of her life in a British school where she tries to preserve her Indian culture and traditional home.

Skill 7.3 Identify characteristics of major movements and periods in world literatures

Below are some of the major movements in world literature:

Greek and Roman

Among the most important authors from the rest of the European continent, ancient Greek philosophers such as Sophocles, Euripides, and Aeschylus wrote many tragedies that have formed the backbone of much of Western literature.

Greek tragedies focus largely on the failings of the main character and on their pride (or hubris) that causes them to subvert the natural order of things and earn the ire of the gods, which eventually leads to their downfall (a catharsis" or cleansing). Most plays contain a mythic or religious component, and many end with direct intervention from the gods themselves (termed a "deus ex machina," a sudden ending where a godlike figure appears and reestablishes order). Significant Greek tragedies include *Oedipus Rex*, *Medea*, and *Antigone*. The epics of Homer are also noteworthy, which include *The Iliad* and *The Odyssey*, epic poems that described the exploits of brave Greek warriors and their struggles against one another and the gods themselves. Homer is sometimes considered the first great European author, and his influence cannot be overstated.

Much of the mythology that produces allusions in world literature is a product of ancient Greece and Rome because Greek and Roman myths have been liberally translated. Some Norse myths are also well known. These stories provide insight into the order and ethics of life. In them, ancient heroes overcome the terrors of the unknown, and explanations are given for thunder and lightning, the changing seasons, the origin and function of magical creatures of the forests and seas, and frightening natural phenomena. There is often a childlike directness in the emotions of supernatural beings. Many good translations of myths exist, but Edith Hamilton's *Mythology* is the definitive choice for adolescents.

Middle English

During the Anglo-Saxon period between the eighth and eleventh centuries, the English language was still coming into its own as a unique dialect separate from Latin or German. Among the earliest works in the English language is *Beowulf*, an epic poem describing the exploits of its titular hero as he attempts to slay the monstrous creature Grendel. Beowulf's author is not known, and the story likely originated as an oral telling that distorted real historical events into the realm of fairy tale.

The medieval period lasted until the fifteenth century and introduced many other stories that have become an essential part of British consciousness. Thomas Malory's *Le Morte d'Arthur* is one of the first Arthurian legends, describing the exploits of King Arthur, Guinevere, Sir Lancelot, and the rest of the Knights of the Round Table, which have made an indelible mark on world literature. But Geoffrey Chaucer's *Canterbury Tales* is the true apex of medieval British literature. The book, which follows a group of pilgrims engaged in a storytelling contest as they travel to a famous shrine, featured an unprecedented mastery of common language and a massive cast of characters from all walks of life who painted an ironic and critical view of English life. Chaucer introduced many new words and phrases into the English language with this novel, and his view of English life as seen through the eyes of worldly lower-class laborers has proven invaluable to historians ever since.

Renaissance

Of course, no mention of British literature is complete without Shakespeare and his contemporaries who worked during the Renaissance of the fourteenth through seventeenth centuries. Considered by many to be the greatest writer in the English language, William Shakespeare produced 39 plays and more than one hundred sonnets, ranging from broad comedies to heartfelt tragedies and bloody historical tellings. Shakespeare was a master of iambic pentameter, a poetical meter with each line having five iambs, or "feet," each containing a stressed and unstressed syllable. This style of verse was said to mimic the beating of the human heart, and it lent Shakespeare's prose much lively energy that has proved attractive to actors and readers for centuries. Shakespeare was also a great wit and an incredible craftsman of language. No other author has contributed more words to the English language than Shakespeare. His contemporaries, such as Christopher Marlowe and John Webster, also experimented wildly with new forms of vernacular storytelling, often repackaging ancient Greek tales for popular consumption.

In the seventeenth century, British literature largely focused on religious concerns. John Milton, a staunch Puritan, gave *Paradise Lost* to the world. The epic poem details the fall of the archangel Lucifer from heaven and his subsequent rebellion against God. The work proved so influential that it is sometimes mistaken for biblical canon. John Bunyan's *Pilgrim's Progress* is also staunchly religious, telling of a man's journey toward heaven after death. For many years, the book was second only to the Bible in terms of sales. John Donne's poetry, meanwhile, was more personal and satirical. Common turns of phrase like "for whom the bell tolls" and "no man is an island" come from his works.

Neoclassicism
Patterned after the greatest writings of classical Greece and Rome, this type of writing is characterized by a balanced, graceful, well-crafted, refined, elevated style. Major proponents of this style are poet laureates John Dryden and Alexander Pope. The eras in which they wrote are called the Ages of Dryden and Pope. The self is not exalted, and focus is on the group, not the individual, in neoclassic writing.

Romanticism
The works of William Blake help usher in an era of romanticism in British literature in the 1800s. These writings emphasize the individual. For example, emotions and feelings are validated and nature acts as an inspiration for creativity; it is a balm of the spirit. Romantics hearken back to medieval, chivalric themes and ambiance. They also emphasize supernatural, Gothic themes and settings, which are characterized by gloom and darkness. Imagination is stressed. New types of writings include detective and horror stories and autobiographical introspection (William Wordsworth).

There are two generations in British literature: The first generation of romantics included William Wordsworth and Samuel Taylor Coleridge, who collaborated on *Lyrical Ballads*, a collection of experimental poems like "Rime of the Ancient Mariner," which epitomized the romantic style and essayed Wordsworth's philosophical belief that men are inherently good but often become corrupted by society. Wordsworth maintained that the scenes and events of everyday life and the speech of ordinary people were the raw material with which poetry could and should be made. Romanticism spread to the United States, where Ralph Waldo Emerson and Henry David Thoreau adopted it in their transcendental romanticism, emphasizing reasoning. Further extensions of this style are found in Edgar Allan Poe's Gothic writings.

The second generation of romantics include John Keats, Lord Byron, and Percy Bysshe Shelley, who churned out sonnets, epics, and narrative poems featuring gorgeous prose and keen wit. Byron's *Don Juan* is a masterpiece of British satire, and his autobiographical *Childe Harold's Pilgrimage* is exceedingly self-deprecating. Shelley's works feature remarkable sensory detail; his poem "Ozymandias" describes a traveler who discovers a monument to some forgotten king whose grand empire has crumbled to dust. Keats's works display maturity far beyond his years, as the poet died at the tender age of 25. The romantics wrote resoundingly in protest against social and political wrongs and in defense of the struggles for liberty in Italy and Greece. The second-generation romantics stressed personal introspection and the love of beauty and nature as requisites of inspiration.

The romantic era also saw the rise of some of the first prominent female authors in British history, creating a feminist perspective that was often missing from literature until that point. Jane Austen is the most popular author from this time, and her works, such as *Pride and Prejudice* and *Mansfield Park*, provided realistic characters and cutting social commentary that have endured in popularity even to the present day. Charlotte and Emily Brontë were sisters and professional rivals, who wrote *Jane Eyre* and *Wuthering Heights* respectively, two grand romantic novels focusing on duplicity and unrequited love among the landed gentry of England. All these authors struggled against societal expectations of women during this time, and many critics were less than generous with their reviews, leading another prominent author of this time, Mary Ann Evans, to write under the alias of George Eliot to get a fairer appraisal of her work.

Victorian
The Victorian period is remarkable for the diversity and proliferation of work. Poets who are typified as Victorians include Alfred Lord Tennyson, who wrote *Idylls of the King*, 12 narrative poems about the Arthurian legend; and Robert Browning, who wrote chilling, dramatic monologues such as "My Last Duchess," as well as long poetic narratives such as *The Pied Piper of Hamlin*. Browning's wife Elizabeth wrote two major works, the epic feminist poem *Aurora Leigh* and the deeply moving and provocative *Sonnets from the Portuguese*, in which she details her deep love for Robert and his startling (to her) reciprocation. Gerard Manley Hopkins, a Catholic priest, wrote poetry using sprung rhythm. A. E. Housman, Matthew Arnold, and the Pre-Raphaelites, especially the brother-and-sister duo Dante Gabriel and Christina Rossetti, contributed much to the Victorian era poetic scene.

During the Victorian period, Robert Louis Stevenson, the great Scottish novelist, wrote his adventure/history lessons for young adults. Victorian prose ranges from the incomparable, keenly woven plot structures of Charles Dickens to the deeply moving Dorset/Wessex novels of Thomas Hardy, in which women are repressed and life is more struggle than euphoria. Rudyard Kipling wrote about colonialism in India in works such as *Kim* and *The Jungle Book*, which re-create exotic locales and dissect the Raj, the British colonial government during Queen Victoria's reign. Victorian drama is a product mainly of Oscar Wilde, whose satirical masterpiece *The Importance of Being Earnest* farcically details and lampoons Victorian social mores.

Realism
Unlike classical and neoclassical writing, which often deal with aristocracies and nobility or the gods, realistic writers deal with the everyday people and their socioeconomic problems in a nonsentimental way. Muckraking, social injustice, domestic abuse, and inner-city conflicts are examples of writings by writers of realism. Realistic writers include Thomas Hardy, George Bernard Shaw, and Henrik Ibsen.

Naturalism
This is realism pushed to the maximum, writing that exposes the underbelly of society, usually the lower-class struggles. Émile Zola was inspired by his readings in history and medicine and attempted to apply methods of scientific observation to the depiction of pathological human character, notably in his series of novels devoted to several generations of one French family.

Modernist
This experimentation and variety has continued in the twentieth century, in which Britain firmly establishes itself as a major force in world literature. Irish authors James Joyce and Samuel Beckett pioneered modernist literature, which remixed and recontextualized existing dramatic forms in absurd, experimental new ways. Beckett's *Waiting for Godot* is among the most influential plays ever written, examining the tragedy and comedy of the human condition via two clownish vagabonds contemplating their own inability to accomplish anything of note. The play is a landmark work of absurdist and postmodern theater, two experimental styles that pushed the limits of what audiences could expect from the stage.

Joyce's *Ulysses* experiments and invents in nearly every literary style, using a dreamlike stream-of-consciousness narrative of a man's madcap journey through Dublin on a single day. The works of George Orwell are more political. A former police officer in English-occupied Burma, Orwell's works are fiercely antifascist, providing stark warnings about the dangers of totalitarianism. His science fiction dystopian novel *1984* is considered his masterpiece, telling the tale of a common man's struggle against his brutally conformist society led by the mysterious dictator "Big Brother."

This is not a complete list of major movements and periods in literatures from around the world. *(For additional information within this text, see Skill 7.2 for more of a focus on authors and literary texts and 7.1 for more of a focus on different parts of the world.)* Please make sure that you are aware of additional movements and characteristics outside of this text as well.

Skill 7.4　Identify characteristics of major literary genres and works in the oral tradition

Mythology and Oral Tradition
Works in the oral tradition have contributed greatly to the body of works on world literature. Oral tradition genres include poetry, drama, epics, ballads, songs, folktales and legends, myths, proverbs, riddles, and myths.

One characteristic of oral literature generally includes a lack of known authorship. Native American Raven, Coyote, or Salmon stories, as well as African Anansi stories, were passed down from generation to generation orally before they were written down. Many of the famous epics such as the Finnish *Kalevala*, the Sumerian *Gilgamesh*, and Homer's *Odyssey*, as well as written fairy tales, were gathered stories from popular oral recountings and traditions.

Below is a table with some of the major genres and characteristics of oral traditions. The epic has been discussed extensively in different parts of this book.

(See Skill 8.1 for more discussion of the influence of these traditions on world literatures.)

Genre	Characteristics
Folktales (including fables)	<ul><li>Short</li><li>Humans, animals, gods, fantastical figures/creatures</li><li>Cross sociopolitical and linguistic boundaries</li></ul>
Songs (including ballads, laments, work songs, praise songs)	<ul><li>Structure of lyric poetry (formal structure)</li><li>Accompanied by an instrument</li><li>Repeated refrains</li></ul>
Dramas	<ul><li>Connected to ritual/religion</li><li>Sometimes a distinction between folk drama and drama for more elite audiences</li></ul>
Myths	<ul><li>Cosmological, explaining phenomena</li><li>Localized and culturally embedded as well as universal</li><li>Multiple versions spread over space and time</li></ul>

| Legends | - Explanations of local peoples, places, and cultures
- Part of ritual traditions of telling |

In addition to the characteristics of the content of these genres, there are also specific characteristics relating to the performance of the tales. Some are recited by parents to children, some in a group ritual setting during specific times of year, and others from one individual to another.

OBJECTIVE 8	HISTORICAL, SOCIAL, CULTURAL, AND POLITICAL ASPECTS OF LITERATURE FROM AROUND THE WORLD

Literatures from around the world have both reflected and influenced major historical, social, cultural, and political events, movements, and issues. Individual authors from countries around the world and from diverse backgrounds within countries have been inspired by and inspire one another. The skills described in this section overlap in many cases because the realms of politics, history, and cultural and social issues are intertwined as they play out in history and the present day. As you read through the skills in this objective, keep this in mind.

Skill 8.1 Understand the ways in which historical, social, cultural, and political events and movements influenced the development of world literatures

Literary allusions are drawn from classic mythology, national folklore, and religious writings that are supposed to have such familiarity that the readers can recognize the comparison between the subject of the allusion and the person, place, or event in the current reading. Children and adolescents who have knowledge of proverbs, fables, myths, epics, and the Bible can understand these allusions and thereby appreciate their reading to a greater degree than those who cannot recognize them.

Fables and Folktales
This literary group of stories and legends was originally orally transmitted to the common populace to provide models of exemplary behavior or deeds worthy of recognition and homage.

In fables, animals talk, feel, and behave like human beings. The fable always has a moral, and the animals illustrate specific people or groups without directly identifying them. For example, in Aesop's *Fables,* the lion is the "king" and the wolf is the cruel, often unfeeling "noble class." In the fable of "The Lion and the Mouse," the moral is "Little friends may prove to be great friends." In "The Lion's Share," it is "Might makes right."

Folktales are stories handed down through a culture. Of unknown origin, they began through the oral tradition and, like fables, they teach moral lessons. Many British folktales—*How Robin Became an Outlaw* and *St. George and the Dragon*—stress the correlation between power and right.

Classical Mythology
Much of the mythology that produces allusions in modern English writings is a product of ancient Greece and Rome because these myths have been more liberally translated. Some Norse myths are also well known. Children are fond of myths because those

ancient people were seeking explanations for those elements in their lives that predated scientific knowledge just as children seek explanations for the occurrences in their lives.

These stories provide insight into the order and ethics of life as ancient heroes overcome the terrors of the unknown and bring meaning to the thunder and lightning, to the changing of the seasons, to the magical creatures of the forests and seas, and to the myriad of natural phenomena that can frighten humankind.

There is often a childlike quality in the emotions of supernatural beings with which children can identify. Many good translations of myths exist for readers of varying abilities, but Edith Hamilton's *Mythology* is the most definitive reading for adolescents.

Fairy Tales
Fairy tales are fictional stories involving children or animals that come in contact with superbeings via magic. The fairy tales of many nations are peopled by trolls, elves, dwarfs, and pixies, child-sized beings capable of fantastic accomplishments.

Among the most famous are "Beauty and the Beast," "Cinderella," "Hansel and Gretel," "Snow White and the Seven Dwarfs," "Rumpelstiltskin," and "Tom Thumb." In many tales, the protagonist survives prejudice, imprisonment, ridicule, and even death to receive justice in a cruel world. In other tales, the protagonist is sacrificed to make a larger point about morality.

Older readers encounter a kind of fairy tale world in Shakespeare's *Tempest* and *A Midsummer Night's Dream*, which use pixies and fairies as characters. Adolescent readers today are as fascinated by the creations of fantasy realms in the works of Piers Anthony, Ursula Le Guin, and Anne McCaffrey. An extension of interest in the supernatural is the popularity of science fiction that allows us to use current knowledge to predict the possible course of the future.

Angels (or sometimes fairy godmothers) play a role in some fairy tales, and Milton in *Paradise Lost* and *Paradise Regained* also used symbolic angels and devils.

Biblical stories provide many allusions. Parables, moralistic-like fables but with human characters, include the stories of the Good Samaritan and the Prodigal Son.

American Folktales
American folktales are divided into two categories: tall tales and legends.

Imaginary tales, also called tall tales, are humorous tales based on fictional characters developed through exaggeration.

- Rip Van Winkle sleeps for 20 years in the Catskill Mountains and upon awakening cannot understand why no one recognizes him.

- Paul Bunyan, a giant lumberjack, owns a great blue ox named Babe and has extraordinary physical strength. He is said to have plowed the Mississippi River while the impression of Babe's hoofprints created the Great Lakes.

Legends about individuals are often based on real persons who accomplished the feats that are attributed to them, even if they are slightly exaggerated.

- For more than 40 years, Johnny Appleseed (John Chapman) roamed Ohio and Indiana planting apple seeds.
- Daniel Boone, scout, adventurer, and pioneer, blazed the Wilderness Trail and made Kentucky safe for settlers.
- Paul Revere, a colonial patriot, rode through the New England countryside warning of the approach of British troops.
- George Washington cut down a cherry tree, which he could not deny. Or did he?

Throughout history, the politics of each culture is reflected in its literature. Developments in technology, philosophy, and language can be charted through familiarity with each culture's body of work. An understanding of major developments in world literature provides insights on the different perspectives and viewpoints of major events both in history and in modern society.

At times of major technological innovation, for example, literature can reflect both anxiety about the changes as well as excitement about what the future holds. Major events such as colonization and wars often highlight contrasting perspectives and can be glimpsed through literature from different countries and cultures.

(See Skills 8.2, 8.3, and 8.4 for major works, authors, and issues in world literatures.)

Skill 8.2 Recognize the ways in which diverse values, attitudes, and ideas are expressed in world literatures

Literature is powerful in influencing the thinking of individual readers and all of society. Waves of philosophical ideas have swept over the reading world almost from the time of the invention of the printing press. It's possible to trace the emergence of a particular set of values over centuries. Feminism is a case in point. While the issue of women's rights didn't reach a boiling point until the 1960s, it can be traced through history for many years.

For example, Empress Theodora of Byzantium was a proponent of legislation that would provide greater protections and freedoms to her female subjects. Christine de Pizan, the first professional female writer, advanced many feminist ideas as early as the 1300s in the face of attempts to restrict female inheritance and guild membership. In 1869, John Stuart Mill published *The Subjection of Women* to demonstrate that "the legal subordination of one sex to the other is wrong…and…one of the chief hindrances to human improvement."

Norwegian playwright Henrik Ibsen wrote the highly controversial play, *A Doll's House,* in 1879, a scathing criticism of the traditional roles of men and women in Victorian marriages. These and many other works with feminist themes led to changes in the way society viewed women throughout the civilized world. The impact of the literature and the changes in thinking on this issue led to many countries' granting the vote to women in the late 1800s and the early years of the twentieth century.

Regional literature has played an important role in the themes of popular literature, particularly in American literature. The best known of the regional American writers is Samuel Langhorne Clemens, better known as Mark Twain, with his stories about the Mississippi River and the state of Missouri.

James A. Michener wrote history as fiction in his many novels: Tales of the South Pacific (for which he won the Pulitzer Prize for fiction in 1948*)*, *Hawaii*, *The Drifters*, *Centennial*, *The Source*, *The Fires of Spring*, *Chesapeake*, Caribbean, Caravans, *Alaska*, Texas, and Poland.

Literature about different time periods has also been popular with American writers. The Civil War has been the focus of several well-known novels including *The Red Badge of Courage,* by Stephen Crane; *Cold Mountain*, by Charles Frazier; and *Lincoln*, by Gore Vidal.

Immigration
This has been a popular topic for literature from the time of the Louisiana Purchase in 1804. The recent *Undaunted Courage*, by Stephen E. Ambrose, is ostensibly the autobiography of Meriwether Lewis but is actually a recounting of the Lewis and Clark expedition. Presented as a scientific mission by President Jefferson, the expedition was actually intended to provide maps and information for the opening up of the West. A well-known novel of the settling of the West by immigrants from other countries is *Giants in the Earth*, by Ole Edvart Rolvaag, himself a descendant of immigrants.

John Steinbeck's *Cannery Row* and *Tortilla Flats* reflect the lives of Mexican migrants in California. Amy Tan's *Joy Luck Club* deals with the problems faced by Chinese immigrants.

The diversity of the American experience has shaped American literature in countless ways. Different writers from different backgrounds have explored themes sometimes closely tied to identity, while others have delved into personal experience. Rich, layered, and powerful works have emerged from some of the biggest challenges to American society. Some of the greatest American novels of the twentieth century have dealt with:

- Racism
- Inequality
- The rights of women
- Slavery and its effects
- The effects of colonization

- The experience of immigrants as they adapted to and shaped American society
- Poverty and class
- The struggle for equality
- Sexual identity

Some examples of renowned American novelists of the twentieth century include:

- Sandra Cisneros: *The House on Mango Street*, short story collections
- Louise Erdrich: *Love Medicine, The Round House*
- William Faulkner: *The Sound and the Fury; Absalom, Absalom*
- F. Scott Fitzgerald: *The Great Gatsby, Tender Is the Night*
- Ernest Hemingway: *A Farewell to Arms, For Whom the Bell Tolls*
- Zora Neale Hurston: *Their Eyes Were Watching God*
- Sinclair Lewis: *Babbitt, Elmer Gantry*
- Cormac McCarthy: *The Border Trilogy*
- Toni Morrison: *Beloved, The Bluest Eye*
- José Saramago: *Blindness*
- Leslie Marmon Silko: *Gardens in the Dunes, Ceremony*
- Gary Soto: *The Tale of Sunlight*
- John Steinbeck: *Cannery Row, The Grapes of Wrath*
- Henry David Thoreau: *Walden*
- John Updike: *Rabbit Run, Rabbit Redux*
- Alice Walker: *The Color Purple, The Temple of My Familiar* Richard Wright: *Native Son; White Man, Listen!*

(Note that here are too many important writers to try to create a comprehensive list.)

Skill 8.3 **Recognize the ways in which writers from diverse backgrounds have commented on major events and issues and influence public understanding of these events through literature**

(See Skill 8.2 for specific novels and issues.)

Worldwide philosophical trends can be traced to the literature that was popular in a particular period of time. America has always been a nation of readers. With the development of theaters, and ultimately movies and TV shows that often dramatized popular novels, the power of the written word has increased.

Early Native American literature was part of a vast oral tradition that spanned most of continental America from as far back as before the fifteenth century. Characteristics of Native American works in the oral tradition include respect for nature and the earth and an appreciation of the interconnectedness of the elements in the life cycle. Themes of Native American works in the literary tradition include place, vision, and identity.

John Steinbeck's *Grapes of Wrath* focused the attention of Americans on the plight of the common people, who suffered more than anyone else during the Great Depression. His revelation that Americans were starving to death in a land of great abundance still resonates with the public. Members of the "establishment" in the farms and towns of California are revealed as callous and greedy. Church members, particularly clergy and leaders, are not caring or compassionate in his revealing story. Steinbeck lived with some of the migrants so that he could write authentically and with firsthand knowledge. Many of the writers who have influenced public opinion write from personal experience.

The feminist movement has virtually been fueled by literature going back several hundred years. Although the organized movement began with the first women's rights convention at Seneca Falls, New York, in 1948, in 1869, John Stuart Mill had already published *The Subjection of Women* to demonstrate that the legal subordination of one sex to the other is wrong. Virginia Woolf's *Room of One's Own*, first published in 1929, and strongly influenced how women were beginning to see their roles.

In the crusade that was ignited by the civil rights movement of the 1960s, however, Betty Friedan's popular book, *The Feminine Mystique*, published in 1963, influenced many women to become involved, both in changing their own outlooks and behaviors but also in becoming activists in the movement at large. Feminism has been so much a part of the thinking throughout the world that it should always be included in the potential themes one looks for when critiquing a literary work.

Writers such as Harriet Beecher Stowe used literature to shine a light on the ills of American society. With *Uncle Tom's Cabin* she sought to highlight the injustice of slavery. By exposing the horrible truth of how the institution of slavery exploited and abused people, she hoped to turn America to the abolitionist cause. Authors such as Kate Chopin and Louisa May Alcott explored essential ideas about the roles of women in society in their compelling novels.

The Vietnam War inspired many novels, although most were written after the war, including *The Things They Carried*, by Tim O'Brien, and *Fallen Angels*, by Walter Dean Myers. The attitudes of Americans about the war, however, have been influenced by these novels, and for many, their viewpoints about the conflict as well.

Colonialism and war also inspired many novels including *Things Fall Apart*, by Chinua Achebe; *Night*, by Elie Wiesel; *Anil's Ghost*, by Michael Ondaatje; *Survival in Auschwitz*, by Primo Levi; *House of the Spirits*, by Isabel Allende; as well as poet Jose Marti's works.

Writers from diverse countries and cultures, from the time of the invention of the printing press, have played essential roles in shaping public opinion, not only in their own countries but also around the world.

Skill 8.4   Analyze the ways in which major sociocultural and sociopolitical issues are addressed in contemporary and classical literature

Below is an incomplete list of sociocultural and sociopolitical issues and some of the authors and works that address them.

Exploitation: Upton Sinclair, *The Jungle*; Emile Zola, *Germinal*

Women's rights: Mary Wollstonecraft, *A Vindication of the Rights of Women*; Alice Walker, *The Color Purple*; Sandra Cisneros, *The House on Mango Street*; Margaret Atwood, *A Handmaid's Tale*; Simone de Beauvoir, *The Second Sex*; Virginia Woolf, *A Room of One's Own*; Isabel Allende, *House of the Spirits*

Bioethics: Mary Shelley, *Frankenstein*; Aldous Huxley, *Brave New World*

Freedom and censorship: Arthur Miller, *The Crucible*; Ray Bradbury, *Fahrenheit 451*; Jerome Lawrence and Robert Edwin Lee, *Inherit the Wind*; Azar Nafisi, *Reading Lolita in Tehran*

Groupthink/mob mentality: Robert Cormier, *The Chocolate War*; William Golding, *Lord of the Flies*; Dai Sijie, *Balzac and The Little Chinese Seamstress*; Lu Xun, *Diary of a Madman and Other Stories*

Mental illness and disability: Ken Kesey, *One Flew over the Cuckoo's Nest*; John Steinbeck, *Of Mice and Men*; the works of Sigmund Freud and Carl Jung

Identity and civil rights: Richard Wright, *Native Son*; Maya Angelou, *I Know Why the Caged Bird Sings*; Malcom X, *Autobiography of Malcolm X*; Amy Tan, *The Joy Luck Club*; Joy Kogawa, *Obasan*; Ralph Ellison, *Invisible Man*; Naguib Mahfouz, *Children of Gebelawi*; Salman Rushdie, *Midnight's Children*; Rohinton Mistry, *A Fine Balance*; Frederick Douglass, *Narrative of the Life of Frederick Douglass, an American Slave*; *My Bondage and My Freedom*; and *The Life and Times of Frederick Douglass*

DOMAIN III	ENGLISH LANGUAGE CONVENTIONS, COMPOSITION, WRITING PROCESS, AND RESEARCH
OBJECTIVE 9	STANDARD AMERICAN ENGLISH AND ELEMENTS OF EFFECTIVE COMPOSITION

Skill 9.1 Understand spelling and capitalization conventions when composing a text

Spelling

Spelling rules are extremely complex, because they are based on rules of phonics and letter doubling, and replete with exceptions. Even adults who have a good command of written English benefit from using a dictionary.

Plurals

Most plurals of nouns that end in hard consonants or hard consonant sounds followed by a silent *e* are made by adding *s*. Some nouns ending in vowels only add *s*. For example, fingers, numerals, banks, bugs, riots, homes, gates, radios, bananas, and so on.

Add an es *for:*

- Nouns that end in the soft consonant sounds: *s, j, x, z, ch,* and *sh*
- Some nouns ending in *o*

Examples: dresses, waxes, churches, brushes, tomatoes, potatoes, and so on

- Nouns ending in *y* preceded by a consonant change. First make sure to change the *y* to an *i*.

Examples: babies, corollaries, frugalities, poppies, and so on

Add an s *for:*
- Nouns ending in *y* preceded by a vowel

Examples: boys, alleys, and so on

- Letters, numbers, and abbreviations

Examples: fives and tens, IBMs, 1990s, *p*'s and *q*'s (Note that letters are italicized.)

Irregular Noun Plurals

Some noun plurals are formed irregularly or are the same as the singular word:

Examples: sheep, deer, children, leaves, oxen, and so on

Derivations

Nouns derived from foreign words, especially Latin, may make their plurals in two different ways, one of them Anglicized. Sometimes, the meanings are the same; other times, the two plurals are used in slightly different contexts. It is always wise to consult the dictionary.

Examples: appendices/appendixes, criterion/criteria, indexes/indices, crisis/crises

Compound Words

Make the plurals of closed (solid) compound words in the usual way except for words ending in -ful, which make their plurals on the root word.

Examples: timelines, hairpins, cupsful, and so on

Make the plurals of open or hyphenated compounds by adding the change in inflection to the word that changes in number.

Examples: fathers-in-law, courts-martial, masters of art, doctors of medicine, and so on

Skill 9.2 Understand capitalization conventions when composing a text

Capitalize all proper names of persons (including specific organizations or agencies of government); places (countries, states, cities, parks, and specific geographical areas); things (political parties, structures, historical and cultural terms, and calendar and time designations); and religious terms (any deity, revered person or group, or sacred writing).

Examples: Percy Bysshe Shelley, Argentina, Mount Rainier National Park, Grand Canyon, League of Nations, the Sears Tower, Birmingham, Lyric Theater, Americans, Democrats, Renaissance, Boy Scouts of America, Easter, God, Bible, Dead Sea Scrolls, Koran

Capitalize proper adjectives and titles used with proper names.

Examples: California Gold Rush, President John Adams, Senator Elizabeth Warren

Note: Some words that represent titles and offices are not capitalized unless used with a proper name.

Capitalized	Not capitalized
Congressman Ellison Commander Alger Queen Elizabeth President George Washington	the congressman from Florida commander of the Pacific Fleet the queen of England the president

English Language Arts

Skill 9.3   Understand punctuation conventions when composing a text

Punctuation can have a big impact on the overall message that you're trying to convey, and it's likely that points will be deducted if punctuation is used incorrectly or omitted within your essay questions. Using improper punctuation in your writing will create incorrect grammar and will confuse the readers of your essay. It can also create inaccurate quotations and names of famous works of literature.

Commas
Commas indicate a brief pause. They are used to set off dependent clauses and long introductory word groups, and they can also separate words in a series.

Commas are used to:

- Set off unimportant material that interrupts the flow of the sentence
- Separate independent clauses joined by conjunctions
- Separate two or more coordinate adjectives modifying the same word and three or more nouns, phrases, or clauses in a list
- Separate antithetical or complementary expressions from the rest of the sentence

Apostrophes
Apostrophes are used to show either contractions or possession. Contractions show the omission of a letter (wouldn't = would + not—the apostrophe takes the place of the *o*), and possession represents ownership (Sam's new car—the apostrophe lets the readers know the new car belongs to Sam).

Terminal Punctuation in Relation to Quotation Marks
In a quoted statement that is either declarative or imperative, place the period inside the closing quotation marks:

"The airplane crashed on the runway during takeoff."

If the quotation is followed by other words in the sentence, place a comma inside the closing quotations marks and a period at the end of the sentence:

"The airplane crashed on the runway during takeoff," said the announcer.

In most instances in which a quoted title or expression occurs at the end of a sentence, the period is placed before either the single or double quotation marks.

"The middle school readers were unprepared to understand Bryant's poem 'Thanatopsis.'"

Early book-length adventure stories like Don Quixote *and* The Three Musketeers *were known as "picaresque novels."*

There is an instance in which the final quotation mark would precede the period: if the content of the sentence were about a speech or quote so that the understanding of the meaning would be confused by the placement of the period.

The first thing out of his mouth was, "Hi, I'm home."

but

The first line of his speech began, "I arrived home to an empty house".

In sentences that are interrogatory or exclamatory, the question mark or exclamation point should be positioned outside the closing quotation marks if the quote itself is a statement, command, or cited title.

Who decided to lead us in the recitation of the "Pledge of Allegiance"?
Why was Tillie shaking as she began her recitation, "Once upon a midnight dreary"?

In sentences that are declarative but in which the quotation is a question or an exclamation, place the question mark or exclamation point inside the quotation marks.

The hall monitor yelled, "Fire! Fire!"
The hall monitor asked, "Where's the fire?"

Periods with Parentheses or Brackets
Place the period inside the parentheses or brackets if they enclose a complete sentence independent of the other sentences around it.

Stephen Crane was a confirmed alcohol and drug addict. (He admitted as much to other journalists in Cuba.)

If the parenthetical expression is a statement inserted within another statement, the period in the enclosure is omitted.

Mark Twain used the character Indian Joe (he also appeared in The Adventures of Tom Sawyer) *as a foil for Jim in* The Adventures of Huckleberry Finn.

When enclosed matter comes at the end of a sentence requiring quotation marks, place the period outside the parentheses or brackets.

"The secretary of state consulted with the ambassador [Madeleine Albright]."

Double Quotation Marks with Other Punctuation
Quotations—whether words, phrases, or clauses—should be punctuated according to the rules of the grammatical function they serve in the sentence.

The works of Shakespeare, "the bard of Avon," have been contested as originating with other authors.

"You'll get my money," the old man warned, "when hell freezes over."

Sheila cited the passage that began "Four score and seven years ago . . .."
(Note the ellipsis followed by an enclosed period.)

Use quotation marks to enclose the titles of shorter works: songs, short poems, short stories, essays, and chapters of books. (For titles of longer works, see "Italics" below.)

"The Tell-Tale Heart"   "Casey at the Bat"   "America the Beautiful"

Semicolons

Semicolons are needed to divide two or more closely related independent sentences and to separate items in a series containing commas.

1. Use semicolons to separate independent clauses when the second clause is introduced by a transitional adverb. (These clauses may also be written as separate sentences, preferably by placing the adverb within the second sentence.)
    a. *Semicolon: The Elizabethans modified the rhyme scheme of the sonnet; thus, it was called the English sonnet.*
    b. *Separate clauses: The Elizabethans modified the rhyme scheme of the sonnet. It thus was called the English sonnet.*

2. Use semicolons to separate items in a series that are long and complex or have internal punctuation.
    a. *The Italian Renaissance produced masters in the fine arts: Dante Alighieri, author of* The Divine Comedy*; Leonardo da Vinci, painter of* The Last Supper*; and Donatello, sculptor of the* Quattro Santi Coronati, the Four Crowned Saints.
    b. *The leading scorers in the WNBA were Haizhou Zheng, averaging 23.9 points per game; Lisa Leslie, 22; and Cynthia Cooper, 19.5.*

Colons

Colons are used to introduce lists and to emphasize what follows. You place a colon at the beginning of a list of items. (Note its use in the sentence about Renaissance Italians under "Semicolons" above.)

The teacher directed us to compare Faulkner's three symbolic novels: Absalom, Absalom!*; As I Lay Dying; and* Light in August.

Do not use a colon if the list is preceded by a verb.

Three of Faulkner's symbolic novels are Absalom, Absalom!; As I Lay Dying; *and* Light in August.

Dashes
Use en dashes (short dashes) to denote a range in numbers.

The Great Depression took place in the years 1929–39.

Use em dashes (long dashes) to denote sudden breaks in thought.

Some periods in literature—the romantic age, for example—spanned different time periods in different countries.

Also use em dashes instead of commas if commas are used elsewhere in the sentence for amplification or explanation.

The Fireside Poets included three Brahmans—James Russell Lowell, Henry Wadsworth Longfellow, Oliver Wendell Holmes—and John Greenleaf Whittier.

Italics
Use italics to style the titles of long works of literature, periodical publications, musical scores, works of art, movies, and television and radio programs.

> *Idylls of the King*　　*Hiawatha*　　*The Sound and the Fury*
> *Mary Poppins*　　*Newsweek*　　*The Nutcracker Suite*

Note: When unable to write in italics, you should underline where italics would be appropriate.

Skill 9.4　Understand and apply appropriate word usage and grammar when composing a text

Parts of Speech
There are eight parts of speech: nouns, verbs, adjectives, adverbs, pronouns, conjunctions, prepositions, and interjections.

Noun	A person, place, or thing (*student, school, textbook*)
Verb	An action word (*study, read, run*)
Adjective	Describes a noun (*smart, beautiful, colorful*)
Adverb	Describes a verb (*quickly, fast, intelligently*)

Pronoun	Substitution for a noun (*he, she, it*)
Conjunction	Joins two phrases (*because, but, so*)
Preposition	Used usually before a noun or pronoun to provide additional details (*before, after, on*)
Interjection	Expresses emotion (*Ha!, Ah!, Yeah!*)

Syntax

Although widely different in many aspects, written and spoken English share a common basic structure or syntax (subject, verb, and object) and the common purpose of fulfilling the need to communicate—but there, the similarities end.

Spoken English follows the basic word order mentioned above (subject, verb object) as does written English. We would write as we would speak: "I sang a song." It is usually only in poetry or music that word order or syntax is altered: "Sang I a song."

Types of Sentences

Declarative	Makes a statement. *I bought a new textbook.*
Interrogative	Asks a question. *Where did you buy the textbook?*
Exclamatory	Expresses strong emotion. *I can't believe it's your birthday today!*
Imperative	Gives a command. *Put the birthday cake on the table.*

Types of Clauses

Clauses are connected word groups that are composed of at least one subject and one verb. (A subject is the doer of an action or the element that is being joined. A verb conveys either the action or the link.)

Students are waiting for the start of the assembly.
subject   verb

At the end of the play, students waited for the curtain to come down.
                        subject   verb

Clauses can be independent or dependent. **Independent clauses** can stand alone or can be joined to other clauses, either independent or dependent. Words that can be used to join clauses include:

- And
- Nor
- But
- Or
- Yet
- So

Dependent clauses, by definition, contain at least one subject and one verb. They cannot, however, stand alone as a complete sentence. They are structurally dependent on the independent clause (the main clause of the sentence). There are two types of dependent clauses: (1) those with a subordinating conjunction and (2) those with a relative pronoun. Coordinating conjunctions include:

- Although
- When
- If
- Unless
- Because

Example: *Unless a cure is discovered, many more people will die of the disease.*
(dependent clause with coordinating conjunction [unless] + independent clause)
Relative pronouns include:

- Who
- Whom
- Which
- That

Example: *The White House has an official Website, which contains press releases, news updates, and biographies of the president and vice president.*
(independent clause + relative pronoun [which] + relative dependent clause)

Sentence Structures
There are simple, compound, complex, and compound-complex sentences. Use dependent (subordinate) and independent clauses correctly to create these sentence structures.

Simple	Joyce wrote a letter.
Compound	Joyce wrote a letter, and Dot drew a picture.
Complex	While Joyce wrote a letter, Dot drew a picture.

Compound/complex	When Mother asked the girls to demonstrate their newfound skills, Joyce wrote a letter and Dot drew a picture.

*Note: Do not confuse compound sentence elements with compound sentences.

Simple sentence with compound subject:

Rosie and Marissa wrote letters.
The girl in row three and the boy next to her were passing notes across the aisle.

Simple sentence with compound predicate:

Sumiyo wrote letters and drew pictures.
The captain of the high school debate team graduated with honors and studied broadcast journalism in college.

Simple sentence with compound object of preposition:

Claudia graded the students' essays for style and mechanical accuracy.

Parallelism
Use phrases (prepositional, gerund, participial, and infinitive) and omissions from sentences to make a sentence parallel.

    Prepositional phrase/single modifier:

Incorrect:	Francesca ate the ice cream with enthusiasm and hurriedly.
Correct:	Francesca ate the ice cream with enthusiasm and in a hurry.
Correct:	Francesca ate the ice cream enthusiastically and hurriedly.

    Participial phrase/infinitive phrase:

Incorrect:	After hiking for hours and to sweat profusely, Mateo sat down to rest and drinking water.
Correct:	After hiking for hours and sweating profusely, Mateo sat down to rest and drink water.

Misplaced and Dangling Phrases
Dangling phrases are attached to sentence parts in such a way that they create ambiguity and an incorrect meaning.

    Participial phrase:

Incorrect:	Hanging from her skirt, Akiko tugged at a loose thread.
Correct:	Akiko tugged at a loose thread hanging from her skirt.

Infinitive phrase:

Incorrect: To improve his behavior, the dean warned Anders.
Correct: The dean warned Anders to improve his behavior.

Prepositional phrase:

Incorrect: On the floor, Suada saw the dog eating table scraps.
Correct: Suada saw the dog eating table scraps on the floor.

Syntactic Omission
These errors occur when keywords have been omitted from a sentence.

Incorrect: Ryan opened his book, recited her textbook, and answered the teacher's subsequent question.

Correct: Ryan opened his book, recited **from the** textbook, and answered the teacher's subsequent question.

Double Negatives
This error occurs from positioning two negatives that cancel each other out (creating a positive statement).

Incorrect: Madeline didn't have no double negatives in her paper.
Correct: Madeline didn't have **any** double negatives in her paper.

Skill 9.5 Demonstrate knowledge of developing an effective introduction for a written text (interest, topic, thesis)

A good piece of writing begins with the main idea early in the first paragraph. This topic paragraph answers a question or expresses the writer's position, presents an argument, and includes brief highlights of how the writer plans to support that argument. This first paragraph makes a claim (statement) and shows how the composition will support it. Typically, this paragraph should only be five or six sentences long, so from the beginning, writers must be well organized. Writers must clearly establish what the rest of the piece will be about and may also include purpose.

The best introductory paragraphs avoid three mistakes. First, they don't restate the question either directly or paraphrased. You need to consider the question and formulate your answer in a manner that simply answers the question. Next, don't write about how you thought about the assignment or how you came to decide what you would write. That's all background that feeds the composition, but is *not* the composition. The final error is to start your paper with what someone else has said, including the author, a dictionary, a character in the book, et cetera. This is about what you have considered and will present, so it should start with your own main idea in your own words.

Remember, if you haven't captured the readers' attention in this first paragraph (or "hooked" them), they will not want to read further. In your first five or six sentences, be certain you have presented an interesting idea and provoked the readers to think about this idea in a new manner.

Skill 9.6 Demonstrate knowledge of how to develop the body of a written text (clearly presents, contrasts, and links ideas)

Body paragraphs elaborate on a topic. The essential thing to remember is that the ideas must be organized so that the readers' knowledge steadily builds. The writer takes care to fully explain one element before moving on to another.

The structure of a piece of writing should be organized to inform the readers by logically explaining different elements of the topic. Each section should contain facts, quotes, and other details to help the readers understand the topic thoroughly.

Transitional words and phrases are designed to lead the readers forward and through a piece of writing. Such words as "therefore," "however," "even so," and "although" are clues to connections between one part of the writing and another. Phrases sometimes substitute for words. Some examples include "in the case of," "in the long run," and "looking back." These transitional words and phrases clarify the nature of the connection as seen in the following examples:

To show time or order: afterward, then, first, finally
To show contrast: however, but, although
To show additional ideas: and, furthermore, moreover
To show example: for instance, for example, as in the case of

Another example of a transitional sentence could be, "Not all projects have been so successful." This could refer to the previous information and prepares the readers for the next paragraph, which will be about an unsuccessful project. This next transitional sentence is a little more forthright: "The cost of these proposed projects—and who will pay for them—may jeopardize their implementation."

Another fairly simple and straightforward transitional device is the use of numbers or their approximation. Words like "first," "initially," and "second" may help to sequence ideas and information, but these should be used cautiously to avoid overuse.

An entire paragraph may be transitional in purpose and form. In *Darwiniana*, Thomas Huxley used a transitional paragraph:

So much, then, by way of proof that the method of establishing laws in science is exactly the same as that pursued in common life. Let us now turn to another matter (though really it is but another phase of the same question), and that is, the method by which, from the relations of certain phenomena, we prove that some stand in the position of causes toward the others.

In music, composers build the momentum of a piece of music to a crescendo just before a finale. This is how you should consider yourself and your writing—the composer (the writer, you) uses phrases and parts to support a melody (your main idea) to a crescendo (the best of your body paragraphs with the strongest examples) just before your finale (conclusion and finish).

Skill 9.7   Demonstrates knowledge of how to develop a conclusion (summary, course of action, or personal commentary)

The final piece of a story is always the most memorable, for good or bad. You want to make sure that your conclusion is *not* a mirror image with only a few word changes. Rather, you want to state your thesis slightly modified, building upon your facts and subpoints. It's strongest when you are able to state your thesis in another manner, summarizing quickly and giving the readers something positive to consider for the future.

Good writers not only lead the readers to a conclusion about the topic at hand but also ask if they had ever considered a topic this way before reading your essay. It should be a graceful closure to a well-organized and considerate presentation of the evidence that supported your main idea.

As you write the critical finishing review of the body of your essay, you need to make sure the whole paragraph clearly makes the readers feel like the discussion or presentation of your argument is complete. You can't have a dangling idea at the end of a great argument.

The conclusion is what the readers will remember. Whether the purpose of a conclusion is to summarize, call readers to action, or make an impactful personal statement, make it count. Restate in a different way why your argument was oriented the way you chose, wrap up the ideas, and complete the ending thought that clearly shows the readers that you had enough time to finish saying everything.

OBJECTIVE 10 — THE WRITING PROCESS

Skill 10.1 Understand and apply methods for matching forms of writing to audience and purpose

The first step in the writing process when writing for an audience is to determine the purpose of your writing. Is it to complain to an airline about the uncomfortable seats, convince a friend to see a six-hour-long opera with you, or review a book? You may be given writing assignments where the purpose is to express yourself creatively and use your imagination.

For most assignments in an academic setting, however, the basic purpose will be to either summarize, synthesize, or analyze/evaluate a text, issue, or event.

Once you determine the purpose of your writing, it's time to consider your audience. The audience may be peers, a teacher, an employer, parents, or any other number of individuals and/or groups. Either way, when writers know why they are writing and whom they are writing for, they can choose the form of their writing. This is an important part of taking students from completing class assignments, where the forms of writing are taught and selected for them, to becoming independent writers, where after identifying the purpose and audience for their composition, they can determine the most appropriate form for themselves. So, for example, they would write a business letter to complain to an airline, an email to convince a friend, and an expository essay to review a book (this one might be different depending on the audience).

Identifying audience, purpose, and form of writing is the first step in the writing process. It will help you with every other step, from generating ideas for writing to choosing sources to proofreading the publication.

Skill 10.2 Understand and apply methods for generating and organizing ideas for writing

When you are writing, you are trying to convey a message to the readers. You need to ensure that certain points are understood and there is a proper order to help the delivery of your information. All the facts or quotes that you can muster—even when they are true and correctly used—cannot help you make your points if they aren't well organized.

Prewriting Strategies
Writers gather ideas before writing. Prewriting may include clustering, listing, brainstorming, mapping, free writing, and charting.

Listed below are the most common prewriting strategies writers use to explore, plan, and write on a topic.

- Keep an idea book for jotting down ideas that come to mind.
- Write in a daily journal.
- Write down whatever comes to mind on a topic; this is called **free writing**.
- Make a list of all ideas connected with the topic; this is called **brainstorming**. After completing the list, analyze the list to see a pattern or a way to group the ideas
- Ask the questions *who, what, when, where, why,* and *how.* This helps writers approach a topic from several perspectives.
- Create a visual map on paper to gather ideas. Use cluster circles and lines to show connections between ideas. Try to identify the relationship that exists between ideas.
- Observe details of sight, hearing, taste, touch, and taste (creative writing).
- Visualize by making mental images of something and write down the details in a list.

Outlining Strategies

As you begin to develop the message that you want the readers to understand, it's best to form an outline, or mind map. Most people need to physically create an outline and not rely on what they can track in their heads.

To create an outline, brainstorm things about the book, author, or subject matter first. You may ask yourself what questions a topic or text raises for you and write the answers down in a list. You may want to write about obvious messages conveyed in a text you are writing about, and you should put those on the list. Don't forget to include any large topics or themes of the subject you are writing about, such as gender issues, good versus evil, or the individual versus society. If you are writing a creative piece, you want to devise a strategy for how you want your plot to unfold.

Skill 10.3   Understand and apply methods for writing an effective draft of a text

With a knowledge of purpose, audience, and form; a solid outline; and sources or examples to use for evidence or elaboration, writers are ready to begin a first draft of a text. Here are some drafting strategies:

1. Leave yourself plenty of time for revising, editing, and proofreading.
2. Keep all the materials that you will need close by so that you don't have to break your flow to find something you might need to make a point.
3. Make sure you have notes that summarize, evaluate, and/or express your thoughts or opinions. If you have only highlighted notes or copied and pasted quotes, it will be hard for you to write a cohesive and focused draft.

4. Start with your body paragraphs. You can write the introduction and conclusions later. They will be easier to write and more relevant when the body of the text is written.
5. Just *write*! Don't overthink everything. Let the words flow. You have an outline to follow, so you know you are on the right track.
6. Don't try to say everything perfectly the first time. It's okay to make mistakes in your first draft, especially if you left yourself lots of time for revision.
7. Stay focused. It might help to write the text in parts, taking a break when you need to refocus before the next part.
8. If you need to find, rephrase, or work on something, you can make a note while you are writing and then come back to it later. Don't break the flow.
9. Write in your own voice. Readers will be interested in your writing if you are interested in what you are writing about. If you decide that your writing needs to be more formal, you can adjust words, transitions, and sentence structure in the revision stage.
10. Take a break before you read your draft. You need a bit of time and space before being able to effectively start the revision process.

Skill 10.4 Understand and apply methods of revising and editing text

Revising and editing a written text involves much more than checking for spelling and grammatical errors. Those are the last steps involved in the writing process and are outlined in Skill 10.5 (proofreading).

It is useful for writers to read and evaluate their compositions to assess style, language, tone, word choice, sentence variety, transitions, meaning, flow, and interest.

An easy way to do this is to ask yourself these questions as you read the text:

- What is the purpose? Is it clear? Is it useful, valuable, and interesting?
- Does the introduction make the readers want to read this discourse?
- What is the thesis? Is it proven?
- Is the point established?
- Is the reasoning coherent?
- Do your ideas need more elaboration?
- Is the style of writing so wordy that it exhausts the readers and interferes with engagement?
- Is the writing so spare that it is boring?
- Are the sentences too uniform in structure?
- Are there too many simple sentences?
- Are too many of the complex sentences the same structure?
- Are the compounds truly compounds, or are they unbalanced?
- Are parallel structures truly parallel?
- If there are characters, are they believable?
- If there is dialogue, is it natural or stilted?

- Is the title appropriate?
- Is the language appropriate? Is it too formal? Too informal? If jargon is used, is it appropriate?
- Does the writing show creativity, or is it boring?

Skill 10.5   Understand and apply methods for proofreading and preparing a text for publication

Writers should proofread drafts, looking for punctuation, spelling, and grammatical errors. These are some areas that proofreaders check for when they are helping to prepare a piece of writing for publication:

- Spelling and capitalization
- Punctuation (including apostrophes, quotation marks, and spacing)
- Grammar
- Word choice (the right word, i.e. no homonyms or homophones)

See all the skills in Objective 9: Standard American English and Elements of Effective Composition for what to look for when proofreading a written text.

OBJECTIVE 11 RESEARCH

Skill 11.1 Demonstrate knowledge of how to select and refine a research topic

Choosing a research topic is a complex process for many writers. Sometimes writers are given a list of topics to choose from, which can help shorten this process as the list is limited and one topic may stand out above all others. At other times, choosing a topic can be a challenging task.

It is useful for writers to choose topics that interest them. If at first even the brainstorming process is challenging, it might help to scan newspapers, journals, or articles in the subject area for topic ideas.

The brainstorming process, which can be mind-mapping or just writing ideas down in a list, is a necessary part of coming up with an initial inspired idea. The next stage is to narrow that topic down. Mind maps are good organizing structures for this activity because they allow you to graphically represent connections between topics and ideas. Narrowing a topic is an important step in the process because if the topic is too broad, it will affect every step of the writing process. The research stage will take a long time, and the writing will not have a clear focus.

Skill 11.2 Demonstrate knowledge of how to compose effective research questions

A good research question:

- Is not too broad or too narrow
- Can be answered relatively objectively, as in, it does not involve the word "should" or "ought," which immediately involves a value judgment but not necessarily any research or evidence
- Can be answered using information that can be answered with data (either collected or read by the author)

As noted in Skill 10.2, during the prewriting and planning stages, writers do initial research on a topic to formulate a thesis (or theses). During this stage the writer must consider whether there is enough evidence to support the topic adequately. Similarly, he or she may determine that a topic needs to be narrowed down or broadened.

For example, if a writer was writing an essay about how solar energy can combat climate change, he or she could start researching solar energy as a method of reducing greenhouse gas emissions but then soon discover that myriad proposals and technologies are being considered. In that case, it would be appropriate to broaden the research question to investigate different approaches. For example, the question might shift from "In what ways will current solar energy plans address climate change concerns?" to "What proposals to address climate change currently being considered are viable?"

Similarly, if the issue is more local, the writer might find that in his or her particular state, only one or two technologies are being seriously considered. In that case he or she would need to jettison much of the previous line of inquiry and focus the research question more specifically.

The key in determining the research question is flexibility and ongoing review of the process. Research into a topic may reveal additional information or that the context warrants greater focus. One way to assure this is through self-evaluation and review with peers. Feedback from another perspective may help you determine the best course of action.

Skill 11.3 Demonstrate knowledge of how to identify and locate resources for research

Access to information on a topic has never been easier than it is today. Libraries continue to be invaluable resources for quality, credible information. Access to the Internet, however, has changed the research process forever. On almost any topic, a writer can find news articles, encyclopedia entries, academic journals, documentary films, interviews with experts, and photographic evidence. In many cases, it is also possible to read primary source documents (historical documents, contracts, first-person accounts, and so on).

For many people, the biggest difficulty in gathering information is wading through the overabundance of material. Determining whether information is credible and current can often be a tremendous challenge.

If library access is available, several tools are recommended for gathering relevant information. Check with library staff for:

- Subscriptions (digital or print) to discipline-specific journals and magazines
- Subscriptions to databases of articles
- Subscriptions to newspapers (digital or print)
- Digital/physical copies of books on the research topic
- Guidance about the credibility of Websites

A focused research question (Skill 11.2) is an essential first step in finding relevant information. Because of the sheer volume of information available, it is easy to be sidetracked and pursue tangents. Regularly referring to the research question is a key way to find relevant information. That said, it is possible that through the research process the writer may decide to change, broaden, or narrow the focus of research.

Primary and Secondary Sources

The resources used to support a piece of writing can be divided into two major groups: primary and secondary. Primary sources are works, records, and the like that were created during the period being studied or immediately after. Secondary sources are works written significantly after the period being studied and are based on primary sources. Primary sources are the basic materials that provide raw data and information. Secondary sources are works that contain the explications of, and judgments on, this primary material.

Primary sources include:

- Documents that reflect the immediate, everyday concerns of people

Examples: memoranda, bills, deeds, charters, newspaper reports, pamphlets, graffiti, popular writings, journals or diaries, records of decision-making bodies, letters, receipts, snapshots, and so on

- Theoretical writings that reflect care and consideration in composition and that attempt to convince or persuade. The topic will generally be deeper and more pervasive than is the case with "immediate" documents.

Examples: newspaper or magazine editorials, sermons, political speeches, or philosophical writings

- Narrative accounts of events, ideas, and trends written with intentionality by someone contemporary with the events described
- Statistical data, although statistics may be misleading
- Literature and nonverbal materials, novels, stories, poetry, and essays from the period, as well as coins, archaeological artifacts, and art produced during the period

Secondary sources include:

- Books written on the basis of primary materials about the period of time
- Books written on the basis of primary materials about persons who played a major role in the events under consideration
- Books and articles written on the basis of primary materials about the culture, social norms, language, and values of the period
- Quotations from primary sources
- Statistical data on the period
- The conclusions and inferences of other historians
- Multiple interpretations of the ethos of the time

Skill 11.4 Demonstrate knowledge of how to assess the credibility and reliability of sources

Writers should be able to synthesize, analyze, and connect logically the main ideas and supporting details in several sources representing different viewpoints on the same topic and be able to point to the texts for support. They must also be able to discern evidence given in support of an argument and whether it is credible, relevant, and of high quality.

Several questions can help determine the validity and point of view of different sources. These include:

- Who is the target audience for this work?
- What is the point of view of the original author?
- What is left out of the text? Is there a point of view deliberately omitted? Facts or ideas?
- Is there language that is exaggerated? Biased?

Similarly, as mentioned in Skill 6.2, libraries and other information professionals can help curate reliable sources of information. Examples might be:

- Newspapers and magazines
- Academic journals
- TED talks
- Interviews with known experts
- Google scholar searches instead of a simple Google search

To determine reliability, you should be able to find the same information in more than one source. If you can't, you need to continue your research until you have resolved any discrepancies. Do not use information that cannot be verified or test results that cannot be repeated.

Skill 11.5 Demonstrate knowledge of how to gather and organize information for research

After gathering sources for research and determining that they are appropriate and credible, it is helpful for writers to decide how they are going to organize their notes. Many writers use graphic organizers and/or index cards to list main ideas, evidence, and bibliographic information about the sources. This part of the process is crucial.

Staying organized helps writers monitor if they have too much information in one argument and not enough in another. In that case, they may need to find new sources or change an argument because they haven't found any information to support it.

Organizing information helps writers focus on their writing and cite their sources. Using the outline of the composition from the planning phase, writers can organize their information so that when it is time to integrate it into the next phase, they know exactly where it's going to go. Part of this organizing stage includes taking notes on the main idea or argument in the text and, when required, noting or writing the part of the text that is going to be quoted in the composition.

Skill 11.6   Demonstrate knowledge of how to paraphrase, summarize, and quote sources and how to integrate these summaries into a written text

Incorporating quotes and information is partly governed by rules and partly by a sense of flow in the writing. The latter takes practice and often revision to ensure that the results of hard work researching a topic fit and do not interrupt the flow of ideas in the piece.

There are various stylistic guides (*MLA, Harvard, Chicago Manual of Style,* and so on) for doing this. The *MLA* rules (one of the most commonly used set of guidelines) for integrating quotes and examples are below.

Short quotes: Short quotes are considered to be those that are fewer than four lines of typed text (or three lines of typed verse). These are included within double quotation marks (" ") and followed by the author's name and page number. If the author's name is referenced within the text, the page number is sufficient. The work mentioned should appear, properly cited, in the complete list of works referenced (bibliography) page.

Examples:

We must consider whether "a right to catch a fish [is] the same thing as owning a piece of land" (Clover 237).

In his book, The End of the Line, *Clover poses the question whether it "is a right to catch a fish the same thing as owning a piece of land" (237).*

In the first example, in order to maintain the proper flow of the text, it was necessary to insert the word "is." Since this is not part of the actual quote, square brackets enclose it ([ ]).

Long quotes: When quotations are more than four lines long (or more than three of verse), they become a freestanding block of text separate from the rest of the writing. The quotation goes on a new line, is double-spaced, and is indented a half inch from the left margin. It does not get quotation marks. The citation should come at the end and be enclosed in parentheses. If the quote covers more than one paragraph, the new paragraph within the quote should be indented an additional quarter inch. Again, a full citation of the work should be added to the bibliography page.

Example:

Fish will remain an important food source for millions of people if we can find sustainable ways of producing it. Raising salmon on land offers a viable solution.

A new system of farming salmon on land, using pumped seawater, claims that it could slash production costs by a quarter. The production centers would be near markets, cutting transportation costs and food miles. The water would be recirculated and purified using bacteria, then sterilized, cutting the 20 percent mortality rate in sea cages, and the waste would become high-value products... (Clover 307)

Omitting words: At times it is necessary or preferable to omit words from a quotation. This may be because of length or to focus only on what is essential. In this case, the writer uses an ellipse (...) where words are omitted.

Example:

Clover suggest that the "water would be recirculated and purified...cutting the 20 percent mortality rate in sea cages... (307).

Paraphrasing: Paraphrasing is the art of rewording text. The goal is to maintain the original purpose of the statement while translating it into your own words. Your newly generated sentence can be longer or shorter than the original. Concentrate on the meaning, not on the words. Do not change concept words, special terms, or proper names.

There are numerous ways to paraphrase effectively:

- Change the keywords' form or part of speech.

Example: "American news coverage is frequently biased in favor of Western views" becomes "When American journalists cover events, they often display a Western bias."

- Use synonyms of "relationship words." Look for a relationship word, such as "contrast," "cause," or "effect," and replace it with a word that conveys a similar meaning, thus creating a different structure for your sentence.

Example: "Unlike many cats, Purrdy can sit on command" becomes "Most cats are not able to be trained, but Purrdy can sit on command."

- Use synonyms of phrases and words.

Example: "The Beatnik writers were relatively unknown at the start of the decade" becomes "Around the early 1950s, the Beatnik writers were still relatively unknown."

- Change passive voice to active voice or move phrases and modifiers.

Example: "Not to be outdone by the third graders, the fourth-grade class added a musical medley to their Christmas performance" becomes "The fourth-grade class added a musical medley to their Christmas performance to avoid being showed up by the third graders."

- Use reversals or negatives that do not change the meaning of the sentence.

Example: "That burger chain is only found in California" becomes "That burger chain is not found on the East Coast."

Skill 11.7   Demonstrate knowledge of how to cite sources in a written text

Documentation is an important skill in incorporating outside information into a piece of writing. Research is more than cutting and pasting from the Internet, and plagiarism is a serious academic offense.

Tips for Documentation

1. Keep a record of all sources consulted during the research process.
2. As you take notes, avoid unintentional plagiarism. Summarize and paraphrase in your own words without the source in front of you. If you use a direct quote, copy it exactly as written and enclose in quotation marks.
3. Cite anything that is not common knowledge. This includes direct quotes as well as ideas or statistics.

Within the body of your document, follow this blueprint for standard attribution following MLA style.

1. Begin the sentence with "According to _____."
2. Proceed with the material being cited, followed by the page number in parentheses.

In-Text Citation Example
According to Steve Mandel, "our average conversational rate of speech is about 125 words per minute" (78).

Once writers have mastered this basic approach, they can learn more sophisticated methods such as embedding information.

Each source used within the document will have a complete citation in a bibliography or works cited page.

Works Cited Entry
Mandel, Steve. Effective Presentation Skills. Menlo Park, California: Crisp Publications, 1993.

Cite anything that is not common knowledge. This includes direct quotes as well as ideas or statistics.

A works-cited page or bibliography should include any source from which the writer found information, quotes, or ideas. This includes text-based sources, Websites, videos, interviews, and so on. Formats for bibliographies vary (but for this guide we suggest MLA) and can be tricky to get right if done by hand. Luckily, many digital tools can make this process simpler and easy to do as an ongoing process. EasyBib, BibMe, and RefME are just three example.

TEACHER CERTIFICATION STUDY GUIDE

DOMAIN IV	MODES OF WRITING
OBJECTIVE 12	NARRATIVE WRITING

Skill 12.1 Apply and understand various purposes and forms of narrative writing

It is important to have a purpose and choose a form when composing a narrative text. *(See Skill 10.1 for the importance of purpose and form in composition.)*

A general definition of narrative writing is that it relates an experience using a temporal structure. The narrative can be a fictional story, or it can convey a personal experience of the author or someone he or she knows or narrate an event that the author or someone he or she knows has experienced.

Narrative writing can be descriptive by centering on a person, place, or object, using sensory words to create a mood or impression and arranging details in a chronological or spatial sequence. Narrative writing can be developed using an incident or anecdote or a related series of events.

Forms of narrative writing include story, novel, autobiography, biography, memoir, personal essay, and so on.

When a writer has a purpose and a narrative form in mind, he or she is ready to choose a topic or subject.

Skill 12.2 Demonstrate knowledge of how to choose and narrow down a subject for narrative writing

Skill 11.1 focuses on some methods for narrowing down a topic. With narrative writing, the subjects may be more personal, even if an author is writing fiction. The idea-generating strategies writers use may depend on the form and purpose of the narrative writing piece.

The following personal essay and descriptive strategies are adapted from *The Truth of the Matter: Art and Craft in Creative Nonfiction*, by Dinty W. Moore.

Personal Essay Strategy
Think about 10 things you care about deeply, choose one, and then narrow the subject down.

Describing an Event/Experience Strategy
Make a list of six to 10 events or circumstances in your life or those close to you that you have strong feelings and/or that you are curious about

Creative Writing Strategies

There are many strategies for coming up with a good story idea:

- Think about your own life or the lives of people you know and fictionalize parts of their stories.
- Scan newspaper and magazine headlines for personal stories that you can fictionalize.
- Think about a story, song, poem, TV show, movie, or book that you know you can tell from an entirely different perspective or in an entirely different time period or setting. If you do this, you have to be thoughtful about why you are doing this. How will you make the story *yours*?
- Go online to find plot, title, conflict, and character generators and choose one to start

General Strategies

Every form of narrative has online writing prompts. Taking a few minutes to look at the prompts is a good way to be inspired. And if that doesn't work, take a walk with a notebook and write down your observations of the world around you.

There are many more strategies for generating ideas and narrowing topics. Just make sure your topic is focused but also flexible enough to allow you to run with it once you get going on the writing. When you choose a good subject or topic, you have to figure out how to tell the story. What kind of organizational structure are you going to use?

Skill 12.3 Apply and understand various organizational structures used in narrative writing

Narrative writing, whether personal essay, memoir, or short story, depends heavily on time as a deeper structure because in all cases the author is conveying a story, fictional or otherwise. Stories have beginnings, middles, and ends. Events and experiences have starting points, midpoints, and endpoints in space and time, even though we may think about them long after they occur.

Writers can choose to tell their stories by starting at the beginning, in chronological order, or in medias res (the middle of the action) and use flashbacks to narrate the backstory.

In deciding which organizational structures to use in narrative texts, writers should consider purpose and audience. Even if a narrative text is related in chronological order, it still needs a hook or a reason for the readers to keep reading. If the audience is older and/or contemplative, vivid descriptions of setting may do the trick. If the audience is in middle school, starting with a provocative line of dialogue or event will make them want to read more.

TEACHER CERTIFICATION STUDY GUIDE

Skill 12.4 Demonstrate knowledge of how to use language to evoke sensory details in narrative writing

Dialogue is one of the most powerful methods at a writer's disposal for creating a character and developing a story. It is the way we "hear" a character and can create subtle impressions about their outlook on the world, sense of humor, intelligence, and even the way they feel about themselves. Dialogue will reflect countless characteristics. The ability to portray the speech of a character can make or break a story.

The kind of person the character is in the minds of the readers is dependent on the impressions created by description and dialogue. How do other characters feel about this one as revealed by their treatment of him or her, their discussions of him or her with one another, or their overt descriptions of the character? For example, "John, of course, can't be trusted with another person's possessions."

Descriptions of people and places shape narratives in powerful ways. Description can be oriented toward sensory input—what the readers would see, hear, feel, and so on—or toward action. Using words that capture the sense of what is happening (e.g., *screamed* versus *said*) helps develop the story as well.

Setting may be visual, temporal, psychological, or social. Descriptive words are often used here also. In Edgar Allan Poe's description of the house in "The Fall of the House of Usher" as the protagonist/narrator approaches it, the air of dread and gloom that pervades the story is caught in the setting and sets the stage for the story. A setting may also be symbolic, as it is in Poe's story, where the house is a symbol of the family that lives in it. As the house disintegrates, so does the family.

The language used in all these aspects of a story—plot, character, and setting—work together to create the story's mood. Poe's first sentence establishes the mood: "During the whole of a dull, dark, and soundless day in the autumn of the year, when the clouds hung oppressively low in the heavens, I had been passing alone, on horseback, through a singularly dreary tract of country; and at length found myself, as the shades of the evening drew on, within view of the melancholy House of Usher."

Multiple plotlines increase the complexity of a narrative. They are also much more like real life in that our lives are shaped by events that happen out of our direct range. For example, the decision to postpone a test in class may change the story of what the students will do after school.

Skill 12.5 Identify ways to choose a style, voice, and tone for a narrative writing purpose and audience

Just as in choosing a subject and organizational structure, the style, voice, and tone a writer uses depends on the writing purpose and audience.

As with any written work, the voice, language, and style of narrative writing must be adapted to fit different contexts and audiences. A narrative work filled with references to early Mayan history may not be well received despite being extremely well written if the audience is not familiar with the background references.

Similarly, dialogue that relies heavily on slang and popular culture references may be popular with a younger audience but seem nonsensical to someone from a different country or age group. Writers must find their own voice, but if they have something to communicate, they must consider the audience they want to reach.

Point of view or voice is essentially the character through whose eyes the readers see the action. There are at least 13 possible choices for point of view (voice) in literature, as demonstrated and explained by Wallace Hildick in *13 Types of Narrative*. For purposes of helping students write essays about literature, however, three, or possibly four, are adequate. Students should think about how a writer's choice of voice impacts the overall effect of the work. *(See Skill 5.3 regarding the use of point of view in literature.)*

OBJECTIVE 13   EXPOSITORY WRITING

Skill 13.1   Apply and understand various purposes and forms of expository writing

The purpose of an expository writing text can be to inform about, explain, or describe an event, person, thing or, place. Facts, examples, statistics, and information are presented in a formal manner. The tone is direct and the delivery objective rather than subjective. There are many forms of expository writing, and each one has a specific structure.

Expository writing forms include but are not limited to:

- Description
- Classification
- Process-based or how-to
- Compare/contrast
- Cause/effect
- Problem/solution

When beginning to write an expository text, writers should have a purpose and a form in mind. This helps readers better understand the main idea in the text and provides a structure for the writer.

For example, a writer who is writing about the freedom of the press, for example, has several choices to make regarding form. The writer will make these choices depending on the purpose of the composition. Here are some possible expository purposes (we are not writing about persuasive texts here):

- To define the concept
- To inform readers of the legal implications and ramifications
- To recount the history of the concept in the United States
- To evaluate current challenges to the concept

When a purpose is selected, writers have to decide on the form. Using the previous examples, the following form choices could be made:

Purpose	Possible forms
Define a concept	Description, classification
Explore the legal implications	Description, problem/solution
Recount the history	Description, classification, cause/effect
Evaluate current challenges	Cause/effect, problem/solution, compare and contrast

Before writing, good writers make careful choices that incorporate the purpose, audience, and form.

Skill 13.2 Demonstrate knowledge of how to choose and narrow down a subject for expository writing

The following suggestions are adapted from *The Craft of Research*.

The first step in choosing a topic is to think about what you might already know about your subject. For example, if the subject is women's rights, you might think about issues that are in the news relating to women's right or you might remember some of the pioneers in the women's rights movement or the issues they addressed.

The second step is to make a list or a word web of words, people, and events. You might write down Gloria Steinem, Angela Davis, Sylvia Pankhurst, and so on. You might write down the right to vote. You might write down equal pay.

Another step is to think about how you view the topic. What do you want to emphasize? Do you want to write about a person or people and what they contributed to the women's rights movement? Do you want to explain how women won the right to vote? Do you want to inform readers about the topic of pay equity?

To develop or narrow down your topic, it helps to list keywords or concepts and connect them to one another. Organize keywords, names, or events around these concepts. Using word webs to show connections between topics might help you organize your writing as well as narrow your topic from a wide subject area.

A good strategy after this is to try to write your topic and purpose in one sentence. For example, "I am exploring the issue of how women in the United States won the right to vote in order to find out what strategies worked and which strategies failed in order to help my readers understand what strategies they can use to work for change."

With purpose, focus, and form, writers are ready to formulate a good essay question and a thesis.

Skill 13.3 Demonstrate knowledge of how to formulate good essay questions and theses in writing expository texts

(See Skill 11.2 for how to formulate a research question.)

Once a topic is assigned or chosen, the next step is to begin preliminary research. Those materials may come from the writer's own experience, and the best way to collect them is in prewriting—simply putting on paper whatever past experiences the writer has relevant to the topic; observations concerning it; newspaper articles or books the writer has read on the topic; and television or radio presentations related to the topic.

The writer needs to keep in mind the need to make a statement about the topic—to declare something about it. Often, once the writer has gone through this exercise, getting his or her own ideas and thoughts down on paper, a thesis or several theses may emerge. If not, then it is time to continue research on the topic.

Skill 13.4 Apply and understand various organizational structures used in expository writing

Each of the forms of expository writing identified in Skill 13.1 influences the organizational structure of the piece. This organization is used in combination with the standard organization of informational texts. *(See Skills 2.2 and 2.3.)*

Below are some common expository writing forms along with some accompanying organizational structures:

Form	Structure
Description	Explain the features of a person, place, thing, or event organized by general features or in chronological order (if an event)
Classification	Break a large topic down into smaller pieces, starting from the general to the specific
How-to	List explanations of how to do something in either numeric (like a recipe) or chronological order (the writing process)
Compare/contrast	Usually compare two ideas, events, people, or things, organized by similarities and differences
Cause/effect	Describe relationship between two events, usually organized by cause and then effect
Problem/solution	Define and explain a problem and then offer one or more solutions

Informative texts share elements in common with persuasive texts. Rather than trying to convince the readers of a particular point of view, however, the writer of an informative text seeks to clearly explain a topic. Beginning with a thesis paragraph, the writer relays the main idea of the essay and introduces the topic. The informative essay introduction may state the importance of the topic or may simply describe the topic.

An essay on measures to combat climate change may begin with a paragraph explaining why researchers feel that taking action to stop climate change is important before going on to explain different proposals to combat it. Though there may be an element of opinion here, the focus is on giving information rather than picking a side.

The first or topic paragraph clearly establishes what the rest of the piece will be about. Typically, this paragraph should only be five or six sentences long, so from the beginning, thoughts must be well organized. The writer must clearly establish what the rest of the piece will be about and may also include purpose.

Subsequent paragraphs elaborate on the topic. Using the previously mentioned example of measures to combat climate change, the paragraphs that follow the introduction would do the following:

- Explain a proposal to deal with climate change.
- Describe the research that has been done regarding that proposal.
- Share information about the result so far.
- Explain another proposal.
- Describe related research regarding that proposal.

The structure continues to build not toward an argument (as in a persuasive piece) but toward a full understanding of what proposals are being considered (again, using this example) to combat climate change. The different sections are linked by the common thread established in the introduction and go on to explain related ideas and information.

The essential thing to remember is that the ideas must be organized so that the readers' knowledge steadily builds. The writer takes care to fully explain one element before moving on to another.

A mark of maturity in writing is the effective use of transitional devices at all levels. For example, a topic sentence can be used to establish continuity, especially if it is positioned at the beginning of a paragraph. The most common device is to refer to what has preceded, repeat or summarize it, and then introduce a new topic.

(See Skill 9.6 for explanations of transitions.)

Conclusions
Aristotle taught that the conclusion should strive to do five things:

1. Inspire the reader with a favorable opinion of the writer.
2. Amplify the force of the points made in the body of the paper.
3. Reinforce the points made in the body.
4. Rouse appropriate emotions in the readers.
5. Restate in a summary way what has been said.

The conclusion may be short or it may be long depending on its purpose in the paper. Recapitulation, a brief restatement of the main points or certainly of the thesis, is a common part of effective conclusions. A good example is a court trial where an attorney would review the main points, tying together all the information previously shared.

In an informative piece, the writer would generally refer back to the main idea and make a larger point about it. Again using the example of the proposals to combat climate change, the conclusion might read something like this:

With competing proposals to tackle climate change, individuals, businesses, and government leaders will have to make some difficult decisions. Costs, feasibility, and the ability of researchers to "sell" their ideas to the public will all play a role in the final outcome. In the meantime, people with beachfront property may be watching the sea warily.

Skill 13.5 Demonstrate knowledge of how to use effective and appropriate supporting details in expository texts

(See also Skills 9.5 and 11.6.)

The structure of an expository composition should be organized to inform the readers by logically explaining different elements of the topic. Each section should contain facts, quotes, and other details to help the readers understand the topic thoroughly. Continuing with the example of proposals to combat climate change, here are some ideas of the type of information that might be incorporated into the different sections:

- Definition of greenhouse gases and its acronym
- Statistics about the amount of greenhouse gases produced by cars in a typical American city
- Cost of electric vehicle
- Quote from a producer of electric vehicles about their potential
- Description of how solar panels work
- Explanation of a particular city that has installed large numbers of solar panels
- And so on

Though a writer could likely explain several different proposals to combat climate change in general terms, the addition of details like statistics, quotes, and examples are necessary to truly inform the readers (and to show that the writer knows what he or she is talking about).

Skill 13.6 Identify ways to make expository writing clear, direct, and succinct

In writing or speaking, you can be convincing if you follow the three basic principles of unity, coherence, and emphasis.

Unity: All ideas must relate to the controlling thesis. At the simplest level, this means that all sentences must develop the topic sentence of a paragraph. By extension, then, all paragraphs must develop the thesis statement of the essay; all chapters must develop the main idea of the book; and all ideas must develop the argument.

Coherence: One way to achieve unity is to show the relationships between ideas by using transitional words, phrases, sentences, and paragraphs. Using coordinating conjunctions (for, and, nor, but, or, yet, so), subordinating conjunctions (because, since, whenever), or transitional adverbs (however, therefore) is an effective way to show logical order and thus create coherence. Another way to show relationships between ideas is to use an appropriate strategy (spatial, chronological, cause/effect, classification, and comparison/contrast) to arrange details.

Emphasis: Use strategic placement of arguments to emphasize the significance of the ideas. In direct order, the main ideas are stated first and then supported by reasons or details. In indirect order, the support is provided first (in either increasing or decreasing order of importance) and leads to a well-defended argument.

Successful informative writing includes words and terminology specifically related to the topic. Just as a writer could likely describe in general terms several proposals related to combating climate change, he or she could do so without using specific terms. The effect, however, would not be particularly interesting or informative, and the readers would likely come away having learned nothing.

As an example, a writer could talk about ways in which humans have impacted the environment, but using the term "Anthropocene" (a term many scientists use to describe the age in which we are living) gives a greater sense of the scale of change that researchers are warning about and more weight to the information being shared.

Successfully using this type of domain-specific language requires learning on the part of the writer, research, and often clear definitions of terms for the readers.

OBJECTIVE 14   PERSUASIVE WRITING

Skill 14.1   Apply and understand various purposes and forms of persuasive writing

A persuasive text can generally be described as a text that is constructed to make you do, think, or want something. Depending on the purpose and the audience, writers choose the appropriate form of persuasive writing to get their points across. Sometimes the form and purpose of a persuasive composition is given to a writer, as in an ad writer or a student in a history class, in which case the writer identifies the audience for the writing and crafts the text to reach them.

Some forms of persuasive writing include editorials, essays, speeches, letters, songs, poems, advertisements, personal opinion writing, and so on.

General features of a persuasive text are that claims are made and supported and appeals are used to convince the readers. Appeals in persuasive texts can be emotional, logical, personal, or stylistic or a combination of any or all of these. The focus in a persuasive piece is trying to convince or persuade the readers, so knowing the audience is an essential aspect of an effective piece of writing.

(See Objective 3 for more on persuasive text features, forms, and purposes.)

Skill 14.2   Demonstrate knowledge of how to choose a position or idea for a subject for persuasive writing

Planning, writing, revising, and rewriting are essential elements of good writing. All successful writers go through these stages. With persuasive writing, this is equally true as the writer refines an argument to be as powerful, concise, and compelling as possible.

In developing the central message of a persuasive piece of writing, it's often best to form an outline (or "mind map"). Any time there is a limited timeframe to finish writing, the few minutes spent organizing one's thoughts are beneficial because it saves time later on. Most people need to write an outline (or type it out) and not rely on what they can track in their head (that makes it too easy for errors, and the hard copy allows you to check off when you complete that discussion area in your essay).

To create an outline, brainstorm things about the topic first. Start with potential thesis statements and try to come up with examples of facts and/or reasons that support that point of view. Successful writers revisit this list, considering better ideas and then finding specific facts or data to elaborate on a claim.

This process is the strongest way to form a persuasive argument. When you have taken a few minutes to draft the outline, when you reach the concluding portion, it is fairly easy to determine if you have indeed identified the correct thesis or you should change it—much simpler to do before you get deep into writing.

After writing, it is common to seek feedback about the clarity of ideas and the efficacy of the supporting arguments. Sometimes additional research is needed to find stronger examples. At other times, a counterpoint may be anticipated, allowing the writer to refine and improve his or her argument. These stages of planning, writing, revising, and rewriting are essential parts of the writing process.

Skill 14.3 Apply and understand various organizational structures used in persuasive writing, including using supporting details

The structure of a persuasive essay, regardless of length, is fairly consistent and expected by readers. Beginning with a thesis paragraph, the writer relays the main idea of the essay and introduces the topic. The next several paragraphs of the essay support the main idea, using examples that give credence to the main idea. At times, writers may use the compare/contrast organizational style that gives "counterpoints" at the end of the supporting paragraphs to show recognition of the opposite argument.

Introduction and Main Idea or "Thesis" of the Essay
The first or topic paragraph answers a question or expresses the writer's position, lays out an argument, and presents brief highlights of how the writer plans to support that argument. This first paragraph makes a claim (statement) and shows how the composition will support it. Typically, this paragraph should only be five or six sentences long, so from the beginning, thoughts must be well organized.

The most common introductory sentences (usually two at the beginning of this paragraph) begin to set the tone and topic for the readers. The writer defines the central idea from the start and then builds support for it. "Frankenstein was not a monster, but rather a representation of the ills in society" is an example of a strong main idea that could be supported by passages in Mary Shelley's book as well as other writings of that time. It clearly and plainly states what the readers will learn in the paper.

The sequencing of arguments in persuasive writing is useful in constructing a logical, compelling claim. Though appeals to emotion can be powerful features of persuasive writing, the structure is expected to be logical and to methodically lay out the writer's reasoning. Without a strong structure, many arguments fall flat or are considered open to criticism.

A common framework involves three arguments and/or reasons or pieces of evidence to support a claim. People are often accustomed to reading lists of three. When considering that studies have shown repeatedly that it takes a person six times to hear a message in order to believe it, this threefold format makes sense. Each of the three supporting ideas has two subsupporting prongs that uphold or illustrate the supporting idea—that adds up to six points to support your main idea.

Writers often include six or seven specific examples to support their central idea. Each then falls into a type of category. This gives three paragraphs in order to support the introductory thesis paragraph, and each of these support paragraphs has two examples to support the topic of each paragraph. Each paragraph should go back to the thesis to address the central point, ensuring that there is support for the main idea (and not just restating it).

With the Frankenstein example, where the generalization of societal ills incorporated the supportive categories of boundaries, grotesqueness, and secrecy/shame, the writer might include two points that helped create these categories:

    Point 1: Boundaries
        Subpoint A: isolation or alienation from society
        Subpoint B: perspectives alter viewpoint(s)' interpretation
    Point 2: Grotesqueness
        Subpoint C: delusions of personal grandeur and lack of self-reflexion
        Subpoint D: personal assumptions based on appearance
    Point 3: Secrecy/shame
        Subpoint E: shame of rejection, which leads to revenge
        Subpoint F: madness compels Victor to create his own reality

Use your knowledge of the book and the subpoints to determine the strongest one (the one you can write about the most easily and with the most confidence). You should shift the order of the list so that this identified strong point is now the last grouping. You may even reorder the subpoints within the point to help ensure the final subpoint in each paragraph is the strongest.

Skill 14.4   Demonstrate knowledge of how to anticipate counterarguments and incorporate responses in a persuasive writing text

Another potential structure in persuasive writing involves point/counterpoint. This structure can be written by alternating supporting points and counterpoints all by explaining all the reasons for and the reasons against (block all of one side of the argument and then block all of the other side of the argument), ensuring that the strongest arguments, just as before, are incorporated at the end of the composition.

If, for example, the writer is comparing two people and how they performed their jobs—authors, politicians, characters, or whoever—the block method is probably best suited for that persuasion. The author takes the points for each, but lists Author A with all of her or his qualities on the topics and then provides Author B with all of her or his qualities on the same points. In this way, the writer blocks points one, two, and three for each person being compared, and the transitions explain the differences in the second person's outline by using such phrases as "compared to Author A, Author B said…" or "unlike Author A, Author B thought it necessary to focus on..." to relate the blocks to each other.

Persuasive arguments always engage readers to follow a train of thought to reach a conclusion, but these two methods take much more energy, focus, and commitment on the part of the author. The block method in this particular style results in a composition that appears "A, A, and A, whereas B, B, and B yield to conclusion that [A or B] was..." and the effort must be focused on showing the differences on these pieces and how or why one is preferred or the other option. The point/counterpoint method requires that the writer keep the readers engaged and wanting to read further as the "argument ball" goes back and forth between support, and the final "shot" is the one that cinches support for the main idea. Once the support pieces are completed, the writer moves to the final step of the essay.

The final piece of a story is always the most memorable—for good or bad. In a persuasive essay it is important that your conclusion is *not* a mirror image of the introduction with only a few word changes. Rather, it is essential to give a slightly modified thesis, building upon facts and subpoints used. It's strongest when the writer is able to state the thesis in another manner, summarizing quickly and giving the readers something positive to consider for the future.

To restate the main idea used with the previous Frankenstein example, we can adjust the main idea to reflect the generalized supportive points. For example, we may wrap the conclusion around the main sentence for this paragraph as "The monster was a manifestation of personal flaws—shame, alienation, outrageous ego—and Shelley compelled the readers to reflect on how environment and nature shape the development of a person and society's acceptance of things that are different."

This statement takes the readers back to what was included in the body, but in a different phrasing, and actually gives the action item of how to read the story without asking a question. (In general using a question is strongly discouraged.) A strong conclusion practically begs the readers to ask themselves if they are smart enough to think of it in the manner in which the persuasive essay has.

The conclusion is what the readers will remember. It is the last thing they see before deciding whether an argument is compelling. Good writing makes it count, restating in a different way why the argument was oriented in such a way and wrapping up the ideas neatly.

Skill 14.5   Identify ways to choose a style, voice, and diction for a persuasive writing purpose and audience

To write a successful persuasive argument, it is essential to understand one's audience. If the anticipated audience has extensive background knowledge in a subject, for example, they will quickly lose interest (or perhaps even feel resentful) if a writer feels it is necessary to include the basic details about a topic. Conversely, if the intended audience is unfamiliar with a topic, the writer can lose the audience by focusing on a high-level, in-depth analysis of a topic.

Similarly, if a writer is trying to persuade an audience that consists of people who work in the oil industry of the need to reduce consumption of fossil fuels to address climate change, he or she must be careful not to be seen as demonizing the oil industry as the cause of the problem. Rather, a successful argument might include calls for a gradual transition to different energy sources while providing support for workers who need retraining. If appealing to politicians, a writer might reference their responsibility to the long-term health and prosperity of the country.

Writers must learn to adapt their writing to the needs of their audiences. One way to do this is to determine the values, needs, constraints, and demographics of their audience.

Values: What matters to this group of people? What is their background, and how will that affect their perception of your arguments?

Needs: Find out in advance what the audience's needs are. Why are they reading your writing? Find a way to satisfy their needs.

Constraints: What might hold the audience back from being fully engaged in what you are saying, agreeing with your point of view, or processing what you are trying to say? These could be political reasons, which make them wary of your ideology from the start, or knowledge reasons, in which the audience lacks the appropriate background information to grasp your ideas. Avoid this last constraint by staying away from technical terminology, slang, or abbreviations that may be unclear to your audience.

Demographic information: Demographics could include age, gender, education, religion, income level, and other such countable characteristics. Arguing for greater support for public schools to an audience of seniors might be more successful if it referenced the need to provide for future generations or noted the strong support for community schools they enjoyed as children. An argument on the same topic to wealthy families who may or may not send their children to public schools might emphasize the shared responsibility of all citizens to ensure an educated populace for the good of society.

After determining the audience, writers should decide which one (or more) of the following appeals will sway the readers:

Personal: using the author's personality
Emotional: using and/or triggering the readers' emotions
Logical: using science, statistics, or logical arguments
Stylistic: using language (figurative, stylistic devices, word choice)

TEACHER CERTIFICATION STUDY GUIDE

OBJECTIVE 15   CRITICAL/ANALYTICAL WRITING

Skill 15.1   Apply and understand various purposes and forms of critical or analytical writing

A critical or analytical text can generally be described as a critique or analysis of a text. The text can be a book, story, video, movie, song, painting, and so on. This type of text is not the same as a review.

It critically evaluates a text by looking at features, passages, or smaller pieces and by doing one or more of the following:

- Evaluating strengths and weaknesses
- Comparing/contrasting with other texts
- Analyzing the ways in which the smaller pieces contribute to the whole
- Connecting/locating the text thematically to movements, events, and so on

The most common form of analytical writing is a critical essay, although that essay may focus on different aspects of the text it is analyzing, such as what the text says, does, or means. Essential elements of the analysis include references to content, language, and structure.

Skill 15.2   Demonstrate knowledge of how to formulate specific critical or analytical questions and an effective thesis statement

With expository, persuasive, and critical/analytical writing, having a good question and thesis statement is an essential element of effective composition. If a topic or question is not assigned, writers can choose topics or questions for analysis using methods similar to those used in expository and persuasive writing.

With critical and analytical writing, the question you pose will become the thesis of your essay. A good way to start thinking about a question or thesis is review your notes and see if you can find patterns or ideas that spark your interest, curiosity, or emotions. Choose a one and flesh it out by expressing it in the form of a question and then answering the question. When you find a question and answer that you feel would work for the purpose, audience, and form of critical or analytical writing that you are doing, just take the answer and phrase it as a thesis.

There are other methods for coming up with central questions and thesis ideas. These include using online resources and/or consulting printed texts relating to writing critical essays.

A thesis statement needs to be a specific, arguable point. In this example, adapted from the Purdue Writing Lab, here are three possible thesis statements about a literary text. Only the last one would make a good thesis for a critical or analytical essay:

- The book *1984* is boring and pointless.
- The book *1984* is about a man living in a futuristic society.
- The book *1984* is about the problem of a totalitarian government trying to control its citizens.

Skill 15.3   Apply and understand various organizational structures used in critical or analytical writing

Critical and analytical essays follow along with the general organizational structure of most informational writing compositions, i.e., introduction, body, conclusion, thesis, supporting details, and transitions.

Some structures that are more specific to critical and analytical writing can be used depending on the purpose and/or main focus of the essay. For example, a writer may choose to use a compare/contrast format when writing about two books by the same author. A writer may also choose to organize elements of the analysis from the simple to the most complex if the focus of the composition is more descriptive. Another way to organize the structure of the critical or analytical essay is by ordering specific examples from a text either chronologically, by importance, from simple to complex, or with another thread that supports your thesis and arguments.

You can organize your composition by text (starting first with one and then moving on to the other) or by point (incorporating analysis of both texts).

Within the body of your essay, each section is organized with a passage or example and an interpretation of that example and how it relates to the central idea of the composition.

Skill 15.4   Demonstrate knowledge of how to develop a solid literary analysis in critical or analytical writing

Other skills in this book identify ways to incorporate quotes and passages into written texts. When writing a critical or analytical essay, it is essential to take detailed notes while reading through the texts you are analyzing. While rereading sections of the text, it is a good idea to paraphrase, summarize, and mark the direct quotations you may want to use in your analysis.

Critical and analytical writing is based on a claim, like persuasive writing, so you should filter the notes and quotes that you highlighted by looking at whether they support your claim. Gather the strongest and most relevant evidence and examples from the text(s) to incorporate into your analysis. Sometimes you will want to include quotes from secondary sources as well as words or phrases from the original text.

The skills for incorporating quotes from a text into a piece of writing can be found in Objective 11.

Skill 15.5 Identify ways to relate or connect characters, themes, and points of view in various literary works

One of the main tasks of critical or analytical literary essays is to relate and connect elements from one literary text to another. These elements for analysis can include character, themes, and points of view.
One step is this process can be to list similarities and differences in these elements. Your essay might focus on similarities, differences, and/or both. Sometimes writers compare two seemingly different texts to uncover similarities, and other times they do the opposite.

Another way to connect themes, characters, and points of view in various literary works is to use one text as a lens through which to view the other. Using one text to understand another can be an effective way to relate two literary texts.

These strategies or frameworks for connecting texts are adapted from Harvard University's writing center and can be broken down into the following stages:

- Frame of reference: What idea, theme, question, problem, or theory connects the texts or textual elements in question?
- Grounds for comparison: Why compare these literary texts? Your essay needs to make it clear to the readers that your grounds for comparison is justified.

If you choose to use one text as a lens for viewing the other text, the organizational structure of your writing might be to discuss one text and then the other. If you are comparing texts, you might use the point-by-point structure for your writing.

TEACHER CERTIFICATION STUDY GUIDE

DOMAIN V   ORAL AND VISUAL COMMUNICATION

OBJECTIVE 16   EFFECTIVE LISTENING AND SPEAKING STRATEGIES (INCLUDING GROUP DISCUSSION)

Skill 16.1   Understand purposes of listening, listening strategies, and challenges to effective listening

Listening is not a skill that is talked about much except when someone clearly does not listen. The truth is, though, that listening is a specific skill for specific circumstances. There are two aspects to listening that warrant attention. The first is comprehension or understanding what someone says, the purposes behind the message, and the contexts in which it is said. The second aspect is purpose. While someone may completely understand a message, what is the listener supposed to do with it—just nod and smile, or go out and take action?

Often, when we understand the purpose of listening in various contexts, comprehension will be much easier. Furthermore, when we know the purpose of listening, we can better adjust our comprehension strategies.

Listening is often done for the purpose of enjoyment, and schools must teach students how to listen and enjoy such work. Teachers can accomplish this by making it fun and giving many possibilities and alternatives to capture the wide array of interests in each classroom.

Students like to listen to stories, poetry, and radio dramas and theater. Listening to literature can also be a great pleasure. In the classrooms of exceptional teachers, we will often find that students are captivated by the reading aloud of good literature.

Strategies for Active Listening
Oral speech can be difficult to follow. When complex or new information is provided to us orally, we must analyze and interpret that information. Often, making sense of this information can be tough when presented orally because students have no place to go back and review material already stated.

Students must have opportunities to listen in large and small group conversations. The difference here is that conversation requires more than just listening. It involves feedback and active involvement.

This can be particularly challenging, as the dominant culture in the United States focuses more on moving conversations along, discouraging silence in a conversation, and always getting the last word in. This poses significant problems for the art of listening. In a discussion, for example, when we are instead preparing our next response—rather than listening to what others are saying—we do a large disservice to the entire discussion.

Students need to learn how listening carefully to others in discussions actually promotes better responses on the part of subsequent speakers. One way teachers can encourage this, in both large and small group discussions, is to expect students to respond directly to the previous student's comments before moving ahead with their new comments. This will encourage them to pose their new comments in light of the comments that came just before them.

Students must also be able to listen for transitions between ideas. Sometimes, in oral speech, this is pretty simple when voice tone or body language changes. Of course, we don't have the luxury of looking at paragraphs in oral language, but we do have the animation that comes along with live speech. Human beings would have to try hard to be completely nonexpressive in their speech. Listeners should take advantage of this and notice how the speaker changes character and voice to signal a transition of ideas. Also, simply looking to see expression on the face of a speaker can do more to signal irony, for example, than trying to extract irony from actual words.

One good way to follow oral speech is to take notes and outline major points. Because oral speech can be more circular (as opposed to linear) than written text, it can extremely helpful to keep track of an author's message.

Other classroom methods can help students learn good listening skills. For example, teachers can have students practice following complex directions. They can also have students orally retell stories—or retell (in writing or in oral speech) oral presentations of stories or other materials. These activities give students direct practice in the essential skills of listening. They provide students with outlets in which they can slowly improve their abilities to comprehend oral language and take decisive action based on oral speech.

Challenges to effective listening can be grouped into three areas: the listener, the person speaking, and the environment in which the speaking and listening is taking place. Each of these areas contains a myriad of factors that can cause listening to be a challenge. It is essential that educators are aware of these challenges so that they can help students make maximum progress in developing effective listening skills.

Skill 16.2 Understand the ways in which interpersonal communication is influenced by social norms/conventions, individual and cultural factors

There are two aspects of interpersonal communication outlined by this skill. One is that a person's communication style is influenced by individual or sociocultural factors. The second is that specific interpersonal situations are characterized by social norms and conventions.

As effective speakers and listeners, we need to realize that some of the listeners and speakers we are communicating with may face challenges in understanding the nuances of what we are saying or trying to communicate. Similarly, we may struggle to get a handle on the nuances of what someone is trying to communicate to us.

Once we take these factors into account, we can more quickly identify barriers to effective communication and try to ameliorate them. As educators, we can actively teach social norms and conventions so that students who struggle with them for whatever reason can practice and develop the skills themselves.

Educators can help students who face challenges communicating (either speaking or listening) by finding out whether these challenges exist due to social, political, environmental, cultural, or individual factors (or a combination of these factors) in order to help students identify what to do to overcome these challenges. Educators should work hard to help all students understand that social norms and conventions are learned and that they should try to understand one another and improve their communication skills.

Skill 16.3   Understand strategies for effective participation in group discussions

Effective listening and speaking skills can be developed with practice and an understanding of the techniques.

Communication skills are crucial in a collaborative society. In particular, a person cannot be a successful communicator without being an active listener. Focus on what others say rather than planning on what to say next. By listening to everything another person is saying, you may pick up on natural cues that lead to the next conversation without needing added effort.

Starting a Discussion
It is quite acceptable to use standard opening lines to facilitate a conversation. Don't agonize trying to come up with witty one-liners—the main obstacle in initiating a conversation is just getting the first statement over with. After that, the real substance begins. A useful technique may be to comment or ask a question about a shared situation. This may be anything from the weather to the food you are eating to a new policy at work. Use an opener you are comfortable with because your partner in conversation will be comfortable with it as well.

Stimulating Higher-Level Critical Thinking through Inquiry
Many people rely on questions to communicate with others. Most, however, fall back on simple clarifying questions rather than open-ended inquiries. For example, if you paraphrase a response by asking "Did you mean this…?" you may receive merely a "yes" or "no" answer. One open-ended inquiry would ask "What did you mean when you said…?"

Try to ask open-ended, deeper-level questions since those tend to have the greatest reward and lead to a greater understanding. With answers to those questions, you can make more complex connections and achieve more significant information.

The following strategies for educators, adapted from The Teaching Center at Washington University, St. Louis, Missouri, can help all students be more effective participants in group discussions:

- Assign some students to encourage other students to speak.
- Vary teaching methods so that shyer students get practice speaking with partners and/or in small groups before larger group discussions.
- Include time for questions after each class or presentation with questions ready in case students don't have them.
- Use verbal and nonverbal cues to encourage speakers and teach these cues to students.
- Wait time can help students—teach this concept to students as well so that they give one another that time in group discussions.
- Encourage listening without interrupting so that listeners can hear the whole thing before speaking or answering.
- Teach students how to ask follow-up questions and model those yourself.
- Encourage constructive responses to disagreement including the use of "I" statements.
- Redirect and teach students how to do this so that more students participate.

Skill 16.4 Understand how to craft and present effective oral presentations including language, style, rhetorical devices, and vocal techniques

Oral discursive forms include debates, speeches, discussions, and conversations. The ability to use language and logic to convince the audience to accept your reasoning and to side with you is an art.

Effective oral presentations are presented in a logically sequenced way and include supporting reasons and evidence. A position statement, evidence, reason, and evaluation and refutation are integral parts of this schema. *(See Skill 8.3 on language and audience.)*

The art of rhetoric was first developed in ancient Greece. Its pioneer was Socrates, who recognized the crucial role that rhetoric played in education, politics, and storytelling. Socrates argued that, presently effectively, speech could evoke any desired emotion or opinion. His method of dialectic syllogism, known today as the Socratic Method, pursued truth through a series of questions.

Today, rhetoric's evolution can be traced back to ancient Athens in many facets of our society. The structure of many governments and judicial systems reflect rhetorical tactics established by the Greeks so long ago.

The media has taken rhetoric to a whole new level and has refined it to a skilled art. Every word, as well as the method of presentation, is carefully planned. The audience is taken into account and speech tailored to their needs and motivations. Though the content has changed, this concept has been around since Socrates contemplated it thousands of years ago.

Posture
Maintain a straight but not stiff posture. Instead of shifting weight from hip to hip, point your feet directly at the audience and distribute your weight evenly. Keep shoulders toward the audience. If you have to turn your body to use a visual aid, turn 45 degrees and continue speaking toward the audience.

Movement
Instead of staying glued to one spot or pacing back and forth, stay within four to eight feet of the front row of your audience. Take a step or half step to the side every once in a while. If you are using a lectern, feel free to move to the front or side of it to engage your audience more. Avoid distancing yourself from the audience; you want them to feel involved and connected.

Gestures
Gestures can help you maintain a natural atmosphere when speaking publicly. Use them just as you would when speaking to a friend. They shouldn't be exaggerated, but they should be used for added emphasis. Avoid keeping your hands in your pockets or locked behind your back, wringing your hands and fidgeting nervously, or keeping your arms crossed.

Eye Contact
Many people are intimidated by using eye contact when speaking to large groups. Interestingly, eye contact usually helps the speaker overcome speech anxiety by connecting with the attentive audience and easing feelings of isolation. Instead of looking at a spot on the back wall or at your notes, scan the room and make eye contact for one to three seconds per person.

Voice
Many people fall into one of two traps when speaking: using a monotone or talking too fast. These are both caused by anxiety. A monotone restricts your natural inflection but can be remedied by releasing tension in the upper- and lower-body muscles. Subtle movement will keep you loose and natural. Talking too fast, on the other hand, is not necessarily bad if you are exceptionally articulate. If you are not a strong speaker or you are talking about technical items, the audience will easily become lost. When you talk too fast and begin tripping over your words, consciously pause after every sentence you say. Don't be afraid of brief silences. The audience needs time to absorb what you are saying.

Volume
Problems with volume, whether too soft or too loud, can usually be overcome with practice. If you tend to speak too softly, have someone stand in the back of the room and signal you when your volume is strong enough. If possible, have someone stand in the front of the room as well to make sure you're not overcompensating with excessive volume. Conversely, if you have a problem with speaking too loudly, have the person in the front of the room signal you when your voice is soft enough and check with the person in the back to make sure it is still loud enough to be heard. In both cases, note your volume level for future reference. Don't be shy about asking your audience, "Can you hear me in the back?" Suitable volume is beneficial for both you and the audience.

Pitch
Pitch refers to the length, tension, and thickness of your vocal bands. As your voice gets higher, the pitch gets higher. In oral performance, pitch reflects emotional arousal level. More variation in pitch typically corresponds to more emotional arousal but can also be used to convey sarcasm or highlight specific words. By encouraging the development of proper techniques for oral presentations, you are enabling your students to develop self-confidence for higher levels of communication.

OBJECTIVE 17 EFFECTIVE MEDIA VIEWING, ANALYZING, AND PRESENTING STRATEGIES

Skill 17.1 Interpret and evaluate visual images in various forms of media (messages, themes, bias, meanings)

Every day, students and teachers "read" and interpret visual images in various forms of media. A basic understanding of media literacy can help readers and viewers understanding the meanings, themes, messages, and biases in these texts.

Media literacy organizations generally agree on five key concepts in media literacy:

1. All forms of media are constructed texts and, as such, are a product of individual and group decisions (ethical, economic, social, cultural, political). Some of these decisions are conscious and some are unconscious.
    a. Key investigative areas for interpretation are authorship, purpose, and the values or beliefs embedded in the text.

2. Readers/viewers negotiate meaning. *(See Skill 17.3.)*
    a. Key investigative areas for interpretation are how different people might interpret the images and texts differently, and what experiences you bring to your viewing or reading experience.

3. Media is tied to economic transactions.
    a. Key investigative areas for interpretation relate to the commercial purpose of the image or text and how this may influence content and presentation.

4. Media communicates values (social, political, and so on).
    a. Key investigative areas for interpretation relate to the ways in which some objects, people, or places in the images or text may be portrayed in a negative or positive way, and some people, places, and objects may be missing from the picture.

5. Each medium has its own form (as do other written and oral texts),
    a. Key investigative areas for interpretation relate to presentation and design techniques, editing/manipulation of images, and organizational structures of the specific form.

An understanding of key media literacy concepts and questions can help readers or viewers interpret and evaluate visual messages in various forms of media.

Skill 17.2 Understand the ways in which visual images can be used as persuasive texts in various forms of media

(See Skill 17.1 for investigative and interpretive questions and concepts.)

Visual images can be used as or incorporated into various media as persuasive texts. The same types of appeal used in oral and written persuasive texts are used in media texts.

Visual images can consist of symbols to announce upcoming events, push ideas, and advertise products. By using attractive photographs, brightly colored cartoon characters, or instructive messages, they increase sales, win votes, or stimulate learning. The graphics are designed to communicate messages clearly, precisely, and efficiently.

Images are used, often in combination with text, in the following persuasive appeals:

Beauty appeal: Beauty attracts us; we are drawn to beautiful people, places, and things.

Celebrity endorsement: This technique associates product use with a well-known person. By purchasing this product we are led to believe that we will attain characteristics similar to the celebrity.

Compliment the consumer: Advertisers flatter the consumer who is willing to purchase their product. By purchasing the product, the consumer is recognized by the advertisers for making a good decision with the selection.

Escape: Getting away from it all is appealing; you can imagine adventures you cannot have. The idea of escape is pleasurable.

Independence/individuality: This technique associates products with people who can think and act for themselves. Products are linked to individual decision making.

Intelligence: This technique associates product with smart people who can't be fooled.

Lifestyle: This technique associates product with a particular style of living or way of doing things.

Nurture: Every time you see an animal or a child, the appeal is to your paternal or maternal instincts, so this technique associates products with taking care of someone.

Peer approval: This technique associates product use with friendship and acceptance. Advertisers can also use this negatively to make you worry that you'll lose friends if you don't use a certain product.

Rebel: This technique associates products with behaviors or lifestyles that oppose society's norms.

Rhetorical question: This technique poses a question to the consumer that demands a response. A question is asked and the consumer is supposed to answer in such a way that affirms the product's goodness.

Scientific/statistical claim: This provides some sort of scientific proof or experiment, specific numbers, or an impressive-sounding mystery ingredient.

Unfinished comparison/claim: This technique uses phrases such as "Works better in poor driving conditions!" Works better than what?

Skill 17.3 Understand the role of the viewer's/reader's background, prior knowledge, and point of view in interpreting visual images in various forms of media

(See Skill 7.5 for the role that readers' prior knowledge, background, and experiences plays in interpreting texts.)

One of the key tenets of media literacy is that audiences negotiate meaning. That is, individuals and groups interpret similar visual images and media messages differently as a result of our different experiences, prior knowledge, backgrounds, and worldviews.

This means that meaning does not exist in a text. Meaning exists in the interplay between viewers and readers and the text. It is negotiated. In order to understand the role that individual viewers and readers play in interpreting various forms of media, we can ask ourselves two questions.

1. How might different individuals and groups see this image or text differently?
2. How does this make you feel, based on how similar or different you are from the people portrayed in the media product? (See Media Smarts.ca.)

Skill 17.4 Demonstrate knowledge of how to craft a presentation for a particular purpose and audience

Preparing to present on a topic should be seen as a process that has three stages: discovery, organization, and editing.

Discovery
There are many possible sources for the information that will be used to create an oral presentation. The first step in the discovery process is to settle on a topic or subject. Answer the question: What is the speech going to be about? For example, the topic or subject could be immigration. In the discovery stage, one's own knowledge, experience, and beliefs should be the first source, and notes should be taken as the speaker probes this source. The second source might be interviews with friends and possibly experts. The third source will be research, what has been written or said publicly on this topic. Research can become overwhelming, so a plan for the collecting of source information that is well organized with set time limits for each part.

Organization

At this point, the presenter needs to make several decisions. The first is what the purpose of the speech is. Does the speaker want to persuade the audience to believe or act on something, or does the speaker simply want to present information the audience might not have? Once that decision is made, a thesis should be developed. What point does the speaker want to make? What are the points that will support that point? In what order will those points be arranged? Introductions and conclusions should be written last. The purpose of the introduction is to draw the audience into the topic. The purpose of the conclusion is to polish off the speech, making sure the thesis is clear, reinforcing the thesis, or summarizing the points that have been made.

Editing

This is the most crucial stage in preparing a speech. Once decisions have been made in the discovery and organization stages, it's good to allow time to let the speech rest for a while and go back to it with fresh eyes. Objectivity is extremely important, and the speaker should be willing to make drastic changes if they are needed. It's difficult to let go of one's own composition, but good speechmakers are able to do that. Editing can get out of hand, however, and it should be limited. The speaker must recognize that at some point, the decisions must be made and he or she must be committed to the speech as it stands to deliver the message with conviction.

The concept of recursiveness is useful to speechwriters. That is, everything must be written at the outset with the full knowledge that it can be changed. The willingness to go backward, even to the discovery stage, is what makes a good speechwriter.

(See Skill 10.1 for the importance of audience in composition.)

Skill 17.5 Demonstrate knowledge of how to incorporate images and effective use of technology into presentations

Students should be able to produce visual images, messages, and meaning to communicate with others using technology, enhance an oral presentation, replace a written assignment they could make or upload a video as an adjunct to an oral presentation, illustrate a point, or add information and interest.

Add media (images, film or video clips and/or sound clips (voices, music, or sound effects) to a presentation:

- To illustrate, explain, or represent an idea
- As evidence to support an idea
- To evoke emotions
- To provide a subtext or commentary

An audiovisual message offers the easiest accessibility for learners. It has the advantages of each, medium: the graphic and the audio. Learners' eyes and ears are engaged. Nonreaders get significant access to content. On the other hand, viewing an audiovisual presentation is an even more passive activity than listening to an audio message because information is coming to learners effortlessly through two senses. Activities to foster a critical perspective on an audiovisual presentation serve as valuable safeguards against any overall and unwelcome passivity.

Students should learn the skills of how to integrate images and media texts seamlessly into presentations so that these images and technology do not distract from the presentation.

Visuals should make a point; they should not just be "thrown in" randomly for distraction. Selection of font color and size when using presentation software, such as Haiku Deck, Google Slides, Keynote, Prezi, or PowerPoint, is part of a necessary oral presentation skill—readability for the audience is the primary consideration. Just as in oral presentations without media, students need to practice to ensure that their presentation, along with the technology, is smooth.

Skill 17.6   Understand the importance of ethical issues relating to using viewing and presenting media (copyright, citation, and so on)

Just as with composing written texts, there are ethical issues related to using and presenting media. It is essential that students are aware of copyright issues and proper citation for legal as well as ethical reasons. Sites like Creative Commons can be good sources for visual images, videos, and audios as well as how to attribute or cite those sources.

Common Sense Education contains an extensive list of digital citizenship resources and lesson plans that can help teachers learn and teach issues such as creative credit and copyright, information literacy, and other ethical and social issues involved in using and presenting media.

ADDITIONAL WORKS CITED

Adams, D. *The Hitchhiker's Guide to the Galaxy.* Pan Books, 1979.

Booth, W. C., et al. *The Craft of Research.* 2nd ed. Chicago: University of Chicago Press, 2003.

Duke, N. K., et al. *Visual Literacy Development in Young Children: An Investigation with Informational Texts.* Paper presented at the annual meeting of the Literacy Research Association. 2009.

Goody, J. "Oral Literature." *Encyclopedia Brittanica.* https://www.britannica.com/art/oral-literature.

Higgins, C. *Harold and Maude.* Chicago: Chicago Review Press, 2015.

"Increasing Student Participation." The Teaching Center, Washington University in St. Louis. https://teachingcenter.wustl.edu/resources/teaching-methods/participation/increasing-student-participation/#Listening.

"Media Literacy Fundamentals." Media Smarts. http://mediasmarts.ca/digital-media-literacy/general-information/digital-media-literacy-fundamentals/media-literacy-fundamentals.

Moore, D. W. *The Truth of the Matter: Art and Craft in Creative Nonfiction.* 1st edition. Pearson, 2006.

Morison, S. E. "The Oxford History of the American People." *Oxford University Press.* December 31, 1965.

Newman, E. J., et al. "Nonprobative Photographs (or Words) Inflate Truthiness." Psychon Bull Rev. 2012, vol. 19: 969. doi:10.3758/s13423-012-0292-0.

Roberts, K., et al. "Diagrams, Timelines, and Tables." *Reading Rockets.* http://www.readingrockets.org/article/diagrams-timelines-and-tables.

Walk, K. *How to Write a Comparative Analysis.* Harvard Writing Centre. http://writingcenter.fas.harvard.edu/pages/how-write-comparative-analysis.

Yothers, B. *Writing a Literary Analysis.* Purdue Online Writing Lab. https://owl.english.purdue.edu/owl/resource/697/1.

SAMPLE TEST

1. Latin words that entered the English language during the Elizabethan age include: *(Objective 1)*

    A. Allusion, education, and esteem
    B. Vogue and mustache
    C. Canoe and cannibal
    D. Alligator, cocoa, and armadillo

2. To understand the origins of a word, one must study the: *(Objective 1)*

    A. Synonyms
    B. Inflections
    C. Phonetics
    D. Etymology

3. Which of the following literary elements and devices describes the human practice of associating emotional effects stemming from the implications of a word beyond its literal meaning? *(Objective 1)*

    A. Connotation
    B. Denotation
    C. Caesura
    D. Conceit

4. Which of the following reading strategies calls for higher-order cognitive skills? *(Objective 1)*

    A. Making predictions
    B. Summarizing
    C. Monitoring
    D. Making inferences

5. Which level of meaning is the hardest aspect of a language to master? *(Objective 1)*

    A. Denotation
    B. Jargon
    C. Connotation
    D. Slang

6. Which of the following is *not* true about the English language? *(Objective 1)*

   A. English is the easiest language to learn.
   B. English is the least inflected language.
   C. English has the most extensive vocabulary of any language.
   D. English originated as a Germanic tongue.

7. Which of the following is an example of an informational text suitable for use in the classroom? *(Objective 2)*

   A. A sonnet
   B. The results of a chemistry experiment
   C. A magazine article on habitat loss
   D. A speech

8. Which of the following is most true of expository writing? *(Objective 2)*

   A. It is mutually exclusive of other forms of discourse.
   B. It can incorporate other forms of discourse in the process of providing supporting details.
   C. It should never employ informal expression.
   D. It should only be scored with a summative evaluation.

9. Which of the following is not one of the four forms of discourse? *(Objective 2)*

   A. Exposition
   B. Description
   C. Rhetoric
   D. Persuasion

10. Sometimes readers are asked to demonstrate their understanding of a text. This might include all of the following except: *(Objective 2)*

    A. Role-playing
    B. Paraphrasing
    C. Storyboarding a part of the story with dialogue bubbles
    D. Reading the story aloud

TEACHER CERTIFICATION STUDY GUIDE

11. Which of the following methods can help readers comprehend the purpose in an informational text? *(Objective 3)*

    A. FRI
    B. SQ3R
    C. VENN
    D. MEME

12. In literature, evoking feelings of pity or compassion is to create: *(Objective 3)*

    A. Colloquy
    B. Irony
    C. Pathos
    D. Paradox

13. What type of reasoning does Henry David Thoreau use in the following excerpt from "Civil Disobedience"? *(Objective 3)*

    Unjust laws exist; shall we be content to obey them, or shall we endeavor to amend them, and obey them until we have succeeded, or shall we transgress them at once? Men generally, under such a government as this, think that they ought to wait until they have persuaded the majority to alter them. They think that, if they should resist, the remedy would be worse than the evil. But it is the fault of the government itself that the remedy is worse than the evil. … Why does it always crucify Christ, and excommunicate Copernicus and Luther, and pronounce Washington and Franklin rebels?

    A. Ethical reasoning
    B. Inductive reasoning
    C. Deductive reasoning
    D. Intellectual reasoning

14. Identify the type of appeal used by Molly Ivins in this excerpt from her essay "Get a Knife, Get a Dog, but Get Rid of Guns." *(Objective 3)*

    As a civil libertarian, I, of course, support the Second Amendment. And I believe it means exactly what it says: "A well-regulated militia being necessary to the security of a free state, the right of the people to keep and bear arms shall not be infringed."

    A. Ethical
    B. Emotional
    C. Rational
    D. Literary

15. What literary device is used in this passage? *(Objective 3)*

   And outside, the silent wilderness surrounding this cleared speck on the earth struck me as something great and invincible, like evil or truth, waiting patiently for the passing away of this fantastic invasion.

   A. Simile
   B. Metaphor
   C. Illusion
   D. Personification

16. Use the image below to answer the question:

   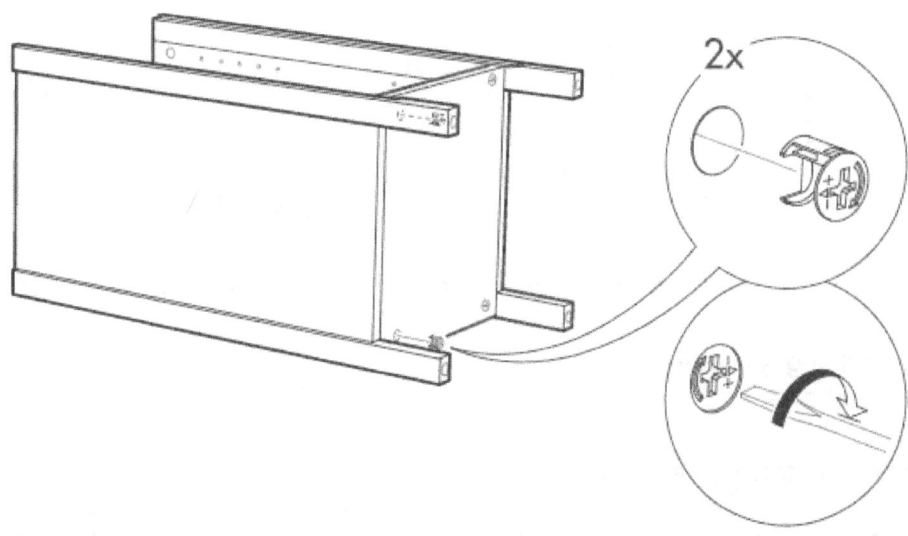

   What is the purpose of this diagram/illustration? *(Objective 4)*

   A. Part of a set of instructions for how to build a piece of furniture from scratch
   B. An illustration to accompany a warranty for a piece of furniture
   C. Part of a set of instructions for how to assemble a piece of furniture
   D. An illustration to accompany a repair manual for a piece of furniture

17. Use the picture below to answer the question: *(Objective 4)*

[Image of IRS Form 1040 showing Filing Status, Exemptions, and Income sections]

What types of clues will help you determine the purpose of this text?

A. Organizing structures
B. Word choice
C. A and B
D. Style and tone of language

18. Which is an untrue statement about a theme in literature? *(Objective 5)*

A. The theme is always stated directly somewhere in the text.
B. The theme is the central idea in a literary work.
C. All parts of the work (such as plot, setting, and mood) should contribute to the theme in some way.
D. By analyzing the various elements of the work, the reader should be able to arrive at an indirectly stated theme.

19. The technique of starting a narrative at a significant point in the action and then developing the story through flashbacks is called: *(Objective 5)*

    A. Octava rima
    B. In medias res
    C. Irony
    D. Suspension of willing disbelief

20. The following passage is written from which point of view? *(Objective 5)*

    As she mused the pitiful vision of her mother's life laid its spell on the very quick of her being—that life of commonplace sacrifices closing in final craziness. She trembled as she heard again her mother's voice saying constantly with foolish insistence: Derevaun Seraun! Derevaun Seraun!*
    * "The end of pleasure is pain!" (Gaelic)

    A. First person, narrator
    B. Second person, direct address
    C. Third person, omniscient
    D. First person, omniscient

21. In the phrase "The cabinet conferred with the president," cabinet is an example of a/an: *(Objective 5)*

    A. Metonym
    B. Synecdoche
    C. Metaphor
    D. Allusion

22. Based on the excerpt below from Kate Chopin's short story "The Story of an Hour," what can students infer about the main character? *(Objective 5)*

    She did not stop to ask if it were or were not a monstrous joy that held her. A clear and exalted perception enabled her to dismiss the suggestion as trivial. She knew that she would weep again when she saw the kind, tender hands folded in death; the face that had never looked save with love upon her, fixed and gray and dead. But she saw beyond that bitter moment a long procession of years to come that would belong to her absolutely. And she opened and spread her arms out to them in welcome.

    A. She dreaded her life as a widow.
    B. Although she loved her husband, she was glad that he was dead for he had never loved her.
    C. She worried that she was too indifferent to her husband's death.
    D. Although they had both loved each other, she was beginning to appreciate that opportunities had opened because of his death.

23. **In classic tragedy, a protagonist's defeat is brought about by a tragic flaw, which is called:** *(Objective 5)*

    A. Hubris
    B. Hamartia
    C. Catharsis
    D. The skene

24. **How will literature help students in a science class understand the following passage?** *(Objective 5)*

    Just as was the case more than three decades ago, we are still sailing between the Scylla of deferring surgery for too long and risking irreversible left ventricular damage and sudden death, and the Charibdas of operating too early and subjecting the patient to the early risks of operation and the later risks resulting from prosthetic valves.
    —E. Braunwald, *European Heart Journal*, July 2000

    A. They will recognize the allusions to Scylla and Charibdas from Greek mythology and understand that the medical community has to select one of two unfavorable choices.
    B. They will recognize the allusion to sailing and understand its analogy to doctors as sailors navigating unknown waters.
    C. They will recognize that the allusions to Scylla and Charibdas refer to the two islands in Norse mythology on which sailors would find themselves shipwrecked and understand how the doctors feel isolated by their choices.
    D. They will recognize the metaphor of the heart and relate it to Eros, the character in Greek mythology who represents love. Eros was the love child of Scylla and Charibdas.

25. **The substitution of "went to his rest" for "died" is an example of a/an:** *(Objective 5)*

    A. Bowdlerism
    B. Jargon
    C. Euphemism
    D. Malapropism

26. Read the first stanza from Edgar Allan Poe's poem "The Bells" to answer the question: *(Objective 6)*

   Hear the sledges with the bells—
   Silver bells!
   What a world of merriment their melody foretells!
   How they tinkle, tinkle, tinkle,
   In the icy air of night!
   While the stars that oversprinkle
   All the heavens, seem to twinkle
   With a crystalline delight;
   Keeping time, time, time,
   In a sort of Runic rhyme,
   To the tintinnabulation that so musically wells
   From the bells, bells, bells, bells
   Bells, bells, bells—
   From the jingling and the tinkling of the bells.

   Words such as "tinkling" and "tintinnabulation" are examples of:

   A. Consonance
   B. Onomatopoeia
   C. Alliteration
   D. Free verse

27. Read the following quotation to answer the question: *(Objective 6)*

   O, pardon me, though
   Bleeding piece of earth
   That I am meek and gentle with
   These butchers.
   —Marc Antony from *Julius Caesar*

   Addressing the dead body of Caesar as though he were still a living being is to employ an:

   A. Apostrophe
   B. Allusion
   C. Antithesis
   D. Anachronism

28. **The literary device of personification is used in which example below?** *(Objective 6)*

    A. "Beg me no beggary by soul or parents, whining dog!"
    B. "Happiness sped through the halls cajoling as it went."
    C. "O wind thy horn, thou proud fellow."
    D. "And that one talent which is death to hide."

29. **An extended metaphor comparing two dissimilar things (one lofty, one lowly) is the definition of a/an:** *(Objective 6)*

    A. Antithesis
    B. Aphorism
    C. Apostrophe
    D. Conceit

30. **Which of the following is a characteristic of blank verse?** *(Objective 6)*

    A. Meter in iambic pentameter
    B. Clearly specified rhyme scheme
    C. Lack of figurative language
    D. Unspecified rhythm

31. **Which is the best definition of free verse, or *vers libre*?** *(Objective 6)*

    A. Poetry, which consists of an unaccented syllable followed by an unaccented sound
    B. Short lyrical poetry written to entertain but with an instructive purpose
    C. Poetry, which does not have a uniform pattern of rhythm
    D. A poem, which tells the story and has a plot

32. What is the salient literary feature of this excerpt from an epic? *(Objective 6)*

   Hither the heroes and the nymphs resorts,
   To taste awhile the pleasures of a court;
   In various talk th'instructive hours they passed,
   Who gave the ball, or paid the visit last;
   One speaks the glory of the English Queen,
   And another describes a charming Indian screen;
   A third interprets motion, looks, and eyes;
   At every word a reputation dies.

   A. Sprung rhythm
   B. Onomatopoeia
   C. Heroic couplets
   D. Motif

33. Which poem is typified as a villanelle? *(Objective 6)*

   A. "Do Not Go Gentle into That Good Night"
   B. "Dover Beach"
   C. "Sir Gawain and the Green Knight"
   D. *The Pilgrim's Progress*

34. **Which term best describes the form of the following poetic excerpt?**
    (Objective 6)

    And more to lulle him in his slumber soft,
    A trickling streake from high rock tumbling downe,
    And ever-drizzling raine upon the loft.
    Mixt with a murmuring winde, much like a swowne
    No other noyse, nor peoples troubles cryes.
    As still we wont t'annoy the walle'd towne,
    Might there be heard: but careless Quiet lyes,
    Wrapt in eternall silence farre from enemyes.

    A. Ballad
    B. Elegy
    C. Spenserian stanza
    D. Octava rima

35. **Which of the writers below wrote "I Know Why the Caged Bird Sings" and received the Presidential Medal of Freedom Award in 2010?**
    (Objectives 5 and 6)

    A. Maya Angelou
    B. Sandra Cisneros
    C. Richard Wilbur
    D. Richard Wright

36. **Charles Dickens, Robert Browning, and Robert Louis Stevenson were:**
    (Objective 7)

    A. Victorians
    B. Medievalists
    C. Elizabethans
    D. Absurdists

37. **The Elizabethans wrote in:** *(Objective 7)*

    A. Celtic
    B. Old English
    C. Middle English
    D. Modern English

38. **Which of the following is the best definition of existentialism?** *(Objective 7)*

    A. The philosophical doctrine that matter is the only reality and that everything in the world, including thought, will, and feeling, can be explained only in terms of matter
    B. A philosophy that views things as they should be or as one would wish them to be
    C. A philosophical and literary movement, variously religious and atheistic, stemming from Kierkegaard and represented by Sartre
    D. The belief that all events are determined by fate and are hence inevitable

39. **What is considered the first work of English literature because it was written in the vernacular of the day?** *(Objectives 1 and 7)*

    A. *Beowulf*
    B. *Le Morte d'Arthur*
    C. "The Faerie Queene"
    D. *Canterbury Tales*

40. **Which choice below best defines naturalism?** *(Objective 7)*

    A. A belief that the writer or artist should apply scientific objectivity in his or her observation and treatment of life without imposing value judgments
    B. The doctrine that teaches that the existing world is the best to be hoped for
    C. The doctrine that teaches that God is not a personality, but that all laws, forces, and manifestations of the universe are God-related
    D. A philosophical doctrine that professes that the truth of all knowledge must always be in question

41. **A traditional anonymous story, ostensibly having a historical basis, usually explaining some phenomenon of nature or aspect of creation, defines a:** *(Objective 7)*

    A. Proverb
    B. Idyll
    C. Myth
    D. Epic

42. In the following poem, what literary movement is reflected? *(Objective 7)*

    "My Heart Leaps Up," by William Wordsworth

    My heart leaps up when I behold
    A rainbow in the sky:
    So was it when my life began;
    So is it now I am a man;
    So be it when I shall grow old,
    Or let me die!
    The Child is father of the Man;
    And I could wish my days to be
    Bound each to each by natural piety

    A. Neoclassicism
    B. Victorian literature
    C. Romanticism
    D. Naturalism

43. Arthur Miller wrote *The Crucible* as a parallel to what twentieth-century event? *(Objective 8)*

    A. Senator McCarthy's House Un-American Activities Committee Hearing
    B. The cold war
    C. The fall of the Berlin Wall
    D. The Persian Gulf War

44. Considered one of the first feminist plays, this Ibsen drama ends with a door slamming, symbolizing the lead character's emancipation from traditional societal norms. *(Objective 8)*

    A. *The Wild Duck*
    B. *Hedda Gabler*
    C. *Ghosts*
    D. *The Doll's House*

45. Which of the following is not a characteristic of a fable? *(Objective 8)*

    A. Features animals that feel and talk like humans
    B. Offers happy solutions to human dilemmas
    C. Teaches a moral or standard for behavior
    D. Illustrates specific people or groups without directly naming them

46. Which of the following is not a common theme of Native American literature? *(Objective 8)*

    A. Emphasis on the relationship of human beings to nature
    B. Belief that everyone can make their dreams come true
    C. Colonialism and/or genocide
    D. Culture and cultural loss

47. Which of the following activities would most effectively familiarize readers with the attitudes and issues of the Depression-era South, the historical period in which *To Kill a Mockingbird* was written? *(Objective 8)*

    A. Construct a detailed timeline of 15 to 20 social, cultural, and political events that focus on race relations in the 1930s
    B. Research and report on the life of author Harper Lee to compare her background with the events in the book
    C. Watch the movie version and note language and dress
    D. Study the stock market crash of 1929 and its effects

48. Read the following passage, "A Vindication of the Rights of Woman," by Mary Wollstonecraft, to answer the question: *(Objective 8)*

    It is impossible for any man, when the most favourable circumstances concur, to acquire sufficient knowledge and strength of mind to discharge the duties of a king, entrusted with uncontrouled power; how then must they be violated when his very elevation is an insuperable bar to the attainment of either wisdom or virtue; when all the feelings of a man are stifled by flattery, and reflection shut out by pleasure! Surely it is madness to make the fate of thousands depend on the caprice of a weak fellow creature, whose very station sinks him necessarily below the meanest of his subjects! But one power should not be thrown down to exalt another—for all power intoxicates weak man; and its abuse proves, that the more equality there is established among men, the more virtue and happiness will reign in society. But this, and any similar maxim deduced from simple reason, raises an outcry—the church or the state is in danger, if faith in the wisdom of antiquity is not implicit; and they who, roused by the sight of human calamity, dare to attack human authority, are reviled as despisers of God, and enemies of man. These are bitter calumnies, yet they reached one of the best of men, whose ashes still preach peace, and whose memory demands a respectful pause, when subjects are discussed that lay so near his heart. After attacking the sacred majesty of Kings, I shall scarcely excite surprise by adding my firm persuasion that every profession, in which great subordination of rank constitutes its power, is highly injurious to morality. A standing army, for instance, is incompatible with freedom; because subordination and rigour are the very sinews of military discipline; and despotism is necessary to give vigour to enterprizes that one will directs. A spirit inspired by romantic notions of honour, a kind of morality founded on the fashion of the age, can only be felt by a few officers, whilst the main body must be moved by command, like the waves of the sea; for the strong wind of authority pushes the crowd of subalterns forward, they scarcely know or care why, with headlong fury.

What impact on the reader does the author have in mentioning kings and common officers?

    A. She explains the divide between the two classes.
    B. She shows that regardless of rank, every profession has downfalls.
    C. She demonstrates the level of respect officers have for their king.
    D. She questions gender roles in professional settings.

49. **Read the following passage from the novel *Beloved*, by Toni Morrison, to answer the question:** *(Objective 8)*

    And if she thought anything, it was No. No. Nono. Nonono. Simple. She just flew. Collected every bit of life she had made, all the parts of her that were precious and fine and beautiful, and carried, pushed, dragged them through the veil, out, away, over there where no one could hurt them. Over there. Outside this place, where they would be safe.

    The author implies that the main character:

        A. Is trying to hide her children from the master
        B. Is planning to escape on the Underground Railroad
        C. Would like to return to Africa
        D. Would rather see her children die than watch them suffer

50. **Which of the following sentences contains a capitalization error?** *(Objective 9)*

        A. The commander of the English navy was Admiral Nelson.
        B. Napoleon was the president of the French First Republic.
        C. Queen Elizabeth II is the Monarch of the British Empire.
        D. William the Conqueror led the Normans to victory over the British.

51. **Select the correct version of the sentence below.** *(Objective 9)*

        A. I climbed to the top of the mountain, it took me three hours.
        B. I climbed to the top of the mountain it took me three hours.
        C. I climbed to the top of the mountain: it took me three hours.
        D. I climbed to the top of the mountain; it took me three hours.

52. Which transition word would show contrast between these two ideas? *(Objective 9)*

   We are confident in our skills to teach English. We welcome new ideas on this subject.

   A. We are confident in our skills to teach English, and we welcome new ideas on this subject.
   B. Because we are confident in our skills to teach English, we welcome new ideas on the subject.
   C. When we are confident in our skills to teach English, we welcome new ideas on the subject.
   D. We are confident in our skills to teach English; however, we welcome new ideas on the subject.

53. The arrangement and relationship of words in sentences or sentence structures best describes: *(Objective 9)*

   A. Syntax
   B. Discourse
   C. Thesis
   D. Style

54. Which of the following sentences contains a subject-verb agreement error? *(Objective 9)*

   A. Both mother and her two sisters were married in a triple ceremony.
   B. Neither the hen nor the rooster is likely to be served for dinner.
   C. My boss, as well as the company's two personnel directors, have been to Spain.
   D. Amanda and the twins are late again.

55. What is the proper way to punctuate the sentence below? *(Objective 9)*

   Wally said with a groan, "Why do I have to do an oral interpretation of "The Raven."

   A. With a groan, "Why… of 'The Raven'?"
   B. With a groan "Why… of "The Raven"?
   C. With a groan ", Why… of "The Raven?"
   D. With a groan, "Why… of "The Raven."

56. Which of the following sentences is properly punctuated? *(Objective 9)*

    A. The more you eat; the more you want.
    B. The authors—John Steinbeck, Ernest Hemingway, and William Faulkner—are staples of modern writing in American literature textbooks.
    C. Handling a wild horse, takes a great deal of skill and patience.
    D. The man who replaced our teacher, is a comedian.

57. Which of the following choices best corrects the error in the sentence below? *(Objective 9)*

    Edward didn't hardly know his cousin Gregor who'd had a rhinoplasty.

    A. Hardly did know his cousin Gregor
    B. Didn't know his cousin Gregor hardly
    C. Hardly knew his cousin Gregor
    D. Didn't know his cousin Gregor

58. A punctuation mark indicating omission, interrupted thought, or an incomplete statement is a/an: *(Objective 9)*

    A. Ellipsis
    B. Anachronism
    C. Colloquy
    D. Idiom

59. Which of the following choices best corrects the underlined error in the sentence below? *(Objective 9)*

    Mixing the batter for cookies, the cat licked the Crisco from the cookie sheet.

    A. While mixing the batter for cookies
    B. While the batter for cookies was mixing
    C. While I mixed the batter for cookies
    D. While I mixed the cookies

60. Which of the following choices best corrects the underlined error in the sentence below? *(Objective 9)*

    Mr. Smith respectfully submitted his resignation and had a new job.

    A. Respectfully submitted his resignation and has
    B. Respectfully submitted his resignation before accepting
    C. Respectfully submitted his resignation because of
    D. Respectfully submitted his resignation and had

61. Which of the following is *not* a technique of prewriting? *(Objective 10)*

    A. Clustering
    B. Listing
    C. Brainstorming
    D. Proofreading

62. Writing ideas quickly without interruption of the flow of thoughts or attention to conventions is called: *(Objective 10)*

    A. Brainstorming
    B. Mapping
    C. Listing
    D. Free writing

63. What is the ideal first step of the writing process? *(Objective 10)*

    A. Choose a writing form for your composition.
    B. Create an outline for your composition.
    C. Identify a purpose of your composition.
    D. Identify the audience for your composition.

64. Why is it helpful to outline ideas through lists or mind-mapping before writing a draft? *(Objective 10)*

    A. Outlines help you organize your text so that you know where you are going.
    B. Outlines help you remember why you are writing.
    C. Outlines can prove to an examiner or teacher that you are doing original work and not plagiarizing.
    D. This question is a trick. Mind-mapping is not a good way to organize your writing as it is graphic instead of a list and will confuse you when you are ready to write your draft.

65. Which of the following do you *not* need before you write your draft? *(Objective 10)*

    A. Knowledge of purpose and audience
    B. Preparation of your conclusion and introduction
    C. Knowledge of form
    D. Preparation of an outline

66. A student is writing a draft of a persuasive essay, and she is using lots of primary and secondary sources. You see her writing her draft without any index cards, notes, or sources. She has only one tab open on her computer, and it's the document she is working on. As a teacher, what do you do in this situation? *(Objective 10)*

   A. Let her be. She is working hard.
   B. Make a note to talk to her after the class ends about the importance of keeping her sources and notes nearby when writing a draft.
   C. Take points off for process. She will probably also write an essay that is full of opinion without evidence to back it up. She clearly chose not to learn from the lesson about how to write a draft.
   D. Encourage her to take a brief break to find her sources.

67. In the writing process, revision means reading through a text to: *(Objective 10)*

   A. Eliminate wordiness, redundancy, and distracting details
   B. Vary sentence length and structure and check for appropriate transition use
   C. Check for spelling, grammatical, and punctuation errors
   D. Check that the text is cohesive; if not, choose a new topic

68. In preparing to write a research paper about a social problem, what can you do to determine the credibility of the information you are gathering? *(Objective 11)*

   A. Rest assured that the information on the Internet has been peer-reviewed and verified for accuracy.
   B. Find one solid source and use that exclusively.
   C. Cross-check your information with another credible source.
   D. Use only primary sources.

69. Which of the following are secondary research materials? *(Objective 11)*

   A. The conclusions and inferences of other historians
   B. Literature and nonverbal materials, novels, stories, poetry, and essays from the period, as well as coins, archaeological artifacts, and art produced during the period
   C. Interviews and surveys conducted by the researcher
   D. Statistics gathered as the result of the research's experiments

Read the following passage to answer questions 70–72: *(Objective 11)*

The brazen, vicious attack occurred in broad daylight. The cowardly action took the lives of 32 innocent victims. So far no single group has claimed responsibility, though several have issued statements noting its importance.

70. Which of the following sentences best incorporates a quote from the passage above?

    A. The writer's description of this as a "vicious attack" reveals bias.
    B. Saying, "The brazen, vicious attack occurred in broad daylight. The cowardly action took the lives of 32 innocent victims" reveals bias.
    C. The characterization of the incident as a "brazen, vicious attack" and a "cowardly action" reveals bias.
    D. When the writer says the brazen, vicious attack, it shows bias.

71. In doing research, a student has second thoughts about using this new story as a source. What is evidence of a flaw with the story?

    A. It is not corroborated by other sources.
    B. The language is inflammatory and biased.
    C. There is no image to accompany the story.
    D. No other point of view is included.

72. Which of the following is *not* an effective research question? *(Objective 11)*

    A. How was Arthur Miller influenced by the politics of his time?
    B. In what ways are adolescents influenced by social media?
    C. What causes some children to become bullies?
    D. What were the major battles of World War II?

73. Read the following passage and answer the question. *(Objective 11)*

When it was first perceived, in early times, that no middle course for America remained between unlimited submission to a foreign legislature and a total independence of its claims, men of reflection were less apprehensive of danger from the formidable power of fleets and armies they must determine to resist than from those contests and dissensions which would certainly arise concerning the forms of government to be instituted over the whole and over the parts of this extensive country. Relying, however, on the purity of their intentions, the justice of their cause, and the integrity and intelligence of the people, under an overruling Providence which had so signally protected this country from the first, the representatives of this nation, then consisting of little more than half its present number, not only broke to pieces the chains which were forging and the rod of iron that was lifted up, but frankly cut asunder the ties which had bound them, and launched into an ocean of uncertainty.

The zeal and ardor of the people during the Revolutionary war, supplying the place of government, commanded a degree of order sufficient at least for the temporary preservation of society. The Confederation which was early felt to be necessary was prepared from the models of the Batavian and Helvetic confederacies, the only examples which remain with any detail and precision in history, and certainly the only ones which the people at large had ever considered. But reflecting on the striking difference in so many particulars between this country and those where a courier may go from the seat of government to the frontier in a single day, it was then certainly foreseen by some who assisted in Congress at the formation of it that it could not be durable.

Negligence of its regulations, inattention to its recommendations, if not disobedience to its authority, not only in individuals but in States, soon appeared with their melancholy consequences—universal languor, jealousies and rivalries of States, decline of navigation and commerce, discouragement of necessary manufactures, universal fall in the value of lands and their produce, contempt of public and private faith, loss of consideration and credit with foreign nations, and at length in discontents, animosities, combinations, partial conventions, and insurrection, threatening some great national calamity.

For which of the following research questions would this passage likely be best suited?

A. How did economic issues influence the causes of the Revolutionary War?
B. What philosophical schools of thought influenced leaders of the Revolution?
C. What were some of the post-Revolutionary challenges facing the country?
D. How did Britain try to influence the economy of the United States after the Revolution?

74. **What is the correct way to include a quotation from *Orange Is the New Black*? *(Objective 11)***

   A. Kerman was terrified but continued with the plan anyway. "Were the authorities closing in on me? Maybe I should try to get through customs and run? Or perhaps the bag really was just delayed, and I would be abandoning a large sum of money that belonged to someone who could probably have killed me with a simple phone call. I decided that the latter choice was slightly more terrifying."

   B. Kerman was terrified but continued with the plan anyway. "Were the authorities closing in on me? Maybe I should try to get through customs and run? Or perhaps the bag really was just delayed, and I would be abandoning a large sum of money that belonged to someone who could probably have killed me with a simple phone call. I decided that the latter choice was slightly more terrifying" (Kerman 1).

   C. Kerman was terrified but continued with the plan anyway.

   "Were the authorities closing in on me? Maybe I should try to get through customs and run? Or perhaps the bag really was just delayed, and I would be abandoning a large sum of money that belonged to someone who could probably have killed me with a simple phone call. I decided that the latter choice was slightly more terrifying." (Kerman 1)

   D. Kerman was terrified but continued with the plan anyway.

   Were the authorities closing in on me? Maybe I should try to get through customs and run? Or perhaps the bag really was just delayed, and I would be abandoning a large sum of money that belonged to someone who could probably have killed me with a simple phone call. I decided that the latter choice was slightly more terrifying. (Kerman 1)

75. **Which definition is the best for defining diction? *(Objective 12)***

   A. The specific word choices of an author to create a particular mood or feeling in the reader
   B. Writing that explains something thoroughly
   C. The background, or exposition, for a short story or drama
   D. Word choices that help teach a truth or moral

76. The following passage is written from which point of view? *(Objective 12)*

   As she mused the pitiful vision of her mother's life laid its spell on the very quick of her being—that life of commonplace sacrifices closing in final craziness. She trembled as she heard again her mother's voice saying constantly with foolish insistence: Dearevaun Seraun! Dearevaun Seraun!* * "The end of pleasure is pain!" (Gaelic)

   A. First person, narrator
   B. Second person, direct address
   C. Third person, omniscient
   D. First person, omniscient

77. Which of the following techniques is an effective tool of characterization? *(Objective 12)*

   A. Dialogue
   B. Denouement
   C. Sensory language
   D. First-person narration

78. Which of the following descriptions most relies on sensory language? *(Objective 12)*

   A. As a child, their frequent arguments tore him apart.
   B. As a child, their frequent arguments were like wounds that never healed.
   C. As a child, he had to put up with the sound of their frequent arguments.
   D. As a child, their frequent arguments echoed through the house.

Read the following passage to answer questions 79–83.

International baggage claim in the Brussels airport was large and airy, with multiple carousels circling endlessly. I scurried from one to another, desperately trying to find my black suitcase. Because it was stuffed with drug money, I was more concerned than one might normally be about lost luggage.

I was 24 in 1993 and probably looked like just another anxious young professional woman. My Doc Martens had been jettisoned in favor of my beautiful handmade black suede heels. I wore black silk pants and a beige jacket, a typical jeune fille, not a big counterculture, unless you spotted the tattoo on my neck. I had done exactly as I had been instructed, checking my bag Chicago through Paris, where I had to switch planes to take a short flight to Brussels.

When I arrived in Belgium, I looked for my black rollie at the baggage claim. It was nowhere to be seen. Fighting a rushing tide of panic, I asked in my mangled high school French what had become of my suitcase. "Bags don't make it onto the right flight sometimes," said the big lug working in baggage handling. "Wait for the next shuttle from Paris—it's probably on that plane."

Had my bag been detected? I knew that carrying more than ten thousand dollars undeclared was illegal, let alone carrying it for a West African drug lord. Were the authorities closing in on me? Maybe I should try to get through customs and run? Or perhaps the bag really was just delayed, and I would be abandoning a large sum of money that belonged to someone who could probably have killed me with a simple phone call. I decided that the latter choice was slightly more terrifying. So I waited.

The next flight from Paris finally arrived. I sidled over to my new "friend" in baggage handling, who was sorting things out. It is hard to flirt when you're frightened. I spotted the suitcase. "Mon bag!" I exclaimed in ecstasy, seizing the Tumi. I thanked him effusively, waving with giddy affection as I sailed through one of the unmanned doors into the terminal, where I spotted my friend Billy waiting for me. I had inadvertently skipped customs.

"I was worried. What happened?" Billy asked.

"Get me into a cab!" I hissed.

I didn't breathe until we had pulled away from the airport and were halfway across Brussels.
—Orange Is the New Black, *Piper Kerman*

79. Why did the author explain her attire?

    A. She wanted the audience to know how much she stood out in Europe.
    B. She used her clothing to try to fit in with the culture she was immersed in.
    C. She wanted to explain that she was a young, hip woman.
    D. She explained how difficult it was to wait around for her bag in heels.

80. Why didn't she breathe until pulling away from the airport?

    A. Tension
    B. Sadness
    C. Health issues
    D. She was talking to Billy

English Language Arts

81. What is the overall message of this passage?

    A. Young professional women can get away with crimes.
    B. Security guards are not always watching every door in the airport.
    C. It's important to blend in when doing something suspicious.
    D. When you have done something illegal, even small mishaps can seem scary.

82. How did she avoid going through customs?

    A. She flirted with the luggage man.
    B. Her friend Billy came to get her.
    C. She slipped through an unmanned door.
    D. She went through customs in Paris and Chicago, so it wasn't required.

83. What part of the plot does "Mon bag!" represent?

    A. Climax
    B. Rising action
    C. Exposition
    D. Falling action

84. Explanatory or informative discourse is best defined as: *(Objective 13)*

    A. Exposition
    B. Narration
    C. Persuasion
    D. Description

85. Of the following statements, which is most true in regards to expository essays? *(Objective 13)*

    A. Summative evaluations work best when scoring.
    B. They should always be formal.
    C. They should incorporate other forms of discourse when providing elaboration.
    D. This type of essay writing is exclusive to other forms of discourse.

86. In this paragraph from a student essay, identify the sentence that provides a detail. *(Objective 13)*

    (1) The poem concerns two different personality types and the human relation between them. (2) Their approach to life is totally different. (3) The neighbor is a conservative person who follows routines. (4) He follows the traditional wisdom of his father and his father's father. (5) The purpose in fixing the wall and keeping their relationship separate is only because it is all he knows.

    A. Sentence 1
    B. Sentence 3
    C. Sentence 4
    D. Sentence 5

87. Which of the following should *not* be included in the opening paragraph of an informative essay? *(Objective 13)*

    A. Thesis sentence
    B. Details and examples supporting the main idea
    C. Broad general introduction to the topic
    D. A style and tone that grabs the reader's attention

88. In the paragraph below, which sentence does *not* contribute to the overall task of supporting the main idea? *(Objective 13)*

    (1) The Springfield City Council met Friday to discuss new zoning restrictions for the land to be developed south of the city. (2) Residents who opposed the new restrictions were granted 15 minutes to present their case. (3) Their argument focused on the dangers that increased traffic would bring to the area. (4) It seemed to me that the Mayor Simpson listened intently. (5) The council agreed to table the new zoning until studies would be performed.

    A. Sentence 2
    B. Sentence 3
    C. Sentence 4
    D. Sentence 5

89. Students have been asked to write a research paper on automobiles and have brainstormed a number of questions they will answer based on their research findings. Which of the following is *not* an interpretive question to guide research? *(Objective 13)*

   A. Who were the first 10 automotive manufacturers in the United States?
   B. What types of vehicles will be used 50 years from now?
   C. How do automobiles manufactured in the United States compare and contrast with each other?
   D. What do you think is the best solution for the fuel shortage?

90. Which of the following should students use to improve coherence of ideas within an argument? *(Objective 13)*

   A. Transitional words or phrases to show relationship of ideas
   B. Conjunctions like "and" to join ideas together
   C. Extensive use of direct quotes to improve credibility
   D. Adjectives and adverbs to provide stronger detail

Read the following passage to answer questions 91–94. *(Objective 13)*

When rays of light pass through a prism, they undergo a change of direction: they are always deflected away from the refractive edge. It is possible to conceive an assembly of prisms whose refractive surfaces progressively become more nearly parallel to each other toward the middle: light rays passing through the outer prisms will undergo the greatest amount of refraction, with consequent deflection of their path toward the center, whereas the middle prism with its two parallel surfaces causes no deflection at all. When a beam of parallel rays passes through these prisms, the rays are all deflected toward the axis and converge at one point. Rays emerging from a point are also deflected by the prisms that they converge. A lens can be conceived as consisting of a large number of such prisms placed close up against one another, so that their surfaces merge into a continuous spherical surface. A lens of this kind, which collects the rays and concentrates them at one point, is called a convergent lens. Since it is thicker in the middle than at the edge, it is known as a convex lens.

In the case of a concave lens, which is thinner in the middle than at the edge, similar considerations show that all rays diverge from the center. Hence such a lens is called a divergent lens. After undergoing refraction, parallel rays appear to come from one point, while rays re-emerging from a point will, after passing through the lens, appear to emerge from another point. Lenses have surfaces in the same direction but having a different radii of curvature, these are known as meniscus lenses and are used more particularly in spectacles.

TEACHER CERTIFICATION STUDY GUIDE

91. **Which of the following is *not* true of convergent lenses?**

    A. They are concave.
    B. They are made of prisms.
    C. They can refract light.
    D. They have different radii.

92. **Parallel surfaces in prisms cause:**

    A. Little refraction
    B. Divergence of light rays
    C. No refraction
    D. Radii to vary

93. **Which of the following would be the best choice of a conclusion for this piece?**

    A. Prisms were used by many ancient civilizations. They must have seemed like a form of magic to the first people who saw them, and they continue to amaze people today. Though perhaps an accidental discovery, they changed the world.
    B. Prisms were an integral part of the study of the different properties of light. The use of prisms allowed people to see the different component colors of the light around them. The discovery of these different properties opened up new fields of research.
    C. There are dispersive prisms, reflective prisms, deflecting prisms, and polarizing prisms. Each type is useful and has different qualities.
    D. We wake up every morning and there is light. We may not know it, but people have always been fascinated by light for many years. Prisms explained how light works.

94. **Spectacles use meniscus lenses, which are:**

    A. Flat
    B. Varying radii of concave lenses
    C. Varying radii of convex lenses
    D. Round on both sides of the lens, meaning they have double refraction

Read the following passage to answer questions 95 and 96. *(Objective 13)*

Ana woke suddenly and peered into the darkness. Something had moved or made some kind of sound; she was sure of it. She reached across the bed to the lamp on the nightstand, but there was nothing there. She fumbled in the dark until her hand came to rest on something solid, something cold, something wet.

"Looking for something?" came a voice out of the darkness.

Without hesitation, Ana replied, "Yes, actually. My glasses."

"You know why I'm here. No need for games," replied the voice.

"No, I suppose you're right," Ana sighed.

95. For what effect does the author repeat "something…, something…"

   A. To show how frustrating it was not to be able to see
   B. To build tension
   C. To show that the character was helpless
   D. To lighten the mood

96. Ana's reply creates what effect?

   A. The reader sees her as confident and calm.
   B. The reader sees her as confused and fearful.
   C. The reader knows that this is not a serious story.
   D. The reader knows that this is the source of conflict.

97. Which part of a classical argument is illustrated in this excerpt from Caryl Rivers's essay "What Should Be Done about Rock Lyrics?" *(Objective 14)*

   But violence against women is greeted by silence. It shouldn't be. This does not mean censorship, or book (or record) burning. In a society that protects free expression, we understand a lot of stuff will float up out of the sewer. Usually, we recognize the ugly stuff that advocates violence against any group as the garbage it is, and we consider its purveyors as moral lepers. We hold our nose and tolerate it, but we speak out against the values it proffers.

   A. Narration
   B. Confirmation
   C. Refutation and concession
   D. Summation

Read the following passage to answer questions 98 and 99. *(Objective 14)*

The history of all hitherto existing society is the history of class struggles. Freeman and slave, patrician and plebeian, lord and serf, guildmaster and journeyman, in a word, oppressor and oppressed, stood in constant opposition to one another, carried on an uninterrupted, now hidden, now open fight, a fight that each time ended, either in a revolutionary reconstitution of society at large, or in the common ruin of the contending classes. In the earlier epochs of history, we find almost everywhere a complicated arrangement of society into various orders, a manifold gradation of social rank. In ancient Rome we have patricians, knights, plebeians, slaves; in the Middle Ages, feudal lords, vassals, guild-masters, journeymen, apprentices, serfs; in almost all of these classes, again, subordinate gradations. The modern bourgeois society that has sprouted from the ruins of feudal society, has not done away with class antagonisms. It has but established new classes, new conditions of oppression, new forms of struggle in place of the old ones. Our epoch, the epoch of the bourgeoisie, possesses, however, this distinctive feature: It has simplified the class antagonisms. Society as a whole is more and more splitting up into two great hostile camps, into two great classes directly facing each other—bourgeoisie and proletariat…

98. The first sentence can best be paraphrased as:

    A. Every future societal shall deal with issues of class.
    B. Struggle between classes is the most important aspect of history.
    C. In the past, class struggles were common.
    D. Society only began to exist with the invention of class.

99. What is the author's attitude toward class as a concept?

    A. It is a tool of oppression.
    B. It is a necessary evil.
    C. It is an inevitability.
    D. It is useful, but often misused.

100. To explore the relationship of literature to modern life, which of these activities would *not* enable students to explore comparable themes? *(Objective 15)*

   A. After studying various world events, such as the Palestinian-Israeli conflict, students write an updated version of *Romeo and Juliet* using modern characters and settings.
   B. Before studying *Romeo and Juliet*, students watch *West Side Story*.
   C. Students research the major themes of *Romeo and Juliet* by studying news stories and finding modern counterparts for the story.
   D. Students would explore compare the romantic themes of *Romeo and Juliet* and *The Taming of the Shrew*.

101. A student wrote the following passage for a short response item about a novel. What is the biggest potential issue in the writing? *(Objective 15)*

   So the theme of the novel is clearly like the struggle of the individual to be good. In the book, the main character guy really wants to be good, you know, but there are all these things stopping. The author, he's trying to show how all of us are like living our lives but these obstacles come up.

   A. Correct grammar
   B. Adapting to audience
   C. Using evidence to support a claim
   D. Organizational strategies

102. Which of the following would likely be the best conclusion for an essay analyzing potential projects to combat climate change? *(Objective 15)*

   A. A variety of projects and technologies exist that may help the country find a way to deal with climate change. The challenge is to decide which projects are viable and which are not. The best path forward may in fact be to provide seed funding to a variety of projects and see which ones thrive. Betting the farm on one proposal is too risky; we must look at all our options.
   B. Given the budget considerations facing the government, there is no clear path forward. Climate change may be a major issue facing different parts of the country. Without substantial increases in revenue, it will be difficult for the current government to move forward.
   C. Climate change is not the threat people make it out to be. Our planet has gone through swings in climate before and will do so again. As a species, we will do what we have always done—adapt.
   D. Climate change is the biggest threat facing our species and many others. We must act now or we will risk losing countless species. The mounting costs will affect all of us to some extent.

103. Which of the following sentences would likely be the best transitional sentence to follow this paragraph? *(Objective 15)*

The main character wrestles with her own moral code. Though she feels a tremendous sense of obligation toward her community, she cannot turn her back on what she feels is right. This internal conflict drives the novel forward.

   A. But the conflict is too much for her and she cannot cope.
   B. While she is torn between two seemingly impossible choices, the world seems to move forward without her.
   C. Impossible choices are everywhere in the novel.
   D. The world seems to move forward, and she is torn between impossible choices.

Read the following selection from Joseph Conrad's *Heart of Darkness* to answer questions 104–109, selecting the best choice of the options presented. *(Objective 15)*

I went to work the next day, turning, so to speak, my back on that station. In that way only it seemed to me I could keep my hold on the redeeming facts of life. Still, one must look about sometimes; and then I saw this station, these men strolling aimlessly about in the sunshine of the yard. I asked myself sometimes what it all meant. They wandered here and there with their absurd long staves in their hands, like a lot of faithless pilgrims bewitched inside a rotten fence. The word "ivory" rang in the air, was whispered, was sighed. You would think they were praying to it. A taint of imbecile rapacity blew through it all, like a whiff from some corpse. By Jove! I've never seen anything so unreal in my life. And outside, the silent wilderness surrounding this cleared speck on the earth struck me as something great and invincible, like evil or truth, waiting patiently for the passing away of this fantastic invasion.

104. What does the following line represent? "I saw this station, these men strolling aimlessly about in the sunshine of the yard."

   A. Soldiers enjoying their day
   B. Men being unaware of the negativity that surrounds them
   C. The station is a happy place
   D. Embracing the weather before a storm hits

105. What does the word "staves" mean?

   A. Machetes
   B. Axes
   C. Guns
   D. Wooden clubs

106. What does the word "ivory" represent?

　A. Death
　B. Jewelry
　C. Prosperity
　D. Trade

107. What literary device is used when describing the ivory?

　A. Allegory
　B. Simile
　C. Personification
　D. Repetition

108. What does the word "rapacity" represent?

　A. Greed
　B. Rapid movement
　C. Intelligent
　D. Affluent

109. *Heart of Darkness* is about a voyage up the Congo River with an ivory trader and raises questions of imperialism and racism. The movie *Apocalypse Now*, by Francis Ford Coppola, was adapted from this story. Comparing the two texts, in an essay, what structure would be best for organizing a coherent comparison based on theme? *(Objective 15)*

　A. Point by point to illustrate the differences between a film and a book
　B. Text to text to show similarities and differences
　C. Point by point to see *Apocalypse Now* through the lens of *Heart of Darkness*
　D. Text to text to see *Apocalypse Now* through the lens of *Heart of Darkness*

110. In preparing for an oral presentation, which is *not* an effective guideline? *(Objective 16)*

　A. Even if you are using a lectern, feel free to move about. This will connect you to the audience.
　B. Your posture should be natural, not stiff. Keep your shoulders toward the audience.
　C. Gestures can help communicate as long as you don't overuse them or make them distracting.
　D. You can avoid eye contact if you focus on your notes. This will make you appear more knowledgeable.

111. Which of the following would *not* be a major concern in an oral presentation? *(Objective 16)*

    A. Establishing the purpose of the presentation
    B. Evaluating the audience's demographics and psychographics
    C. Creating a slide for each point
    D. Developing the content to fit the occasion

112. Oral debate is most closely associated with which form of discourse? *(Objective 16)*

    A. Description
    B. Exposition
    C. Narration
    D. Persuasion

113. The purpose of presenting a formal report to the class is to explain where acid rain comes from and what it has done to the environment. What is the most likely form of organizational structure for this presentation? *(Objective 16)*

    A. Cause and effect
    B. Problem and solution
    C. Exposition
    D. Definition

114. For a speech on actions the school board should take to reduce energy use, which strategy or approach would be the most successful? *(Objective 16)*

    A. Explain in detail the different uses of energy at schools.
    B. Link reduced energy use to reduced costs and greater environmental responsibility.
    C. Complain about the board's lack of environmental responsibility.
    D. Read letters from other students.

115. Which of the following strategies will likely increase participation by shy students in class discussion? *(Objective 16)*

    A. Requiring each participant to join in at least twice
    B. Giving participants something to read before the discussion
    C. Increasing wait time
    D. Not allowing participants who talk a lot to join in

116. In which context might it not be a good idea to use jargon or technical language to discuss curriculum? *(Objective 16)*

   A. At back-to-school night
   B. A staff meeting
   C. A discussion of teaching materials
   D. A professional development conference

Read the following excerpt to answer questions 117 and 118. *(Objective 15)*

Excerpt from a speech to the Council on Foreign Relations, Tony Blair, December 3, 2008

> *The past 40 years are littered with initiatives, signposts to various potential breakthroughs, unsatisfactory compromises, new dawns that swiftly turned to dusk and failed negotiations. Along the way, there have been immense gains that sometimes are obscured by the central impasse. Egypt and Jordan are at peace with Israel. The Arab Peace Initiative of the then Crown Prince Abdullah in 2002 signaled a new pan-Arab approach. The contours of the final status issues, if not their outcomes, have been clarified.*
>
> *The Annapolis process and the limited but nonetheless real change on the West Bank during the past year—for which the president and Secretary Rice deserve much credit—have yielded a genuine platform for the future.*
>
> *But the central impasse does indeed remain. My view—formed since I came to Jerusalem and refining much of what I thought when I tussled intermittently with the issue for 10 years as British prime minister—is that it remains because the reality on the ground does not, as yet, sufficiently support the compromises necessary to secure a final, negotiated settlement. In other words, we have tended to proceed on the basis that if we could only agree on the terms of the two-state solution—territory, refugees, Jerusalem (i.e., the theory—we would then be able to change the reality of what was happening on the ground (i.e., the practice). In my view, it is as much the other way around. The political process and changing the reality have to march in lock-step. Until recently, they haven't.*
>
> *The reason this is critical to resolving this dispute is as follows. The problem is not that reasonable people do not agree, roughly, what the two states look like. I don't minimize the negotiation challenge. But listen to sensible Palestinians and sensible Israelis and you will quickly find the gaps are not that big; certainly are not unbridgeable.*

117. In what way(s) does Tony Blair demonstrate that he acknowledges the different perspectives of Palestinians and Israelis?

   A. He addresses the importance of peace for both sides.
   B. He talks about past failed negotiations.
   C. He does not blame either side for the lack of results.
   D. He makes an emotional appeal to both sides.

118. In this speech, how did Blair organize his ideas?

   A. He linked past events to the present state of negotiations.
   B. He described past peace proposals and gave evidence of why they make sense.
   C. He thanked people for their past work and showed why it was necessary to continue what they had started.
   D. He analyzed the issue point by point.

119. What is the common advertising technique used by these advertising slogans? *(Objective 17)*

   "It's everywhere you want to be." (Visa)
   "Have it your way." (Burger King)
   "When you care enough to send the very best." (Hallmark)
   "Be all you can be." (U.S. Army)

   A. Peer approval
   B. Rebel
   C. Individuality
   D. Escape

120. In presenting a report to peers about the effects of Hurricane Katrina on New Orleans, the students wanted to use various media in their argument to persuade their peers that more needed to be done. Which of these would be the most effective? *(Objective 17)*

   A. A PowerPoint presentation showing the blueprints of the levees before the flood and redesigned now for current construction
   B. A collection of music clips made by the street performers in the French Quarter before and after the flood
   C. A recent video showing the areas devastated by the floods and the current state of rebuilding
   D. A collection of recordings of interviews made by the various government officials and local citizens affected by the flooding

121. Which of the following statements indicates an instructional goal for using multimedia in the classroom? *(Objective 17)*

   A. Audio messages invite the listener to form mental images consistent with the topic of the audio.
   B. Print messages appeal almost exclusively to the mind and push students to read with more thought.
   C. Listening to an audio message is more passive than reading a print message.
   D. Teachers who develop activities to foster a critical perspective on audiovisual presentation will decrease passivity.

122. Which of the following situations is *not* an ethical violation of intellectual property? *(Objective 17)*

   A. A student visits 10 different Websites and writes a report to compare the costs of downloading music. He uses the names of the Websites without their permission.
   B. A student copies and pastes a chart verbatim from the Internet but does not document it because it is available on a public site.
   C. From an online article found in a subscription database, a student paraphrases a section on the problems of music piracy. She includes the source in her Works Cited but does not provide an in-text citation.
   D. A student uses a comment from M. Night Shyamalan without attribution claiming the information is common knowledge.

Read the following passage to answer questions 123–130.

Most people who bother with the matter at all would admit that the English language is in a bad way, but it is generally assumed that we cannot by conscious action do anything about it. Our civilization is decadent and our language—so the argument runs—must inevitably share in the general collapse. It follows that any struggle against the abuse of language is a sentimental archaism, like preferring candles to electric light or hansom cabs to aeroplanes. Underneath this lies the half-conscious belief that language is a natural growth and not an instrument which we shape for our own purposes.

Now, it is clear that the decline of a language must ultimately have political and economic causes: it is not due simply to the bad influence of this or that individual writer. But an effect can become a cause, reinforcing the original cause and producing the same effect in an intensified form, and so on indefinitely. A man may take to drink because he feels himself to be a failure, and then fail all the more completely because he drinks. It is rather the same thing that is happening to the English language. It becomes ugly and inaccurate because our thoughts are foolish, but the slovenliness of our language makes it easier for us to have foolish thoughts. The point is that the process is reversible. Modern English, especially written English, is full of bad habits which spread by imitation and which can be avoided if one is willing to take the necessary trouble. If one gets rid of these habits one can think more clearly, and to think clearly is a necessary first step toward political regeneration: so that the fight against bad English is not frivolous and is not the exclusive concern of professional writers. I will come back to this presently, and I hope that by that time the meaning of what I have said here will have become clearer. Meanwhile, here are five specimens of the English language as it is now habitually written.

123. What does the author mean by "archaism"? *(Objective 1)*

    A. Mystery
    B. Misidentification
    C. Anachronism
    D. Ignorance

124. "A man may take to drink because he feels himself to be a failure, and then fail all the more completely because he drinks." In context, this sentence is best described as a/an: *(Objective 5)*

    A. Analogy
    B. Metaphor
    C. Simile
    D. Allusion

125. What does this author think of the English language? *(Objective 2)*

    A. It is in unavoidable decline.
    B. It should not be altered.
    C. Its rules are subject to the whims of speakers.
    D. It can be improved through good habits.

126. What can we assume will follow this passage? *(Objectives 2 and 13)*

    A. A screed on the decline of English
    B. Further evidence that English is being destroyed
    C. Names of authors who have contributed to the decline of English
    D. Specific examples of bad English in use

127. What is the subject of the verb "lies" in the last sentence of the first paragraph? *(Objective 9)*

   A. Language
   B. Growth
   C. This
   D. Underneath

128. The author believes the decline of English is due to: *(Objectives 2 and 3)*

   A. The imitation of bad habits
   B. Societal decadence
   C. People preferring what is simple
   D. Political quibbling

129. By characterizing language as a "natural growth," the author emphasizes its: *(Objectives 2 and 3)*

   A. Personified qualities
   B. Duplicitous nature
   C. Inconsistency
   D. Changeability

130. What tone is the author striving for in this piece? *(Objective 5)*

   A. Humorous
   B. Academic
   C. Angry
   D. Disappointed

Read the following passage to answer questions 131–138.

On the domestic front, life was not easy. England was not a wealthy country and its people endured relatively poor living standards. The landed classes—many of them enriched by the confiscated wealth of former monasteries—were determined in the interests of profile to convert their arable land into pasture for sheep, so as to produce the wool that supported the country's chief economic asset, the woolen cloth trade. But the enclosing of the land only added to the misery of the poor, many of whom, evicted and displaced, left their decaying villages and gravitated to the towns where they joined the growing army of beggars and vagabonds that would become such a feature of Elizabethan life. Once, the religious houses would have dispensed charity to the destitute, but Henry VIII had dissolved them all in the 1530s, and many former monks and nuns were now themselves beggars. Nor did the civic authorities help: they passed laws in an attempt to ban the poor from towns and cities, but to little avail. It was a common sight to see men and women lying in the dusty streets, often dying in the dirt like dogs or beasts, without human compassion being shown to them. 'Certainly, wrote a Spanish observer in 1558, 'the state of England lay now most afflicted.' And although people looked to the new Queen Elizabeth to put matters right, there were so many who doubted if she could overcome the seemingly insurmountable problems she faced, or even remain queen long enough to begin tacking them. Some, both at home and abroad, were the opinion that her title to the throne rested on precarious foundations. Many regarded the daughter of Henry VII and Anne Boleyn as a bastard from the time of her birth on 7 September 1533, although, ignoring such slurs on the validity of his second marriage, Henry had declared Elizabeth his heir.

131. Why was land confiscated from the poor? *(Objective 2)*

   A. To build a new monastery
   B. To create pastures for sheep, ultimately increasing the export of wool
   C. To create housing for monks and nuns
   D. Queen Elizabeth wanted to expand her property.

132. A vagabond is a: *(Objective 1)*

   A. Wanderer
   B. Prisoner
   C. Poor person
   D. Rich person

133. Why didn't the poor have shelter with the churches? *(Objective 2)*

   A. They were already filled with beggars.
   B. Religious houses have never offered shelter to the poor.
   C. They were also being used to raise sheep.
   D. Henry VIII had dissolved them all in the 1530s.

134. How were civic authorities unsuccessful? *(Objective 1)*

   A. Poor people remained within city limits.
   B. Public service funds ran out.
   C. Public housing plans extended deadlines.
   D. Churches did not open their doors to the poor.

135. What is a synonym for the word "precarious"? *(Objective 1)*

   A. Strong
   B. Illegitimate
   C. Risky
   D. Determined

136. What is the author's view toward Queen Elizabeth? *(Objective 2)*

   A. Doubtful
   B. Vengeful
   C. Resentful
   D. Supportive

137. How is the English culture portrayed in this passage? *(Objective 2)*

   A. Religious
   B. Elitist
   C. Racist
   D. Diverse

138. What is Elizabeth's relationship to Henry? *(Objective 2)*

   A. Wife
   B. Cousin
   C. Lover
   D. Daughter

Read the following passage to answer questions 139–143.

I have often thought of it as one of the most barbarous customs in the world, considering us as a civilized and a Christian country, that we deny the advantages of learning to women. We reproach the sex every day with folly and impertinence; while I am confident, had they the advantages of education equal to us, they would be guilty of less than ourselves. One would wonder, indeed, how it should happen that women are conversible at all; since they are only beholden to natural parts, for all their knowledge. Their youth is spent to teach them to stitch and sew or make baubles. They are taught to read, indeed, and perhaps to write their names, or so; and that is the height of a woman's education. And I would but ask any who slight the sex for their understanding, what is a man (a gentleman, I mean) good for, that is taught no more? I need not give instances, or examine the character of a gentleman, with a good estate, or a good family, and with tolerable parts; and examine what figure he makes for want of education. The soul is placed in the body like a rough diamond; and must be polished, or the luster of it will never appear. And 'tis manifest, that as the rational soul distinguishes us from brutes; so education carries on the distinction, and makes some less brutish than others. This is too evident to need any demonstration. But why then should women be denied the benefit of instruction? If knowledge and understanding had been useless additions to the sex, GOD Almighty would never have given them capacities; for he made nothing needless. Besides, I would ask such, What they can see in ignorance, that they should think it a necessary ornament to a woman?

139. **What is the best synonym for "reproach" in the second sentence of this piece?** *(Objective 1)*

    A. Attack
    B. Demean
    C. Move toward
    D. Ignore

140. **What is the author saying with the second sentence of the first paragraph?** *(Objective 3)*

    A. Education for women is a necessity, and the fact that we deny it to them is a national disgrace.
    B. If women possessed education, they would be able to give men a taste of their own medicine.
    C. Men often oppress women, and if women were educated, they likely would not do the same.
    D. Education is a privilege, one that women must earn for themselves.

141. **With the last sentence of paragraph two, the author is implying that:** *(Objectives 3 and 14)*

    A. A man with no education is hardly impressive, even if he has other advantages.
    B. Certain qualities of upbringing handily offset the downsides of no education.
    C. Upper-class men have little need for education.
    D. Education is only one facet of many that makes a man worthy.

142. **The author primarily supports his argument with:** *(Objectives 3 and 14)*

    A. Citations
    B. Direct observation
    C. Common sense
    D. Examples

143. **Throughout the piece, the author makes frequent use of:** *(Objectives 3 and 14)*

    A. Rhetorical questions
    B. Hyperbole
    C. Direct quotation
    D. Appeals to authority

TEACHER CERTIFICATION STUDY GUIDE

144. **What are the five key concepts of media literacy based upon?** *(Objective 17)*

    A. All forms of media are designed to trick the viewer.
    B. All forms of media are texts and all texts are constructs.
    C. All forms of media are distracting, so students need to be vigilant.
    D. All forms of media improve learning in the classroom.

145. **What are the three main types of appeal in a persuasive text, whether an advertisement or a persuasive essay?** *(Objectives 3, 14, and 17)*

    A. Pathos, logos, gyros
    B. Bathos, logos, ethos
    C. Pathos, logos, ethos
    D. Pathos, media res, ethos

146. **In choosing images for a campaign for mouthwash, which advertising appeal would be the most effective?** *(Objective 17)*

    A. Beauty
    B. Lifestyle
    C. Independence
    D. Peer approval

147. **What is a key question to ask when interpreting images and/or various forms of media for stereotypes or audience focus?** *(Objective 17)*

    A. How might different individuals or groups see this text differently?
    B. Who paid for this media?
    C. What design choices did the creator of this media make?
    D. How would this work if the creator used a different media?

148. **Which of the following is *not* an essential part of crafting a presentation for a particular purpose and audience?** *(Objective 17)*

    A. Discover—choose a topic you and your audience care about.
    B. Gather feedback—make sure you have forms ready to distribute to get some feedback on your presentation, otherwise, how are you going to learn?
    C. Organize—start off with a hook, organize the body of what you are going to say, and end with a strong finish
    D. Edit—make sure your presentation is polished and practiced, your images are clear, your technology works.

149. Which of the following statements about copyright issues is true?
(Objective 17)

- A. Copyright is a legal and ethical issue.
- B. Copyright issues are important for everyone and not just professionals.
- C. Copyright issues are useful to teach in school because attribution and citation are complicated.
- D. All of the above.

150. Which of the following is not a good reason to add media to a presentation?
(Objective 17)

- A. As something to keep the audience from being bored
- B. To illustrate, explain, or represent an idea
- C. As evidence to support an idea
- D. To evoke emotions, to provide a subtext or commentary

ANSWER KEY

1.A	2.D	3.A	4.D	5.C	6.A	7.C	8.B	9.C	10.D
11.B	12.C	13.C	14.A	15.B	16.C	17.C	18.A	19.B	20.C
21.B	22.D	23.B	24.A	25.C	26.B	27.A	28.B	29.D	30.A
31.C	32.C	33.A	34.D	35.A	36.A	37.D	38.C	39.D	40.A
41.C	42.C	43.A	44.D	45.B	46.B	47.A	48.B	49.D	50.C
51.D	52.D	53.A	54.B	55.A	56.B	57.C	58.A	59.C	60.C
61.D	62.D	63.C	64.A	65.B	66.D	67.A	68.C	69.A	70.C
71.B	72.D	73.C	74.D	75.A	76.C	77.A	78.D	79.B	80.A
81.D	82.C	83.A	84.A	85.C	86.C	87.B	88.C	89.A	90.B
91.A	92.C	93.B	94.B	95.B	96.A	97.C	98.C	99.A	100.D
101.B	102.A	103.B	104.B	105.D	106.C	107.A	108.A	109.D	110.D
111.C	112.D	113.A	114.B	115.C	116.A	117.C	118.A	119.C	120.C
121.D	122.A	123.C	124.A	125.D	126.D	127.C	128.A	129.D	130.B
131.B	132.A	133.D	134.A	135.C	136.A	137.B	138.D	139.B	140.C
141.A	142.C	143.A	144.B	145.C	146.D	147.A	148.B	149.D	150.A

TEACHER CERTIFICATION STUDY GUIDE

RATIONALES

1. Latin words that entered the English language during the Elizabethan age include: *(Objective 1)*

    A. Allusion, education, and esteem
    B. Vogue and mustache
    C. Canoe and cannibal
    D. Alligator, cocoa, and armadillo

The correct answer is A. Allusion, education and esteem
These words reflect the Renaissance interest in the classical world and the study of ideas. The words in Answer B are of French derivation, the words in Answer C are of Carib (indigenous American) origins, and the words in Answer D are derived from Spanish.

2. To understand the origins of a word, one must study the: *(Objective 1)*

    A. Synonyms
    B. Inflections
    C. Phonetics
    D. Etymology

The correct answer is D. Etymology
Etymology is the study of word origins. A synonym is an equivalent of another word and can substitute for it in certain contexts. Inflection is a modification of words according to their grammatical functions, usually by employing variant word endings to indicate such qualities as tense, gender, case, and number. Phonetics is the science devoted to the physical analysis of the sounds of human speech, including their production, transmission, and perception.

3. Which of the following literary elements and devices describes the human practice of associating emotional effects stemming from the implications of a word, beyond its literal meaning? *(Objective 1)*

    A. Connotation
    B. Denotation
    C. Caesura
    D. Conceit

The correct answer is A. Connotation
Connotation is the attached personal meaning of a word as opposed to its literal definition.

TEACHER CERTIFICATION STUDY GUIDE

4. **Which of the following reading strategies calls for higher-order cognitive skills?** *(Objective 1)*

    A. Making predictions
    B. Summarizing
    C. Monitoring
    D. Making inferences

The correct answer is D. Making inferences
Making inferences involves using other reading skills such as making predictions, skimming, scanning, summarizing, and then coming to conclusions or making inferences that are not directly stated in the text.

5. **Which level of meaning is the hardest aspect of a language to master?** *(Objective 1)*

    A. Denotation
    B. Jargon
    C. Connotation
    D. Slang

The correct answer is C. Connotation
Connotation refers to the meanings suggested by a word rather than the dictionary definition of the word. For example, the word "slim" means thin, and it is usually used with a positive connotation, to compliment or admire someone's figure. The word "skinny" also means thin, but its connotations are not as flattering as those of the word "slim." The connotative aspect of language is more difficult to master than the denotative aspect (dictionary definition), as the former requires a mastery of the social aspects of language, not just the linguistic rules.

6. **Which of the following is *not* true about the English language?** *(Objective 1)*

    A. English is the easiest language to learn.
    B. English is the least inflected language.
    C. English has the most extensive vocabulary of any language.
    D. English originated as a Germanic tongue.

The correct answer is A. English is the easiest language to learn
Just like any other language, English has inherent peculiarities that make it difficult to learn, even though English has no declensions, such as those found in Latin, Greek, or contemporary Russian, and no tonal system, such as those found in Chinese.

English Language Arts

7. Which of the following is an example of an informational text suitable for use in the classroom? *(Objective 2)*

   A. A sonnet
   B. The results of a chemistry experiment
   C. A magazine article on habitat loss
   D. A speech

The correct answer is C. A magazine article on habitat loss
Expository content is informative in nature. The results of a chemistry experiment are highly technical. A sonnet is a form of poetry, and a speech may not be informative in nature.

8. Which of the following is most true of expository writing? *(Objective 2)*

   A. It is mutually exclusive of other forms of discourse.
   B. It can incorporate other forms of discourse in the process of providing supporting details.
   C. It should never employ informal expression.
   D. It should only be scored with a summative evaluation.

The correct answer is B. It can incorporate other forms of discourse in the process of providing supporting details
Expository writing sets forth an explanation or an argument about any subject and can use distinct or combined forms of discourse, a sign of academic literacy. This directly contradicts Answer A. Writing can use formal and informal language and can be evaluated in many subjective and objective ways.

9. Which of the following is not one of the four forms of discourse? *(Objective 2)*

   A. Exposition
   B. Description
   C. Rhetoric
   D. Persuasion

The correct answer is C. Rhetoric
Rhetoric is an umbrella term for techniques of expressive and effective speech. Rhetorical figures are ornaments of speech such as anaphora, antithesis, metaphor, and so on. The other three choices are specific forms of discourse.

10. **Sometimes readers are asked to demonstrate their understanding of a text. This might include all of the following except:** *(Objective 2)*

    A. Role-playing
    B. Paraphrasing
    C. Storyboarding a part of the story with dialogue bubbles
    D. Reading the story aloud

The correct answer is D. Reading the story aloud
Reading the text aloud may help readers understand the text, but it won't demonstrate their understanding of it. By role-playing, paraphrasing, or storyboarding, readers will convey their understanding of the purpose and main ideas of the text.

11. **Which of the following methods can help readers comprehend the purpose in an informational text?** *(Objective 3)*

    A. FRI
    B. SQ3R
    C. VENN
    D. MEME

The correct answer is B. SQ3R
The Survey, Question, Read, Recite, and Review method assists readers in following a logical thought process when assessing and reviewing an informational text. It is a good reading comprehension strategy to use with expository, persuasive, and even functional and technical texts.

12. **In literature, evoking feelings of pity or compassion is to create:** *(Objective 3)*

    A. Colloquy
    B. Irony
    C. Pathos
    D. Paradox

The correct answer is C. Pathos
A well-known example of pathos is Desdemona's death in *Othello*, but there are many other examples of pathos.

13. **What type of reasoning does Henry David Thoreau use in the following excerpt from "Civil Disobedience"?** *(Objective 3)*

   Unjust laws exist; shall we be content to obey them, or shall we endeavor to amend them, and obey them until we have succeeded, or shall we transgress them at once? Men generally, under such a government as this, think that they ought to wait until they have persuaded the majority to alter them. They think that, if they should resist, the remedy would be worse than the evil. But it is the fault of the government itself that the remedy is worse than the evil. … Why does it always crucify Christ, and excommunicate Copernicus and Luther, and pronounce Washington and Franklin rebels?

   A. Ethical reasoning
   B. Inductive reasoning
   C. Deductive reasoning
   D. Intellectual reasoning

The correct answer is C. Deductive reasoning
Deductive reasoning begins with a general statement that leads to the particulars. In this essay, Thoreau begins with the general question about what should be done about unjust laws. His argument leads to the government's role in suppressing dissent.

14. **Identify the type of appeal used by Molly Ivins in this excerpt from her essay "Get a Knife, Get a Dog, but Get Rid of Guns."** *(Objective 3)*

   As a civil libertarian, I, of course, support the Second Amendment. And I believe it means exactly what it says: "A well-regulated militia being necessary to the security of a free state, the right of the people to keep and bear arms shall not be infringed."

   A. Ethical
   B. Emotional
   C. Rational
   D. Literary

The correct answer is A. Ethical
An ethical appeal is using the credentials of a reliable and trustworthy authority. In this case, Ivins cites the Constitution. Pathos is an emotional appeal, and logos is a rational appeal. Literature might appeal to you, but it's not a rhetorical appeal.

15. **What literary device is used in this passage?** *(Objective 3)*

And outside, the silent wilderness surrounding this cleared speck on the earth struck me as something great and invincible, like evil or truth, waiting patiently for the passing away of this fantastic invasion.

   A. Simile
   B. Metaphor
   C. Illusion
   D. Personification

The correct answer is B. Metaphor
A simile is a comparison or description that uses "like" or "as." Because this passage uses "like evil or truth" to describe the wilderness, Answer B is the best answer.

16. Use the image below to answer the question:

5

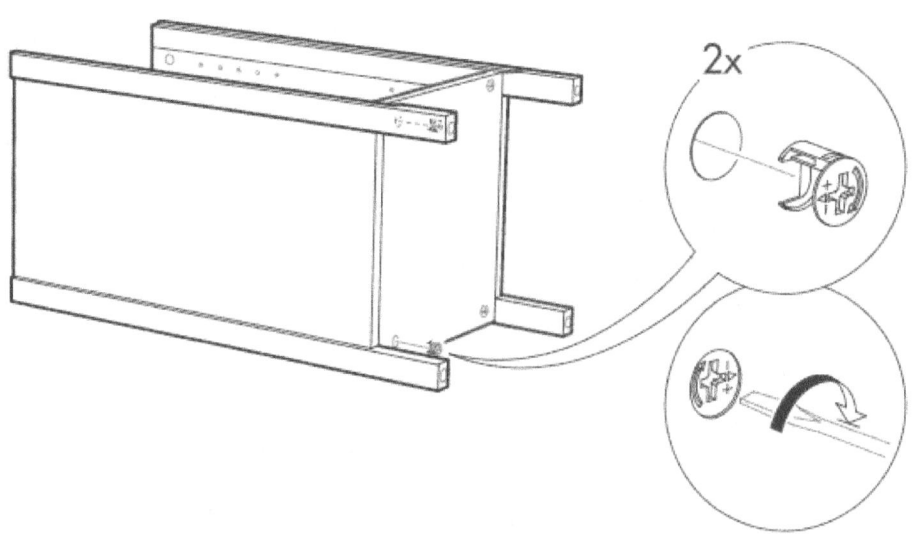

What is the purpose of this diagram/illustration? *(Objective 4)*

A. Part of a set of instructions for how to build a piece of furniture from scratch
B. An illustration to accompany a warranty for a piece of furniture
C. Part of a set of instructions for how to assemble a piece of furniture
D. An illustration to accompany a repair manual for a piece of furniture

The correct answer is C. Part of a set of instructions for how to assemble a piece of furniture
It's an assembly question. You can tell because of the parts included. It's part of a set because you can see the number 5, which indicates that there are other steps. There is nothing to indicate that the furniture is broken, so it cannot be D.

17. Use the picture below to answer the question: *(Objective 4)*

[Image of IRS tax form 1040 showing Filing Status, Exemptions, and Income sections]

What types of clues will help you determine the purpose of this text?

A. Organizing structures
B. Word choice
C. A and B
D. Style and tone of language

The correct answer is C. A and B
The organizing structure shows numbered lists of items to fill out so that you know that it is a form of some kind. The language used such as filing, exemptions, and income indicate that this is a form to collect information for tax purposes.

TEACHER CERTIFICATION STUDY GUIDE

18. **Which is an untrue statement about a theme in literature?** *(Objective 5)*

    A. The theme is always stated directly somewhere in the text.
    B. The theme is the central idea in a literary work.
    C. All parts of the work (such as plot, setting, and mood) should contribute to the theme in some way.
    D. By analyzing the various elements of the work, the reader should be able to arrive at an indirectly stated theme.

The correct answer is A. The theme is always stated directly somewhere in the text
The theme may be stated directly, but it can also be implicit in various aspects of the work, such as the interaction between characters, symbolism, or description.

19. **The technique of starting a narrative at a significant point in the action and then developing the story through flashbacks is called:** *(Objective 5)*

    A. Octava rima
    B. In medias res
    C. Irony
    D. Suspension of willing disbelief

The correct answer is B. In medias res
As its Latin translation suggests: in the middle of things. An octava rima is a specific eight-line stanza of poetry whose rhyme scheme is abababcc. Lord Byron's *Don Juan* is written in octava rima. Irony is an unexpected disparity between what is stated and what is really implied by the author. Benjamin Franklin's "Rules by Which a Great Empire May Be Reduced to a Small One" and Voltaire's tales are texts that are written using irony. Drama is what Coleridge calls "the willing suspension of disbelief for the moment, which constitutes poetic faith."

20. The following passage is written from which point of view? *(Objective 5)*

As she mused the pitiful vision of her mother's life laid its spell on the very quick of her being—that life of commonplace sacrifices closing in final craziness. She trembled as she heard again her mother's voice saying constantly with foolish insistence: Derevaun Seraun! Derevaun Seraun!*

* "The end of pleasure is pain!" (Gaelic)

- A. First person, narrator
- B. Second person, direct address
- C. Third person, omniscient
- D. First person, omniscient

The correct answer is C. Third person, omniscient
The passage is clearly in the third person (the subject is "she"), and it is omniscient since it gives the characters' inner thoughts.

21. In the phrase "The cabinet conferred with the president," cabinet is an example of a/an: *(Objective 5)*

- A. Metonym
- B. Synecdoche
- C. Metaphor
- D. Allusion

The correct answer is B. Synecdoche
In a synecdoche, a whole is referred to by naming a part of it. A synecdoche can stand for a whole of which it is a part.

22. Based on the excerpt below from Kate Chopin's short story "The Story of an Hour," what can students infer about the main character? *(Objective 5)*

   She did not stop to ask if it were or were not a monstrous joy that held her. A clear and exalted perception enabled her to dismiss the suggestion as trivial. She knew that she would weep again when she saw the kind, tender hands folded in death; the face that had never looked save with love upon her, fixed and gray and dead. But she saw beyond that bitter moment a long procession of years to come that would belong to her absolutely. And she opened and spread her arms out to them in welcome.

   A. She dreaded her life as a widow.
   B. Although she loved her husband, she was glad that he was dead for he had never loved her.
   C. She worried that she was too indifferent to her husband's death.
   D. Although they had both loved each other, she was beginning to appreciate that opportunities had opened because of his death.

The correct answer is D. Although they had both loved each other, she was beginning to appreciate that opportunities had opened because of his death
Dismissing her feeling of "monstrous joy" as insignificant, the young woman realizes that she will mourn her husband, who had been good to her and had loved her. But that "long procession of years" does not frighten her; instead she recognizes that this new life belongs to her alone and she welcomes it with open arms.

23. In classic tragedy, a protagonist's defeat is brought about by a tragic flaw, which is called: *(Objective 5)*

   A. Hubris
   B. Hamartia
   C. Catharsis
   D. The skene

The correct answer is B. Hamartia
Hubris is excessive pride, a type of tragic flaw. Catharsis is an emotional purging felt by the character. Skene is the Greek word for scene. All these terms come from Greek drama.

24. **How will literature help students in a science class understand the following passage?** *(Objective 5)*

   Just as was the case more than three decades ago, we are still sailing between the Scylla of deferring surgery for too long and risking irreversible left ventricular damage and sudden death, and the Charibdas of operating too early and subjecting the patient to the early risks of operation and the later risks resulting from prosthetic valves.
   —E. Braunwald, *European Heart Journal*, July 2000

   A. They will recognize the allusions to Scylla and Charibdas from Greek mythology and understand that the medical community has to select one of two unfavorable choices.
   B. They will recognize the allusion to sailing and understand its analogy to doctors as sailors navigating unknown waters.
   C. They will recognize that the allusions to Scylla and Charibdas refer to the two islands in Norse mythology on which sailors would find themselves shipwrecked and understand how the doctors feel isolated by their choices.
   D. They will recognize the metaphor of the heart and relate it to Eros, the character in Greek mythology who represents love. Eros was the love child of Scylla and Charibdas.

The correct answer is A. They will recognize the allusions to Scylla and Charibdas from Greek mythology and understand that the medical community has to select one of two unfavorable choices.
Scylla and Charibdas were two sea monsters guarding a narrow channel of water. Sailors trying to elude one side would face danger by sailing too close to the other side. The allusion indicates two equally undesirable choices.

25. The substitution of "went to his rest" for "died" is an example of a/an: *(Objective 5)*

   A. Bowdlerism
   B. Jargon
   C. Euphemism
   D. Malapropism

The correct answer is C. Euphemism
A euphemism replaces an unpleasant or offensive word or expression with a more agreeable one. A euphemism also alludes to distasteful things in a pleasant manner, and it can even be used to paraphrase offensive texts. Bowdlerism is named after Thomas Bowdler, who excised from Shakespeare what he considered vulgar and offensive. Jargon is a specialized language used by a particular group. What was groovy to one generation has become awesome to another. Named after Mrs. Malaprop, a character in a play by Richard Sheridan, a malapropism is a misuse of words, often to comical effect. Mrs. Malaprop once said, "...she's as headstrong as an allegory on the banks of the Nile," misusing allegory for alligator.

26. Read the first stanza from Edgar Allan Poe's poem, "The Bells," to answer the question: *(Objective 6)*

   Hear the sledges with the bells—
   Silver bells!
   What a world of merriment their melody foretells!
   How they tinkle, tinkle, tinkle,
   In the icy air of night!
   While the stars that oversprinkle
   All the heavens, seem to twinkle
   With a crystalline delight;
   Keeping time, time, time,
   In a sort of Runic rhyme,
   To the tintinnabulation that so musically wells
   From the bells, bells, bells, bells
   Bells, bells, bells—
   From the jingling and the tinkling of the bells.

   Words such as "tinkling" and "tintinnabulation" are examples of:

   A. Consonance
   B. Onomatopoeia
   C. Alliteration
   D. Free verse

The correct answer is B. Onomatopoeia
Onomatopoeia is figurative language that imitates the sound it describes. The poet actually uses twanging and tintinnabulation to convey the feeling of movement and sound of the bells.

27. Read the following quotation to answer the question: *(Objective 6)*

   O, pardon me, though
   Bleeding piece of earth
   That I am meek and gentle with
   These butchers.
   —Marc Antony from *Julius Caesar*

   Addressing the dead body of Caesar as though he were still a living being is to employ an:

   A. Apostrophe
   B. Allusion
   C. Antithesis
   D. Anachronism

The correct answer is A. Apostrophe
This rhetorical figure addresses personified things, absent people, or gods. An allusion, on the other hand, is a quick reference to a character or event known to the public. An antithesis is a contrast between two opposing viewpoints, ideas, or presentation of characters. An anachronism is the placing of an object or person out of its time with the time of the text. The best-known example is the clock in Shakespeare's *Julius Caesar*.

28. **The literary device of personification is used in which example below?** *(Objective 6)*

   A. "Beg me no beggary by soul or parents, whining dog!"
   B. "Happiness sped through the halls cajoling as it went."
   C. "O wind thy horn, thou proud fellow."
   D. "And that one talent which is death to hide."

The correct answer is B. "Happiness sped through the halls cajoling as it went."
"Happiness," an abstract concept, is described as if it were a person with the words "sped" and "cajoling."

29. **An extended metaphor comparing two dissimilar things (one lofty one lowly) is the definition of a/an:** *(Objective 6)*

    A. Antithesis
    B. Aphorism
    C. Apostrophe
    D. Conceit

The correct answer is D. Conceit
A conceit is an unusually far-fetched metaphor in which an object, person, or situation is presented in a parallel and simpler analogue between two apparently different things or feelings, one sophisticated and one ordinary, usually taken from either nature or a well-known everyday concept, familiar to both reader and author alike. The conceit was first developed by Petrarch and spread to England in the sixteenth century.

30. **Which of the following is a characteristic of blank verse?** *(Objective 6)*

    A. Meter in iambic pentameter
    B. Clearly specified rhyme scheme
    C. Lack of figurative language
    D. Unspecified rhythm

The correct answer is A. Meter in iambic pentameter
An iamb is a metrical unit of verse having one unstressed syllable followed by one stressed syllable. This is the most commonly used metrical verse in English and American poetry. An iambic pentameter is a 10-syllable verse made of five of these metrical units, either rhymed as in sonnets, or unrhymed as in free, or blank, verse.

31. **Which is the best definition of free verse, or *vers libre*?** *(Objective 6)*

    A. Poetry, which consists of an unaccented syllable followed by an unaccented sound
    B. Short lyrical poetry written to entertain but with an instructive purpose
    C. Poetry, which does not have a uniform pattern of rhythm
    D. A poem, which tells the story and has a plot

The correct answer is C. Poetry, which does not have a uniform pattern of rhythm
Free verse has lines of irregular length (but it does not run on like prose).

32. What is the salient literary feature of this excerpt from an epic? *(Objective 6)*

Hither the heroes and the nymphs resorts,
To taste awhile the pleasures of a court;
In various talk th'instructive hours they passed,
Who gave the ball, or paid the visit last;
One speaks the glory of the English Queen,
And another describes a charming Indian screen;
A third interprets motion, looks, and eyes;
At every word a reputation dies.

   A. Sprung rhythm
   B. Onomatopoeia
   C. Heroic couplets
   D. Motif

The correct answer is C. Heroic couplets
A couplet is a pair of rhyming verse lines, usually of the same length. It is one of the most widely used verse forms in European poetry. Chaucer established the use of couplets in English, notably in *The Canterbury Tales,* using rhymed iambic pentameters (a metrical unit of verse having one unstressed syllable followed by one stressed syllable) later known as heroic couplets. Other authors who used heroic couplets include Ben Jonson, Dryden, and especially Alexander Pope, who became the master of them.

33. Which poem is typified as a villanelle? *(Objective 6)*

   A. "Do Not Go Gentle into That Good Night"
   B. "Dover Beach"
   C. "Sir Gawain and the Green Knight"
   D. *The Pilgrim's Progress*

The correct answer is A. "Do Not Go Gentle into That Good Night"
This poem by Dylan Thomas typifies the villanelle because it was written as such. A villanelle is a form that was invented in France in the sixteenth century and used mostly for pastoral songs. It has an uneven number (usually five) of tercets rhyming aba, with a final quatrain rhyming abaa. This poem is the most famous villanelle written in English. "Dover Beach," by Matthew Arnold, is not a villanelle, while "Sir Gawain and the Green Knight" was written in alliterative verse by an unknown author usually referred to as The Pearl Poet around 1370. *The Pilgrim's Progress* is a prose allegory by John Bunyan.

34. Which term best describes the form of the following poetic excerpt? *(Objective 6)*

> And more to lulle him in his slumber soft,
> A trickling streake from high rock tumbling downe,
> And ever-drizzling raine upon the loft.
> Mixt with a murmuring winde, much like a swowne
> No other noyse, nor peoples troubles cryes.
> As still we wont t'annoy the walle'd towne,
> Might there be heard: but careless Quiet lyes,
> Wrapt in eternall silence farre from enemyes.

   A. Ballad
   B. Elegy
   C. Spenserian stanza
   D. Octava rima

The correct answer is D. Octava rima
The octava rima is a specific eight-line stanza whose rhyme scheme is abababcc. A ballad is a narrative poem. An elegy is a form of lyric poetry typically used to mourn someone who has died. A form of the English sonnet created by Sir Edmund Spenser combines the English form and the Italian. The Spenserian sonnet follows the English quatrain and couplet pattern but resembles the Italian in its rhyme scheme, which is linked: abab bcbc cdcd ee.

TEACHER CERTIFICATION STUDY GUIDE

35. Which of the writers below wrote *I Know Why the Caged Bird Sings* and received the Presidential Medal of Freedom Award in 2010?
    (Objectives 5 and 6)

    A. Maya Angelou
    B. Sandra Cisneros
    C. Richard Wilbur
    D. Richard Wright

The correct answer is A. Maya Angelou
Among her most famous works are *I Know Why the Caged Bird Sings, And Still I Rise*, and *All God's Children Need Traveling Shoes*. Richard Wilbur is a poet and a translator of French dramatists Jean Racine and Jean-Baptiste Molière, but he is not African-American. Richard Wright is a well-known African-American author of novels such as *Native Son* and *Black Boy*. He was not a poet, however. Sandra Cisneros is the author of *The House on Mango Street*.

36. Charles Dickens, Robert Browning, and Robert Louis Stevenson were:
    (Objective 7)

    A. Victorians
    B. Medievalists
    C. Elizabethans
    D. Absurdists

The correct answer is A. Victorians
The Victorian period is remarkable for the diversity and quality of its literature. Robert Browning wrote chilling monologues such as "My Last Duchess" and long poetic narratives such as *The Pied Piper of Hamlin*. Robert Louis Stevenson wrote his works partly for young adults, whose imaginations were quite taken by his *Treasure Island* and *The Case of Dr. Jekyll and Mr. Hyde*. Charles Dickens tells of the misery of the times and the complexities of Victorian society in novels such as *Oliver Twist* and *Great Expectations*.

37. The Elizabethans wrote in: *(Objective 7)*

    A. Celtic
    B. Old English
    C. Middle English
    D. Modern English

The correct answer is D. Modern English
There is no document written in Celtic in England, and a work such as *Beowulf* is representative of Old English in the eighth century. It is also the earliest Teutonic written document. Before the fourteenth century, little literature is known to have appeared in Middle English, which had absorbed many words from the Norman French spoken by the ruling class, but at the end of the fourteenth century there appeared the works of Chaucer, John Gower, and the story "Sir Gawain and the Green Knight." The Elizabethans wrote in modern English, and their legacy is important: They imported the Petrarchan, or Italian, sonnet, which Sir Thomas Wyatt and Sir Philip Sydney illustrated in their works. Sir Edmund Spenser invented his own version of the Italian sonnet and wrote "The Faerie Queene." Other literature of the time includes the hugely influential works of Shakespeare and Marlowe.

38. Which of the following is the best definition of existentialism? *(Objective 7)*

    A. The philosophical doctrine that matter is the only reality and that everything in the world, including thought, will, and feeling, can be explained only in terms of matter
    B. A philosophy that views things as they should be or as one would wish them to be
    C. A philosophical and literary movement, variously religious and atheistic, stemming from Kierkegaard and represented by Sartre
    D. The belief that all events are determined by fate and are hence inevitable

The correct answer is C. A philosophical and literary movement, variously religious and atheistic, stemming from Kierkegaard and represented by Sartre
Even though there are other prominent thinkers in the movement known as existentialism, such as Albert Camus and Maurice Merleau-Ponty, Sartre remains the main figure in this movement.

39. **What is considered the first work of English literature because it was written in the vernacular of the day?** *(Objectives 1 and 7)*

    A. *Beowulf*
    B. *Le Morte d'Arthur*
    C. "The Faerie Queene"
    D. *The Canterbury Tales*

The correct answer is D. *The Canterbury Tales*
Chaucer wrote *The Canterbury Tales* in the street language of medieval England. *Beowulf* was written during the Anglo-Saxon period and is a Teutonic saga. *Le Morte d'Arthur*, by Thomas Malory, was written after Chaucer. Sir Edmund Spenser's "Faerie Queene" was written during the Renaissance under the reign of Queen Elizabeth I.

40. **Which choice below best defines naturalism?** *(Objective 7)*

    A. A belief that the writer or artist should apply scientific objectivity in his or her observation and treatment of life without imposing value judgments
    B. The doctrine that teaches that the existing world is the best to be hoped for
    C. The doctrine that teaches that God is not a personality, but that all laws, forces, and manifestations of the universe are God-related
    D. A philosophical doctrine that professes that the truth of all knowledge must always be in question

The correct answer is A. A belief that the writer or artist should apply scientific objectivity in his or her observation and treatment of life without imposing value judgements
Naturalism is a movement that was started by French writers Jules and Edmond de Goncourt with their novel *Germinie Lacerteux*, but its real leader is Émile Zola, who wanted to bring "a slice of life" to his readers. His saga, *Les Rougon-Macquart*, consists of 22 novels depicting various aspects of social life. Authors writing in English representative of this movement include George Moore and George Gissing in England, but the most important naturalist novel in English is Theodore Dreiser's *Sister Carrie*.

41. A traditional anonymous story, ostensibly having a historical basis, usually explaining some phenomenon of nature or aspect of creation, defines a: *(Objective 7)*

   A. Proverb
   B. Idyll
   C. Myth
   D. Epic

The correct answer is C. Myth
A myth is usually traditional and anonymous and explains natural and supernatural phenomena. Myths are usually about creation, divinity, the significance of life and death, and natural phenomena.

42. In the following poem, what literary movement is reflected? *(Objective 7)*

   "My Heart Leaps Up," by William Wordsworth

   My heart leaps up when I behold
   A rainbow in the sky:
   So was it when my life began;
   So is it now I am a man;
   So be it when I shall grow old,
   Or let me die!
   The Child is father of the Man;
   And I could wish my days to be
   Bound each to each by natural piety

   A. Neoclassicism
   B. Victorian literature
   C. Romanticism
   D. Naturalism

The correct answer is C. Romanticism
The romantic period of the nineteenth century is known for its emphasis on feelings, emotions, and passions. William Wordsworth and William Blake were two notable poets from this period. In the neoclassicism of the previous period, the literature echoed the classical ideals of proportion, common sense, and reason over raw emotion and imagination, and the purpose was more didactic than celebratory. The Victorian period of the late nineteenth century exerted more restraint on emotions and feelings. In naturalistic writing, authors depict the world more harshly and more objectively.

43. Arthur Miller wrote *The Crucible* as a parallel to what twentieth-century event? *(Objective 8)*

   A. Senator McCarthy's House Un-American Activities Committee Hearing
   B. The cold war
   C. The fall of the Berlin Wall
   D. The Persian Gulf War

The correct answer is A. Senator McCarthy's House Un-American Activities Committee Hearing
The episode of the seventeenth century witch hunt in Salem, Massachusetts, gave Miller a story line that was comparable to what was happening to persons suspected of communist beliefs in the 1950s.

44. Considered one of the first feminist plays, this Ibsen drama ends with a door slamming, symbolizing the lead character's emancipation from traditional societal norms. *(Objective 8)*

   A. *The Wild Duck*
   B. *Hedda Gabler*
   C. *Ghosts*
   D. *The Doll's House*

The correct answer is D. *The Doll's House*
Nora in *The Doll's House* leaves her husband and children when she realizes her husband is not the man she thought he was. Hedda Gabler, another feminist icon, shoots herself. *The Wild Duck* deals with the conflict between idealism and family secrets. *Ghosts,* considered one of Ibsen's most controversial plays, deals with many social ills, some of which include alcoholism, incest, and religious hypocrisy.

45. Which of the following is not a characteristic of a fable? *(Objective 8)*

   A. Features animals that feel and talk like humans
   B. Offers happy solutions to human dilemmas
   C. Teaches a moral or standard for behavior
   D. Illustrates specific people or groups without directly naming them

The correct answer is B. Offers happy solutions to human dilemmas
Fables do not present a happy solution to a human dilemma. A fable is a short tale with animals, humans, gods, or even inanimate objects as characters. Fables often conclude with a moral, delivered in the form of an epigram (a short, witty, and ingenious statement in verse). Fables are among the oldest forms of writing in human history: They appear in Egyptian papyri from 1500 BCE. The most famous fables are those of Aesop, a Greek slave living in about 600 BCE. In India, the Panchatantra appeared in the third century BCE. The most famous modern fables are those of seventeenth-century French poet Jean de La Fontaine.

TEACHER CERTIFICATION STUDY GUIDE

46. Which of the following is not a common theme of Native American literature? *(Objective 8)*

   A. Emphasis on the relationship of human beings to nature
   B. Belief that everyone can make their dreams come true
   C. Colonialism and/or genocide
   D. Culture and cultural loss

The correct answer is B. Belief that everyone can make their dreams come true
Native American literature was first a vast body of oral traditions from as early as before the fifteenth century. The characteristics include reverence for nature and the interconnectedness of the elements in the life cycle. The themes often reflect the harsh reality of the destruction of the Native American way of life and the genocide of many tribes by European Americans. These themes are still present in today's contemporary Native American literature, such as in the works of Duane Niatum, Paula Gunn Allen, Sherman Alexie, Louise Erdrich, and N. Scott Momaday.

47. Which of the following activities would most effectively familiarize readers with the attitudes and issues of the Depression-era South, the historical period in which *To Kill a Mockingbird* was written? *(Objective 8)*

   A. Construct a detailed timeline of 15 to 20 social, cultural, and political events that focus on race relations in the 1930s
   B. Research and report on the life of author Harper Lee to compare her background with the events in the book
   C. Watch the movie version and note language and dress
   D. Study the stock market crash of 1929 and its effects

The correct answer is A. Construct a detailed timeline of 15 to 20 social, cultural, and political events that focus on race relations in the 1930s
By identifying the social, cultural, and political events of the 1930s, readers will better understand the attitudes and values of the United States during the time of the novel. While researching the author's life could add depth to readers' understanding of the novel, it is unnecessary to the more comprehensive understanding of the novel itself. The movie version may portray an accurate depiction of the novel's setting, but it focuses on the events in the novel, not the external factors that fostered the conflict. The stock market crash and the subsequent Great Depression would be useful to note on the timeline, but readers would be distracted from the themes of the book by narrowing their focus to only these two events.

48. Read the following passage, "A Vindication of the Rights of Woman," by Mary Wollstonecraft, to answer the question: *(Objective 8)*

It is impossible for any man, when the most favourable circumstances concur, to acquire sufficient knowledge and strength of mind to discharge the duties of a king, entrusted with uncontrouled power; how then must they be violated when his very elevation is an insuperable bar to the attainment of either wisdom or virtue; when all the feelings of a man are stifled by flattery, and reflection shut out by pleasure! Surely it is madness to make the fate of thousands depend on the caprice of a weak fellow creature, whose very station sinks him necessarily below the meanest of his subjects! But one power should not be thrown down to exalt another—for all power intoxicates weak man; and its abuse proves, that the more equality there is established among men, the more virtue and happiness will reign in society. But this, and any similar maxim deduced from simple reason, raises an outcry—the church or the state is in danger, if faith in the wisdom of antiquity is not implicit; and they who, roused by the sight of human calamity, dare to attack human authority, are reviled as despisers of God, and enemies of man. These are bitter calumnies, yet they reached one of the best of men, whose ashes still preach peace, and whose memory demands a respectful pause, when subjects are discussed that lay so near his heart. After attacking the sacred majesty of Kings, I shall scarcely excite surprise by adding my firm persuasion that every profession, in which great subordination of rank constitutes its power, is highly injurious to morality. A standing army, for instance, is incompatible with freedom; because subordination and rigour are the very sinews of military discipline; and despotism is necessary to give vigour to enterprizes that one will directs. A spirit inspired by romantic notions of honour, a kind of morality founded on the fashion of the age, can only be felt by a few officers, whilst the main body must be moved by command, like the waves of the sea; for the strong wind of authority pushes the crowd of subalterns forward, they scarcely know or care why, with headlong fury.

What impact on the reader does the author have in mentioning kings and common officers?

A. She explains the divide between the two classes.
B. She shows that regardless of rank, every profession has downfalls.
C. She demonstrates the level of respect officers have for their king.
D. She questions gender roles in professional settings.

The correct answer is B. She shows that regardless of rank, every profession has downfalls
Many of the options in this question go against the message that's being portrayed in this passage. She does not mention respect that officers have for their king. While she does give examples of the divisions of classes and questions gender roles, the intention

behind mentioning of kings and common officers was to display the downfalls that each profession has, regardless of rank.

49. Read the following passage from the novel, *Beloved*, by Toni Morrison, to answer the question. *(Objective 8)*

   And if she thought anything, it was No. No. Nono. Nonono. Simple. She just flew. Collected every bit of life she had made, all the parts of her that were precious and fine and beautiful, and carried, pushed, dragged them through the veil, out, away, over there where no one could hurt them. Over there. Outside this place, where they would be safe.

   The author implies that the main character:

   A. Is trying to hide her children from the master
   B. Is planning to escape on the Underground Railroad
   C. Would like to return to Africa
   D. Would rather see her children die than watch them suffer

The correct answer is D. Would rather see her children die than watch them suffer
The symbolism points to the main character considering death for her children instead of watching them go through horrid tragedies. This makes Answer D the best answer.

50. Which of the following sentences contains a capitalization error? *(Objective 9)*

   A. The commander of the English navy was Admiral Nelson.
   B. Napoleon was the president of the French First Republic.
   C. Queen Elizabeth II is the Monarch of the British Empire.
   D. William the Conqueror led the Normans to victory over the British.

The correct answer is C. Queen Elizabeth II is the Monarch of the British Empire
Words that represent titles and offices are not capitalized unless used with a proper name. This is not the case here.

51. Select the correct version of the sentence below. *(Objective 9)*

   A. I climbed to the top of the mountain, it took me three hours.
   B. I climbed to the top of the mountain it took me three hours.
   C. I climbed to the top of the mountain: it took me three hours.
   D. I climbed to the top of the mountain; it took me three hours.

The correct answer is D. I climbed to the top of the mountain; it took me three hours.
A comma alone cannot separate two independent clauses. Instead a semicolon is needed to separate two related sentences.

52. **Which transition word would show contrast between these two ideas?** *(Objective 9)*

   We are confident in our skills to teach English. We welcome new ideas on this subject.

   A. We are confident in our skills to teach English, and we welcome new ideas on this subject.
   B. Because we are confident in our skills to teach English, we welcome new ideas on the subject.
   C. When we are confident in our skills to teach English, we welcome new ideas on the subject.
   D. We are confident in our skills to teach English; however, we welcome new ideas on the subject.

The correct answer is D. We are confident in our skills to teach English; however, we welcome new ideas on the subject.
Transitional words, phrases, and sentences help clarify meanings. In Answer A, the transition word "and" introduces another equal idea. In Answer B, the transition word "because" indicates cause and effect. In Answer C, the transition word "when" indicates order or chronology. Answer D, "however," shows that these two ideas contrast with each other.

53. **The arrangement and relationship of words in sentences or sentence structures best describes** *(Objective 9)*

   A. Syntax
   B. Discourse
   C. Thesis
   D. Style

The correct answer is A. Syntax
Syntax is the grammatical structure of sentences. Style is the manner of expression of writing or speaking. Discourse is an extended expression of thought through either oral or written communication. A thesis is the unifying main idea that can be either explicit or implicit.

54. **Which of the following sentences contains a subject-verb agreement error?** *(Objective 9)*

    A. Both mother and her two sisters were married in a triple ceremony.
    B. Neither the hen nor the rooster is likely to be served for dinner.
    C. My boss, as well as the company's two personnel directors, have been to Spain.
    D. Amanda and the twins are late again.

The correct answer is B. Neither the hen nor the rooster is likely to be served for dinner.
The reason for this is that the true subject of the verb is "My boss," not "two personnel directors."

55. **What is the proper way to punctuate the sentence below?** *(Objective 9)*

    Wally said with a groan, "Why do I have to do an oral interpretation of "The Raven."

    A. With a groan, "Why... of 'The Raven'?"
    B. With a groan "Why... of "The Raven"?
    C. With a groan ", Why... of "The Raven?"
    D. With a groan, "Why... of "The Raven."

The correct answer is A. With a groan, "Why... of 'The Raven'?"
The question mark in a quotation that is an interrogation should be within the quotation marks. Also, when quoting a work of literature within another quotation, one should use single quotation marks ('...') for the title of this work, and they should close before the final quotation mark.

56. **Which of the following sentences is properly punctuated?** *(Objective 9)*

    A. The more you eat; the more you want.
    B. The authors—John Steinbeck, Ernest Hemingway, and William Faulkner—are staples of modern writing in American literature textbooks.
    C. Handling a wild horse, takes a great deal of skill and patience.
    D. The man who replaced our teacher, is a comedian.

The correct answer is B. The authors—John Steinbeck, Ernest Hemingway, and William Faulkner—are staples of modern writing in American literature textbooks.
Dashes should be used instead of commas when commas are used elsewhere in the sentence for amplification or explanation—here within the dashes.

TEACHER CERTIFICATION STUDY GUIDE

57. **Which of the following choices best corrects the error in the sentence below?** *(Objective 9)*

    Edward didn't hardly know his cousin Gregor who'd had a rhinoplasty.

    A. Hardly did know his cousin Gregor
    B. Didn't know his cousin Gregor hardly
    C. Hardly knew his cousin Gregor
    D. Didn't know his cousin Gregor

The correct answer is C. Hardly knew his cousin Gregor
Using the adverb "hardly" to modify the verb creates a negative, and adding "not" creates the dreaded double negative.

58. **A punctuation mark indicating omission, interrupted thought, or an incomplete statement is a/an:** *(Objective 9)*

    A. Ellipsis
    B. Anachronism
    C. Colloquy
    D. Idiom

The correct answer is A. Ellipsis
In an ellipsis, word or words that would clarify the sentence's message are missing, yet it is still possible to understand them from the context.

59. **Which of the following choices best corrects the underlined error in the sentence below?** *(Objective 9)*

    <u>Mixing the batter for cookies</u>, the cat licked the Crisco from the cookie sheet.

    A. While mixing the batter for cookies
    B. While the batter for cookies was mixing
    C. While I mixed the batter for cookies
    D. While I mixed the cookies

The correct answer is C. While I mixed the batter for cookies
Answer A gives the impression that the cat was mixing the batter (the underlined phrase is a dangling modifier). Answer B implies that the batter was mixing itself, and Answer D lacks precision: It is the batter that was being mixed, not the cookies themselves.

TEACHER CERTIFICATION STUDY GUIDE

60. Which of the following choices best corrects the underlined error in the sentence below? *(Objective 9)*

    Mr. Smith <u>respectfully submitted his resignation and had</u> a new job.

    A. Respectfully submitted his resignation and has
    B. Respectfully submitted his resignation before accepting
    C. Respectfully submitted his resignation because of
    D. Respectfully submitted his resignation and had

The correct answer is C. Respectfully submitted his resignation because of
Answer A eliminates any relationship of causality between submitting the resignation and having the new job. Answer B just changes the sentence and, by omission, does not indicate the fact that Mr. Smith had a new job before submitting his resignation. Answer D means that Mr. Smith first submitted his resignation, and then got a new job.

61. Which of the following is *not* a technique of prewriting? *(Objective 10)*

    A. Clustering
    B. Listing
    C. Brainstorming
    D. Proofreading

The correct answer is D. Proofreading
Proofreading cannot be a method of prewriting, since it is done on already written texts only. Clustering, listing, and brainstorming are all prewriting strategies.

62. Writing ideas quickly without interruption of the flow of thoughts or attention to conventions is called: *(Objective 10)*

    A. Brainstorming
    B. Mapping
    C. Listing
    D. Free writing

The correct answer is D. Free writing
Free writing for 10 or 15 minutes allows students to write out their thoughts about a subject. This technique allows the students to develop ideas that they are conscious of, but it also helps them develop ideas that are lurking in the subconscious. It is useful to let the flow of ideas run through the head. If the students get stuck, they can write the last sentence over again until inspiration returns.

TEACHER CERTIFICATION STUDY GUIDE

63. What is the ideal first step of the writing process? *(Objective 10)*

   A. Choose a writing form for your composition.
   B. Create an outline for your composition.
   C. Identify a purpose of your composition.
   D. Identify the audience for your composition.

The correct answer is C. Identify a purpose of your composition.
Knowing the purpose of your writing. Without a purpose, it will be difficult for you to consider your audience, make an outline, or choose the best form for your writing.

64. Why is it helpful to outline ideas through lists or mind-mapping before writing a draft? *(Objective 10)*

   A. Outlines help you organize your text so that you know where you are going.
   B. Outlines help you remember why you are writing.
   C. Outlines can prove to an examiner or teacher that you are doing original work and not plagiarizing.
   D. This question is a trick. Mind-mapping is not a good way to organize your writing as it is graphic instead of a list and will confuse you when you are ready to write your draft.

The correct answer is A. Outlines help you organize your text so that you know where you are going.
Outlines help you organize your text so that you know where you are going.
All the facts or quotes that you can muster—even when they are true and correctly used—cannot help you make your points if they aren't well organized. Mind-mapping is the perfect way for some writers to outline, while others prefer more of a structured list.

65. Which of the following do you *not* need before you write your draft? *(Objective 10)*

   A. Knowledge of purpose and audience
   B. Preparation of your conclusion and introduction
   C. Knowledge of form
   D. Preparation of an outline

The correct answer is B. Preparation of your conclusion and introduction
It's actually a good idea to start with your body paragraphs. You can write the introduction and conclusions later. They will be easier to write and more relevant when the body of the text is written.

English Language Arts

66. A student is writing a draft of a persuasive essay, and she is using lots of primary and secondary sources. You see her writing her draft without any index cards, notes, or sources. She has only one tab open on her computer, and it's the document she is working on. As a teacher, what do you do in this situation? *(Objective 10)*

   A. Let her be. She is working hard.
   B. Make a note to talk to her after the class ends about the importance of keeping her sources and notes nearby when writing a draft.
   C. Take points off for process. She will probably also write an essay that is full of opinion without evidence to back it up. She clearly chose not to learn from the lesson about how to write a draft.
   D. Encourage her to take a brief break to find her sources

The correct answer is D. Encourage her to take a brief break to find her sources
Take the time to encourage her to find her sources. Keep all materials that you will need close by so that you don't have to break your flow to find something that you might need to make a point. It will be better to interrupt her now rather than during the monumental task she will have ahead of trying to integrate evidence, quotes, and citations when she finishes writing.

67. In the writing process, revision means reading through a text to: *(Objective 10)*

   A. Eliminate wordiness, redundancy, and distracting details
   B. Vary sentence length and structure and check for appropriate transition use
   C. Check for spelling, grammatical, and punctuation errors
   D. Check that the text is cohesive; if not, choose a new topic

The correct answer is A. Eliminate wordiness, redundancy, and distracting details
Revising a text is the first step in the last part of the writing process. It is best to focus on language before looking at sentence structure and transitions and grammar and spelling. If you are eliminating words, then you won't need to check their spelling. It may also end up saving you time when you edit for sentence length and transitions. As for Answer D, by the revision stage it's too late to change topics.

68. In preparing to write a research paper about a social problem, what can you do to determine the credibility of the information you are gathering? *(Objective 11)*

    A. Rest assured that the information on the Internet has been peer-reviewed and verified for accuracy.
    B. Find one solid source and use that exclusively.
    C. Cross-check your information with another credible source.
    D. Use only primary sources.

The correct answer is C. Cross-check your information with another credible source
When researchers find the same information in multiple reputable sources, the information is considered credible. Using the Internet for research requires strong critical evaluation of the source. Nothing from the Internet should be taken without careful scrutiny of the source. To rely on only one source is dangerous and shortsighted. Most people would find it a challenge to conduct primary research for a paper about a social problem.

69. Which of the following are secondary research materials? *(Objective 11)*

    A. The conclusions and inferences of other historians
    B. Literature and nonverbal materials, novels, stories, poetry, and essays from the period, as well as coins, archaeological artifacts, and art produced during the period
    C. Interviews and surveys conducted by the researcher
    D. Statistics gathered as the result of the research's experiments

The correct answer is A. The conclusions and inferences of other historians
Secondary sources are works written significantly after the period being studied and based upon primary sources. In this case, historians have studied artifacts of the time and drawn their conclusion and inferences. Primary sources are the basic materials that provide raw data and information. Students or researchers may use literature and other data they have collected to draw their own conclusions or inferences.

Read the following passage to answer questions 70 and 71: *(Objective 11)*

The brazen, vicious attack occurred in broad daylight. The cowardly action took the lives of 32 innocent victims. So far no single group has claimed responsibility, though several have issued statements noting its importance.

70. **Which of the following sentences best incorporates a quote from the passage above?**

    A. The writer's description of this as a "vicious attack" reveals bias.
    B. Saying, "The brazen, vicious attack occurred in broad daylight. The cowardly action took the lives of 32 innocent victims" reveals bias.
    C. The characterization of the incident as a "brazen, vicious attack" and a "cowardly action" reveals bias.
    D. When the writer says the brazen, vicious attack, it shows bias.

The correct answer is C. The characterization of the incident as a "brazen, vicious attack" and a "cowardly action" reveals bias.
Answer B is awkward, and Answer D does not use quotation marks. Answer A leaves out two potentially valid pieces of evidence.

71. **In doing research, a student has second thoughts about using this new story as a source. What is evidence of a flaw with the story?**

    A. It is not corroborated by other sources.
    B. The language is inflammatory and biased.
    C. There is no image to accompany the story.
    D. No other point of view is included.

The correct answer is B. The language is inflammatory and biased
The language used in this excerpt shows the bias of the writer. Words like "brazen," "vicious," and "cowardly" reveal that this may be a problematic source.

72. **Which of the following is *not* an effective research question?** *(Objective 11)*

    A. How was Arthur Miller influenced by the politics of his time?
    B. In what ways are adolescents influenced by social media?
    C. What causes some children to become bullies?
    D. What were the major battles of World War II?

The correct answer is D. What were the major battles of World War II?
All the other questions generate answers that are multifaceted and complex. There are multiple answers and perspectives that must be supported by evidence. Answer D results in a list that could likely be found with a quick Internet search.

73. Read the following passage to answer the question. *(Objective 11)*

When it was first perceived, in early times, that no middle course for America remained between unlimited submission to a foreign legislature and a total independence of its claims, men of reflection were less apprehensive of danger from the formidable power of fleets and armies they must determine to resist than from those contests and dissensions which would certainly arise concerning the forms of government to be instituted over the whole and over the parts of this extensive country. Relying, however, on the purity of their intentions, the justice of their cause, and the integrity and intelligence of the people, under an overruling Providence which had so signally protected this country from the first, the representatives of this nation, then consisting of little more than half its present number, not only broke to pieces the chains which were forging and the rod of iron that was lifted up, but frankly cut asunder the ties which had bound them, and launched into an ocean of uncertainty.

The zeal and ardor of the people during the Revolutionary war, supplying the place of government, commanded a degree of order sufficient at least for the temporary preservation of society. The Confederation which was early felt to be necessary was prepared from the models of the Batavian and Helvetic confederacies, the only examples which remain with any detail and precision in history, and certainly the only ones which the people at large had ever considered. But reflecting on the striking difference in so many particulars between this country and those where a courier may go from the seat of government to the frontier in a single day, it was then certainly foreseen by some who assisted in Congress at the formation of it that it could not be durable.

Negligence of its regulations, inattention to its recommendations, if not disobedience to its authority, not only in individuals but in States, soon appeared with their melancholy consequences—universal languor, jealousies and rivalries of States, decline of navigation and commerce, discouragement of necessary manufactures, universal fall in the value of lands and their produce, contempt of public and private faith, loss of consideration and credit with foreign nations, and at length in discontents, animosities, combinations, partial conventions, and insurrection, threatening some great national calamity.

TEACHER CERTIFICATION STUDY GUIDE

For which of the following research questions would this passage likely be best suited?

    A. How did economic issues influence the causes of the Revolutionary War?
    B. What philosophical schools of thought influenced leaders of the Revolution?
    C. What were some of the post-Revolutionary challenges facing the country?
    D. How did Britain try to influence the economy of the United States after the Revolution?

The correct answer is C. What were some of the post-Revolutionary challenges facing the country?
In the passage the writer addresses economic, political, and policy challenges facing the country after the Revolutionary War.

74. What is the correct way to include a quotation from *Orange Is the New Black*? (Objective 11)

    A. Kerman was terrified but continued with the plan anyway. "Were the authorities closing in on me? Maybe I should try to get through customs and run? Or perhaps the bag really was just delayed, and I would be abandoning a large sum of money that belonged to someone who could probably have killed me with a simple phone call. I decided that the latter choice was slightly more terrifying."

    B. Kerman was terrified but continued with the plan anyway. "Were the authorities closing in on me? Maybe I should try to get through customs and run? Or perhaps the bag really was just delayed, and I would be abandoning a large sum of money that belonged to someone who could probably have killed me with a simple phone call. I decided that the latter choice was slightly more terrifying" (Kerman 1).

    C. Kerman was terrified but continued with the plan anyway.

    "Were the authorities closing in on me? Maybe I should try to get through customs and run? Or perhaps the bag really was just delayed, and I would be abandoning a large sum of money that belonged to someone who could probably have killed me with a simple phone call. I decided that the latter choice was slightly more terrifying." (Kerman 1)

    D. Kerman was terrified but continued with the plan anyway.

    Were the authorities closing in on me? Maybe I should try to get through customs and run? Or perhaps the bag really was just delayed, and I would be abandoning a large sum of money that belonged to someone who could probably have killed me with a simple phone call. I decided that the latter choice was slightly more terrifying. (Kerman 1)

English Language Arts

The correct answer is D.
In Answers A and B, the quote should be included as a block quote because it is more than four lines long. In Answer C it does not need quotation marks because it is a block quote.

75. **Which definition is the best for defining diction?** *(Objective 12)*

    A. The specific word choices of an author to create a particular mood or feeling in the reader
    B. Writing that explains something thoroughly
    C. The background, or exposition, for a short story or drama
    D. Word choices that help teach a truth or moral

The correct answer is A. The specific word choices of an author to create a particular mood or feeling in the reader.
Diction refers to an author's choice of words, expressions, and style to convey his or her meaning.

76. **The following passage is written from which point of view?** *(Objective 12)*

    As she mused the pitiful vision of her mother's life laid its spell on the very quick of her being—that life of commonplace sacrifices closing in final craziness. She trembled as she heard again her mother's voice saying constantly with foolish insistence: Dearevaun Seraun! Dearevaun Seraun!* * "The end of pleasure is pain!" (Gaelic)

    A. First person, narrator
    B. Second person, direct address
    C. Third person, omniscient
    D. First person, omniscient

The correct answer is C. Third person, omniscient
The passage is clearly in the third person (the subject is "she"), and it is omniscient because it gives the character's inner thoughts.

77. **Which of the following techniques is an effective tool of characterization?** *(Objective 12)*

    A. Dialogue
    B. Denouement
    C. Sensory language
    D. First-person narration

The correct answer is A. Dialogue
Dialogue reveals a great deal about a character. The way in which characters speak and interact with others shows what a character is like.

78. **Which of the following descriptions most relies on sensory language? *(Objective 12)***

    A. As a child, their frequent arguments tore him apart.
    B. As a child, their frequent arguments were like wounds that never healed.
    C. As a child, he had to put up with the sound of their frequent arguments.
    D. As a child, their frequent arguments echoed through the house.

The correct answer is D. As a child, their frequent arguments echoed through the house.
Answers A and B include figurative language, but Answer D uses sensory language (the way the arguments sounded) to describe the situation.

Read the following passage to answer questions 79–83. *(Objective 12)*

International baggage claim in the Brussels airport was large and airy, with multiple carousels circling endlessly. I scurried from one to another, desperately trying to find my black suitcase. Because it was stuffed with drug money, I was more concerned than one might normally be about lost luggage.

I was 24 in 1993 and probably looked like just another anxious young professional woman. My Doc Martens had been jettisoned in favor of my beautiful handmade black suede heels. I wore black silk pants and a beige jacket, a typical jeune fille, *not a big counterculture, unless you spotted the tattoo on my neck. I had done exactly as I had been instructed, checking my bag Chicago through Paris, where I had to switch planes to take a short flight to Brussels.*

When I arrived in Belgium, I looked for my black rollie at the baggage claim. It was nowhere to be seen. Fighting a rushing tide of panic, I asked in my mangled high school French what had become of my suitcase. "Bags don't make it onto the right flight sometimes," said the big lug working in baggage handling. "Wait for the next shuttle from Paris—it's probably on that plane."

Had my bag been detected? I knew that carrying more than ten thousand dollars undeclared was illegal, let alone carrying it for a West African drug lord. Were the authorities closing in on me? Maybe I should try to get through customs and run? Or perhaps the bag really was just delayed, and I would be abandoning a large sum of money that belonged to someone who could probably have killed me with a simple phone call. I decided that the latter choice was slightly more terrifying. So I waited.

The next flight from Paris finally arrived. I sidled over to my new "friend" in baggage handling, who was sorting things out. It is hard to flirt when you're frightened. I spotted the suitcase. "Mon bag!" I exclaimed in ecstasy, seizing the Tumi. I thanked him effusively, waving with giddy affection as I sailed

*through one of the unmanned doors into the terminal, where I spotted my friend Billy waiting for me. I had inadvertently skipped customs.
"I was worried. What happened?" Billy asked.*

"Get me into a cab!" I hissed.

I didn't breathe until we had pulled away from the airport and were halfway across Brussels.

—Orange Is the New Black, *Piper Kerman*

79. Why did the author explain her attire?

   A. She wanted the audience to know how much she stood out in Europe.
   B. She used her clothing to try to fit in with the culture she was immersed in.
   C. She wanted to explain that she was a young, hip woman.
   D. She explained how difficult it was to wait around for her bag in heels.

The correct answer is B. She used her clothing to try to fit in with the culture she was immersed in.
The author used her attire to make herself mesh with the setting that she was immersed in. She was out of the country and trying her best to fit in, particularly because she was involved in illegal activity. Because she was trying to use her clothing to fit in, Answer B is the best answer.

80. Why didn't she breathe until pulling away from the airport?

   A. Tension
   B. Sadness
   C. Health issues
   D. She was talking to Billy

The correct answer is A. Tension
She had just gotten away with illegal activity, making her adrenaline at an all-time high. It's clear that she was not sad, and there's no mention of health issues in this passage. Answer A is the best answer.

TEACHER CERTIFICATION STUDY GUIDE

81. **What is the overall message of this passage?**

    A. Young professional women can get away with crimes.
    B. Security guards are not always watching every door in the airport.
    C. It's important to blend in when doing something suspicious.
    D. When you have done something illegal, even small mishaps can seem scary.

The correct answer is D. When you have done something illegal, even small mishaps can seem scary.
The author left plenty of room in the passage for the readers to think she might get caught. Because she portrays the emotions involved in doing something illegal in the airport, and her thoughts of how she might get caught, Answer D is the best answer.

82. **How did she avoid going through customs?**

    A. She flirted with the luggage man.
    B. Her friend Billy came to get her.
    C. She slipped through an unmanned door.
    D. She went through customs in Paris and Chicago, so it wasn't required.

The correct answer is C. She slipped through an unmanned door.
Using the details in the passage, it's easy to zero in on Answer C as the correct answer.

83. **What part of the plot does "Mon bag!" represent?**

    A. Climax
    B. Rising action
    C. Exposition
    D. Falling action

The correct answer is A. Climax
This statement represents the main character getting away with the crime that she was committing, making it the climax.

84. **Explanatory or informative discourse is best defined as:** *(Objective 13)*

    A. Exposition
    B. Narration
    C. Persuasion
    D. Description

The correct answer is A. Exposition
Exposition sets forth a systematic explanation of any subject. It can also introduce the characters of a literary work and their situations in the story. Narration relates a sequence of events (the story) told through a process of narration (discourse), in which events are recounted in a certain order (the plot). Persuasion strives to convince either a character in the story or the reader.

85. **Of the following statements, which is most true in regards to expository essays?** *(Objective 13)*

    A. Summative evaluations work best when scoring.
    B. They should always be formal.
    C. They should incorporate other forms of discourse when providing elaboration.
    D. This type of essay writing is exclusive to other forms of discourse.

The correct answer is C. They should incorporate other forms of discourse when providing elaboration.
Involving other forms of discourse will allow the reader to become involved with the text, as well as the writer.

86. In this paragraph from a student essay, identify the sentence that provides a detail. *(Objective 13)*

   (1) The poem concerns two different personality types and the human relation between them. (2) Their approach to life is totally different. (3) The neighbor is a conservative person who follows routines. (4) He follows the traditional wisdom of his father and his father's father. (5) The purpose in fixing the wall and keeping their relationship separate is only because it is all he knows.

   A. Sentence 1
   B. Sentence 3
   C. Sentence 4
   D. Sentence 5

The correct answer is C. Sentence 4
Sentence 4 provides a detail to sentence 3 by explaining how the neighbor follows routine. Sentence 1 is the thesis sentence, which is the main idea of the paragraph. Sentence 3 provides an example to develop that thesis. Sentence 4 is a reason that explains why.

87. Which of the following should *not* be included in the opening paragraph of an informative essay? *(Objective 13)*

   A. Thesis sentence
   B. Details and examples supporting the main idea
   C. Broad general introduction to the topic
   D. A style and tone that grabs the reader's attention

The correct answer is B. Details and examples supporting the main idea
The introductory paragraph should introduce the topic, capture the readers' interest, state the thesis, and prepare the readers for the main points in the essay. Details and examples, however, should be given in the second part of the essay, so as to help develop the thesis presented at the end of the introductory paragraph, following the inverted triangle method consisting of a broad general statement followed by some information, and then the thesis at the end of the paragraph.

88. In the paragraph below, which sentence does *not* contribute to the overall task of supporting the main idea? *(Objective 13)*

   (1) The Springfield City Council met Friday to discuss new zoning restrictions for the land to be developed south of the city. (2) Residents who opposed the new restrictions were granted 15 minutes to present their case. (3) Their argument focused on the dangers that increased traffic would bring to the area. (4) It seemed to me that the Mayor Simpson listened intently. (5) The council agreed to table the new zoning until studies would be performed.

   A. Sentence 2
   B. Sentence 3
   C. Sentence 4
   D. Sentence 5

The correct answer is C. Sentence 4
The other sentences provide detail to the main idea of the new zoning restrictions. Because sentence 4 provides no example or relevant detail, it should be omitted.

89. Students have been asked to write a research paper on automobiles and have brainstormed a number of questions they will answer based on their research findings. Which of the following is *not* an interpretive question to guide research? *(Objective 13)*

   A. Who were the first 10 automotive manufacturers in the United States?
   B. What types of vehicles will be used 50 years from now?
   C. How do automobiles manufactured in the United States compare and contrast with each other?
   D. What do you think is the best solution for the fuel shortage?

The correct answer is A. Who were the first 10 automotive manufacturers in the United States?
The question asks for objective facts. Answer B is a prediction that asks how something will look or be in the future, based on the way it is now. Answer C asks for similarities and differences, which is a higher-level research activity that requires analysis. Answer D is a judgment question that requires informed opinion.

90. Which of the following should students use to improve coherence of ideas within an argument? *(Objective 13)*

    A. Conjunctions like "and" to join ideas together
    B. Transitional words or phrases to show relationship of ideas
    C. Extensive use of direct quotes to improve credibility
    D. Adjectives and adverbs to provide stronger detail

The correct answer is B. Transitional words or phrases to show relationship of ideas
Transitional words and phrases are two-way indicators that connect the previous idea to the following idea. Sophisticated writers use transitional devices to clarify text (for example), show contrast (despite), show sequence (first, next), or show cause (because).

Read the following passage to answer questions 91–94. *(Objective 13)*

When rays of light pass through a prism, they undergo a change of direction: they are always deflected away from the refractive edge. It is possible to conceive an assembly of prisms whose refractive surfaces progressively become more nearly parallel to each other toward the middle: light rays passing through the outer prisms will undergo the greatest amount of refraction, with consequent deflection of their path toward the center, whereas the middle prism with its two parallel surfaces causes no deflection at all. When a beam of parallel rays passes through these prisms, the rays are all deflected toward the axis and converge at one point. Rays emerging from a point are also deflected by the prisms that they converge. A lens can be conceived as consisting of a large number of such prisms placed close up against one another, so that their surfaces merge into a continuous spherical surface. A lens of this kind, which collects the rays and concentrates them at one point, is called a convergent lens. Since it is thicker in the middle than at the edge, it is known as a convex lens.

In the case of a concave lens, which is thinner in the middle than at the edge, similar considerations show that all rays diverge from the center. Hence such a lens is called a divergent lens. After undergoing refraction, parallel rays appear to come from one point, while rays re-emerging from a point will, after passing through the lens, appear to emerge from another point. Lenses have surfaces in the same direction but having a different radii of curvature, these are known as meniscus lenses and are used more particularly in spectacles.

TEACHER CERTIFICATION STUDY GUIDE

91. Which of the following is *not* true of convergent lenses?

    A. They are concave.
    B. They are made of prisms.
    C. They can refract light.
    D. They have different radii.

The correct answer is A. They are concave.
Convergent lenses are stated to be convex, not concave.

92. Parallel surfaces in prisms cause:

    A. Little refraction
    B. Divergence of light rays
    C. No refraction
    D. Radii to vary

The correct answer is C. No refraction
The answer is in the first paragraph: "whereas parallel surfaces cause no deflection at all."

93. Which of the following would be the best choice of a conclusion for this piece?

    A. Prisms were used by many ancient civilizations. They must have seemed like a form of magic to the first people who saw them, and they continue to amaze people today. Though perhaps an accidental discovery, they changed the world.
    B. Prisms were an integral part of the study of the different properties of light. The use of prisms allowed people to see the different component colors of the light around them. The discovery of these different properties opened up new fields of research.
    C. There are dispersive prisms, reflective prisms, deflecting prisms, and polarizing prisms. Each type is useful and has different qualities.
    D. We wake up every morning and there is light. We may not know it, but people have always been fascinated by light for many years. Prisms explained how light works.

The correct answer is B. Prisms were an integral part of the study of the different properties of light. The use of prisms allowed people to see the different component colors of the light around them. The discovery of these different properties opened up new fields of research.
Answer B links together what prisms do with what they might be used for. Answer A talks primarily about the history of prisms, Answer C only addresses the types of prisms, and Answer D does not link prisms to how we might explain and understand light.

English Language Arts

94. Spectacles use meniscus lenses, which are:

   A. Flat
   B. Varying radii of concave lenses
   C. Varying radii of convex lenses
   D. Round on both sides of the lens, meaning they have double refraction

The correct answer is B. Varying radii of concave lenses
Answer B is indicated in the last sentence of the selection.

Read the following passage to answer questions 95 and 96. *(Objective 13)*

Ana woke suddenly and peered into the darkness. Something had moved or made some kind of sound; she was sure of it. She reached across the bed to the lamp on the nightstand, but there was nothing there. She fumbled in the dark until her hand came to rest on something solid, something cold, something wet.

"Looking for something?" came a voice out of the darkness.

Without hesitation, Ana replied, "Yes, actually. My glasses."

"You know why I'm here. No need for games," replied the voice.

"No, I suppose you're right," Ana sighed.

95. For what effect does the author repeat "something…, something…"

   A. To show how frustrating it was not to be able to see
   B. To build tension
   C. To show that the character was helpless
   D. To lighten the mood

The correct answer is B. To build tension
Repeating this phrase gives the impression of Ana's hand frantically feeling around in the dark.

96. **Ana's reply creates what effect?**

    A. The reader sees her as confident and calm.
    B. The reader sees her as confused and fearful.
    C. The reader knows that this is not a serious story.
    D. The reader knows that this is the source of conflict.

The correct answer is A. The reader sees her as confident and calm.
After creating tension, Ana's response is casual. Though we cannot be sure what will happen next, she seems confident and calm.

97. **Which part of a classical argument is illustrated in this excerpt from Caryl Rivers's essay "What Should Be Done about Rock Lyrics?"** *(Objective 14)*

    But violence against women is greeted by silence. It shouldn't be. This does not mean censorship, or book (or record) burning. In a society that protects free expression, we understand a lot of stuff will float up out of the sewer. Usually, we recognize the ugly stuff that advocates violence against any group as the garbage it is, and we consider its purveyors as moral lepers. We hold our nose and tolerate it, but we speak out against the values it proffers.

    A. Narration
    B. Confirmation
    C. Refutation and concession
    D. Summation

The correct answer is C. Refutation and concession
The author refutes the idea of censorship and concedes that society tolerates offensive lyrics as part of our freedom of speech. Narration provides background material to produce an argument. In confirmation, the author details the argument with claims that support the thesis. In summation, the author concludes the argument by offering the strongest solution.

Read the following passage to answer questions 98 and 99. *(Objective 14)*

The history of all hitherto existing society is the history of class struggles. Freeman and slave, patrician and plebeian, lord and serf, guildmaster and journeyman, in a word, oppressor and oppressed, stood in constant opposition to one another, carried on an uninterrupted, now hidden, now open fight, a fight that each time ended, either in a revolutionary reconstitution of society at large, or in the common ruin of the contending classes. In the earlier epochs of history, we find almost everywhere a complicated arrangement of society into various orders, a manifold gradation of social rank. In ancient Rome we have patricians, knights, plebeians, slaves; in the Middle Ages, feudal lords, vassals, guild- masters, journeymen, apprentices, serfs; in almost all of these classes, again, subordinate gradations. The modern bourgeois society that has sprouted from the ruins of feudal society, has not done away with class antagonisms. It has but established new classes, new conditions of oppression, new forms of struggle in place of the old ones. Our epoch, the epoch of the bourgeoisie, possesses, however, this distinctive feature: It has simplified the class antagonisms. Society as a whole is more and more splitting up into two great hostile camps, into two great classes directly facing each other—bourgeoisie and proletariat...

98. The first sentence can best be paraphrased as:

    A. Every future societal shall deal with issues of class.
    B. Struggle between classes is the most important aspect of history.
    C. In the past, class struggles were common.
    D. Society only began to exist with the invention of class.

The correct answer is C. In the past, class struggles were common
With the opening line, the author is explaining that class struggles have defined history. Answer C is the best answer.

99. What is the author's attitude toward class as a concept?

    A. It is a tool of oppression.
    B. It is a necessary evil.
    C. It is an inevitability.
    D. It is useful, but often misused.

The correct answer is A. It is a tool of oppression
The author is primarily concerned with class hierarchies as a tool of oppression, stating how the modern era of bourgeoisie versus proletariat struggle is simplified in its antagonism. He feels class struggle is oppressive.

TEACHER CERTIFICATION STUDY GUIDE

100. To explore the relationship of literature to modern life, which of these activities would *not* enable students to explore comparable themes? *(Objective 15)*

   A. After studying various world events, such as the Palestinian-Israeli conflict, students write an updated version of *Romeo and Juliet* using modern characters and settings.
   B. Before studying *Romeo and Juliet*, students watch *West Side Story*.
   C. Students research the major themes of *Romeo and Juliet* by studying news stories and finding modern counterparts for the story.
   D. Students would explore compare the romantic themes of *Romeo and Juliet* and *The Taming of the Shrew*.

The correct answer is D. Students would explore compare the romantic themes of *Romeo and Juliet* and *The Taming of the Shrew*
By comparing the two plays by Shakespeare, students will be focusing on the culture of the period in which the plays were written. In Answer A, students should be able to recognize modern parallels with current culture clashes. By comparing the *Romeo and Juliet* to the 1950s update of *West Side Story,* students can study how themes are similar in two completely different historical periods. In Answer C, students can study local, national, and international news for comparable stories and themes.

101. A student wrote the following passage for a short response item about a novel. What is the biggest potential issue in the writing? *(Objective 15)*

   So the theme of the novel is clearly like the struggle of the individual to be good. In the book, the main character guy really wants to be good, you know, but there are all these things stopping. The author, he's trying to show how all of us are like living our lives but these obstacles come up.

   A. Correct grammar
   B. Adapting to audience
   C. Using evidence to support a claim
   D. Organizational strategies

The correct answer is B. Adapting to audience
Since this appears to be an introduction, it wouldn't likely have many examples to support an argument. The grammar is not good, but the student's biggest issue seems to be a lack of understanding of audience. This is written in a casual style that undermines the main point of the writing.

102. **Which of the following would likely be the best conclusion for an essay analyzing potential projects to combat climate change?** *(Objective 15)*

   A. A variety of projects and technologies exist that may help the country find a way to deal with climate change. The challenge is to decide which projects are viable and which are not. The best path forward may in fact be to provide seed funding to a variety of projects and see which ones thrive. Betting the farm on one proposal is too risky; we must look at all our options.
   B. Given the budget considerations facing the government, there is no clear path forward. Climate change may be a major issue facing different parts of the country. Without substantial increases in revenue, it will be difficult for the current government to move forward.
   C. Climate change is not the threat people make it out to be. Our planet has gone through swings in climate before and will do so again. As a species, we will do what we have always done—adapt.
   D. Climate change is the biggest threat facing our species and many others. We must act now or we will risk losing countless species. The mounting costs will affect all of us to some extent.

The correct answer is A. A variety of projects and technologies exist that may help the country find a way to deal with climate change. The challenge is to decide which projects are viable and which are not. The best path forward may in fact be to provide seed funding to a variety of projects and see which ones thrive. Betting the farm on one proposal is too risky; we must look at all our options. Since the essay in question is supposed to be analyzing projects, Answer A addresses the idea of the quality of the proposals. Answer B addresses budgets instead of the projects. Answers C and D are opinions about climate change.

103. Which of the following sentences would likely be the best transitional sentence to follow this paragraph? *(Objective 15)*

The main character wrestles with her own moral code. Though she feels a tremendous sense of obligation toward her community, she cannot turn her back on what she feels is right. This internal conflict drives the novel forward.

   A. But the conflict is too much for her and she cannot cope.
   B. While she is torn between two seemingly impossible choices, the world seems to move forward without her.
   C. Impossible choices are everywhere in the novel.
   D. The world seems to move forward, and she is torn between impossible choices.

The correct answer is B. While she is torn between two seemingly impossible choices, the world seems to move forward without her.
This sentence best illustrates the dilemma faced by the main character and emphasizes it with the word *while*. Answer A is awkward but does try to address the conflict. Answer D includes the same idea but does not transition as well. Answer C does not flow well.

Read the following selection from Joseph Conrad's *Heart of Darkness* to answer questions 104–109, selecting the best choice of the options presented. *(Objective 15)*

I went to work the next day, turning, so to speak, my back on that station. In that way only it seemed to me I could keep my hold on the redeeming facts of life. Still, one must look about sometimes; and then I saw this station, these men strolling aimlessly about in the sunshine of the yard. I asked myself sometimes what it all meant. They wandered here and there with their absurd long staves in their hands, like a lot of faithless pilgrims bewitched inside a rotten fence. The word "ivory" rang in the air, was whispered, was sighed. You would think they were praying to it. A taint of imbecile rapacity blew through it all, like a whiff from some corpse. By Jove! I've never seen anything so unreal in my life. And outside, the silent wilderness surrounding this cleared speck on the earth struck me as something great and invincible, like evil or truth, waiting patiently for the passing away of this fantastic invasion.

TEACHER CERTIFICATION STUDY GUIDE

104. What does the following line represent? "I saw this station, these men strolling aimlessly about in the sunshine of the yard." *(Objective 15)*

    A. Soldiers enjoying their day
    B. Men being unaware of the negativity that surrounds them
    C. The station is a happy place
    D. Embracing the weather before a storm hits

The correct answer is B. Men being unaware of the negativity that surrounds them
The sunshine represents happiness and the fact that they are strolling around aimlessly implies they are unaware of their surroundings. Given the representation of this symbolism, Answer B is the best option for this question.

105. What does the word "staves" mean? *(Objective 15)*

    A. Machetes
    B. Axe
    C. Guns
    D. Wooden clubs

The correct answer is D. Wooden clubs
Because of the invasion mentioned, it can be determined that the characters are walking around with staves in order to protect themselves. Although each of the options for this question are weapons, Answer D is the correct answer. It's a word that is most common to the time period in which this book was written.

106. What does the word "ivory" represent? *(Objective 15)*

    A. Death
    B. Jewelry
    C. Prosperity
    D. Trade

The correct answer is C. Prosperity
Ivory has historically been valuable. While it can be viewed as representing trade, Answer C is the best answer because ivory best represents prosperity.

107. What literary device is used when describing the ivory? *(Objective 15)*

    A. Allegory
    B. Simile
    C. Personification
    D. Repetition

The correct answer is A. Allegory
An allegory represents a piece of writing with hidden meaning or significant hidden symbolism. This is the only option that makes sense for this question.

108. What does the word "rapacity" represent? *(Objective 15)*

    A. Greed
    B. Rapid movement
    C. Intelligent
    D. Affluent

The correct answer is A. Greed
Rapacity represents greed; therefore, Answer A is the correct answer.

109. *Heart of Darkness* **is about a voyage up the Congo River with an ivory trader and raises questions of imperialism and racism. The movie** *Apocalypse Now*, **by Francis Ford Coppola, was adapted from this story. Comparing the two texts, in an essay, what structure would be best for organizing a coherent comparison based on theme?** *(Objective 15)*

    A. Point by point to illustrate the differences between a film and a book
    B. Text to text to show similarities and differences
    C. Point by point to see *Apocalypse Now* through the lens of *Heart of Darkness*
    D. Text to text to see *Apocalypse Now* through the lens of *Heart of Darkness*

The correct answer is D. Text to text to see *Apocalypse Now* **through the lens of** *Heart of Darkness*
Heart of Darkness was written in 1899. Eighty years later, Francis Ford Coppola made a move updating the time and the setting to Vietnam to make a point. Seeing the movie through the lens of the book would allow readers to focus on the major themes and issues that both texts have in common. Analyzing *Heart of Darkness* first would introduce these ideas, and a comparison with *Apocalypse Now* would reinforce their relevancy in a different medium and setting.

TEACHER CERTIFICATION STUDY GUIDE

110. In preparing for an oral presentation, which is *not* an effective guideline?
(Objective 16)

   A. Even if you are using a lectern, feel free to move about. This will connect you to the audience.
   B. Your posture should be natural, not stiff. Keep your shoulders toward the audience.
   C. Gestures can help communicate as long as you don't overuse them or make them distracting.
   D. You can avoid eye contact if you focus on your notes. This will make you appear more knowledgeable.

The correct answer is D. You can avoid eye contact if you focus on your notes. This will make you appear more knowledgeable.
Although many people are nervous about making eye contact, they should focus on two or three people at a time. Body language, such as movement, posture, and gestures, helps the speaker connect to the audience.

111. Which of the following would *not* be a major concern in an oral presentation?
(Objective 16)

   A. Establishing the purpose of the presentation
   B. Evaluating the audience's demographics and psychographics
   C. Creating a slide for each point
   D. Developing the content to fit the occasion

The correct answer is C. Creating a slide for each point
Slides should be kept to a minimum of one slide per minute and should not overwhelm the presentation. The slides should be a supplement so that the speaker can accomplish the purpose. To reach that goal, the speaker should understand the makeup of the audience: demographics, such as age, education level, or other quantifiable characteristic; and psychographics, such as attitudes or values. Knowing the purpose and the audience will enable the speaker to develop the content to fit the occasion.

112. Oral debate is most closely associated with which form of discourse?
(Objective 16)

   A. Description
   B. Exposition
   C. Narration
   D. Persuasion

The correct answer is D. Persuasion
It is extremely important to be convincing while having an oral debate. This is why persuasion is so essential, because this is the way that you can influence your audience.

TEACHER CERTIFICATION STUDY GUIDE

113. The purpose of presenting a formal report to the class is to explain where acid rain comes from and what it has done to the environment. What is the most likely form of organizational structure for this presentation? *(Objective 16)*

    A. Cause and effect
    B. Problem and solution
    C. Exposition
    D. Definition

The correct answer is A. Cause and effect
Although it could offer a solution, the presentation would not focus on that. Most reports are expository because they provide information and an explanation, but that would not be the primary structure of this presentation. While a definition might be an important detail, it would not be the major organizational structure. This presentation would discuss what has caused acid rain and what effects acid rain has had on the environment, therefore, Answer A is correct.

114. For a speech on actions the school board should take to reduce energy use, which strategy or approach would be the most successful? *(Objective 16)*

    A. Explain in detail the different uses of energy at schools.
    B. Link reduced energy use to reduced costs and greater environmental responsibility.
    C. Complain about the board's lack of environmental responsibility.
    D. Read letters from other students.

The correct answer is B. Link reduced energy use to reduced costs and greater environmental responsibility
Strategy provides concrete strategies and gives the board reasons for their adoption.

115. Which of the following strategies will likely increase participation by shy students in class discussion? *(Objective 16)*

    A. Requiring each participant to join in at least twice
    B. Giving participants something to read before the discussion
    C. Increasing wait time
    D. Not allowing participants who talk a lot to join in

The correct answer is C. Increasing wait time
Increasing the amount of time between the time a question is asked and the time you start taking answers will give more participants time to formulate a response.

TEACHER CERTIFICATION STUDY GUIDE

116. In which context might it not be a good idea to use jargon or technical language to discuss curriculum? *(Objective 16)*

   A. At back-to-school night
   B. A staff meeting
   C. A discussion of teaching materials
   D. A professional development conference

The correct answer is A. At back-to-school night
Back-to-school night is generally an opportunity to meet parents and talk about general curricular plans. Using technical language may overcomplicate the topic and actually cause parents to lose interest.

Read the following excerpt to answer questions 117 and 118. *(Objective 15)*

Excerpt from a speech to the Council on Foreign Relations, Tony Blair, December 3, 2008

The past 40 years are littered with initiatives, signposts to various potential breakthroughs, unsatisfactory compromises, new dawns that swiftly turned to dusk and failed negotiations. Along the way, there have been immense gains that sometimes are obscured by the central impasse. Egypt and Jordan are at peace with Israel. The Arab Peace Initiative of the then Crown Prince Abdullah in 2002 signaled a new pan-Arab approach. The contours of the final status issues, if not their outcomes, have been clarified.

The Annapolis process and the limited but nonetheless real change on the West Bank during the past year—for which the president and Secretary Rice deserve much credit—have yielded a genuine platform for the future.

But the central impasse does indeed remain. My view—formed since I came to Jerusalem and refining much of what I thought when I tussled intermittently with the issue for 10 years as British prime minister—is that it remains because the reality on the ground does not, as yet, sufficiently support the compromises necessary to secure a final, negotiated settlement. In other words, we have tended to proceed on the basis that if we could only agree on the terms of the two-state solution—territory, refugees, Jerusalem (i.e., the theory—we would then be able to change the reality of what was happening on the ground (i.e., the practice). In my view, it is as much the other way around. The political process and changing the reality have to march in lock-step. Until recently, they haven't.

The reason this is critical to resolving this dispute is as follows. The problem is not that reasonable people do not agree, roughly, what the two states look like. I don't minimize the negotiation challenge. But listen to sensible

Palestinians and sensible Israelis and you will quickly find the gaps are not that big; certainly are not unbridgeable.

117. In what way(s) does Tony Blair demonstrate that he acknowledges the different perspectives of Palestinians and Israelis?

    A. He addresses the importance of peace for both sides.
    B. He talks about past failed negotiations.
    C. He does not blame either side for the lack of results.
    D. He makes an emotional appeal to both sides.

The correct answer is C. He does not blame either side for the lack of results.
Though Blair does talk about past failed negotiations, he does not blame either side for the lack of a peace agreement. He instead talks about the things many people from both sides agree on. The speech was not an emotional appeal and did not focus on the importance of peace. Instead he made peace seem like a logical step.

118. In this speech, how did Blair organize his ideas?

    A. He linked past events to the present state of negotiations.
    B. He described past peace proposals and gave evidence of why they make sense.
    C. He thanked people for their past work and showed why it was necessary to continue what they had started.
    D. He analyzed the issue point by point.

The correct answer is A. He linked past events to the present state of negotiations.
Blair outlined some of the past negotiations and the agreements they reached and then connected those to the current state of negotiations.

119. **What is the common advertising technique used by these advertising slogans?** *(Objective 17)*

   "It's everywhere you want to be." (Visa)
   "Have it your way." (Burger King)
   "When you care enough to send the very best." (Hallmark)
   "Be all you can be." (U.S. Army)

   A. Peer approval
   B. Rebel
   C. Individuality
   D. Escape

The correct answer is C. Individuality
All of these ads associate products with people who can think and act for themselves. Products are linked to individual decision making. With peer approval, the ads would associate their products with friends and acceptance. For rebelling, the ads would associates products with behaviors or lifestyles that oppose society's norms. Escape would suggest the appeal of getting away from it all.

120. **In presenting a report to peers about the effects of Hurricane Katrina on New Orleans, the students wanted to use various media in their argument to persuade their peers that more needed to be done. Which of these would be the most effective?** *(Objective 17)*

   A. A PowerPoint presentation showing the blueprints of the levees before the flood and redesigned now for current construction
   B. A collection of music clips made by the street performers in the French Quarter before and after the flood
   C. A recent video showing the areas devastated by the floods and the current state of rebuilding
   D. A collection of recordings of interviews made by the various government officials and local citizens affected by the flooding

The correct answer is C. A recent video showing the areas devastated by the floods and the current state of rebuilding.
For maximum impact, a video would offer dramatic scenes of the devastated areas. A video by its very nature is more dynamic than a static PowerPoint presentation. Further, the condition of the levees would not provide as much impetus for change as seeing the devastated areas. Oral messages such as music clips and interviews provide another way of supplementing the message but, again, they are not as dynamic as video.

TEACHER CERTIFICATION STUDY GUIDE

121. **Which of the following statements indicates an instructional goal for using multimedia in the classroom?** *(Objective 17)*

    A. Audio messages invite the listener to form mental images consistent with the topic of the audio.
    B. Print messages appeal almost exclusively to the mind and push students to read with more thought.
    C. Listening to an audio message is more passive than reading a print message.
    D. Teachers who develop activities to foster a critical perspective on audiovisual presentation will decrease passivity.

The correct answer is D. Teachers who develop activities to foster a critical perspective on audiovisual presentation will decrease passivity.
Each of the statements is true, but only the last one establishes a goal for using multimedia in the classroom.

122. **Which of the following situations is *not* an ethical violation of intellectual property?** *(Objective 17)*

    A. A student visits 10 different Websites and writes a report to compare the costs of downloading music. He uses the names of the Websites without their permission.
    B. A student copies and pastes a chart verbatim from the Internet but does not document it because it is available on a public site.
    C. From an online article found in a subscription database, a student paraphrases a section on the problems of music piracy. She includes the source in her Works Cited but does not provide an in-text citation.
    D. A student uses a comment from M. Night Shyamalan without attribution claiming the information is common knowledge.

The correct answer is A. A student visits 10 different Websites and writes a report to compare the costs of downloading music. He uses the names of the Websites without their permission.
In this scenario, the student is conducting primary research by gathering the data and using it for his own purposes. He is not violating any principle by using the names of the Websites. In Answer B, students who copy and paste from the Internet without documenting the sources of their information are committing plagiarism, a serious violation of intellectual property. Even when a student puts information in her own words by paraphrasing or summarizing as in Answer C, the information is still secondary and must be documented. While dedicated movie buffs might consider anything that M. Night Shyamalan says to be common knowledge in Answer D, his comments are not necessarily known in numerous places or known by a lot of people.

Read the following passage to answer questions 123–130.

Most people who bother with the matter at all would admit that the English language is in a bad way, but it is generally assumed that we cannot by conscious action do anything about it. Our civilization is decadent and our language—so the argument runs—must inevitably share in the general collapse. It follows that any struggle against the abuse of language is a sentimental archaism, like preferring candles to electric light or hansom cabs to aeroplanes. Underneath this lies the half-conscious belief that language is a natural growth and not an instrument which we shape for our own purposes.

Now, it is clear that the decline of a language must ultimately have political and economic causes: it is not due simply to the bad influence of this or that individual writer. But an effect can become a cause, reinforcing the original cause and producing the same effect in an intensified form, and so on indefinitely. A man may take to drink because he feels himself to be a failure, and then fail all the more completely because he drinks. It is rather the same thing that is happening to the English language. It becomes ugly and inaccurate because our thoughts are foolish, but the slovenliness of our language makes it easier for us to have foolish thoughts. The point is that the process is reversible. Modern English, especially written English, is full of bad habits which spread by imitation and which can be avoided if one is willing to take the necessary trouble. If one gets rid of these habits one can think more clearly, and to think clearly is a necessary first step toward political regeneration: so that the fight against bad English is not frivolous and is not the exclusive concern of professional writers. I will come back to this presently, and I hope that by that time the meaning of what I have said here will have become clearer. Meanwhile, here are five specimens of the English language as it is now habitually written.

123. What does the author mean by "archaism"? *(Objective 1)*

    A. Mystery
    B. Misidentification
    C. Anachronism
    D. Ignorance

The correct answer is C. Anachronism
"Archaism" is an outdated term or phrase, a synonym of "anachronism."

124. "A man may take to drink because he feels himself to be a failure, and then fail all the more completely because he drinks." In context, this sentence is best described as a/an: *(Objective 5)*

   A. Analogy
   B. Metaphor
   C. Simile
   D. Allusion

The correct answer is A. Analogy
The author uses the idiom to describe the degradation of the English language. He goes on to explain this more explicitly in the next sentence.

125. What does this author think of the English language? *(Objective 2)*

   A. It is in unavoidable decline.
   B. It should not be altered.
   C. Its rules are subject to the whims of speakers.
   D. It can be improved through good habits.

The correct answer is D. It can be improved through good habits.
The author states that English can be improved through positive action. He states the direct opposite of the other answers in the selection.

126. What can we assume will follow this passage? *(Objectives 2 and 13)*

   A. A screed on the decline of English
   B. Further evidence that English is being destroyed
   C. Names of authors who have contributed to the decline of English
   D. Specific examples of bad English in use

The correct answer is D. Specific examples of bad English in use
The last sentence states the author's intention to illustrate some examples of misused English.

127. What is the subject of the verb "lies" in the last sentence of the first paragraph? *(Objective 9)*

   A. Language
   B. Growth
   C. This
   D. Underneath

The correct answer is C. This
"This" is the subject of "lies," and "belief" is the object.

128. The author believes the decline of English is due to: *(Objectives 2 and 3)*

   A. The imitation of bad habits
   B. Societal decadence
   C. People preferring what is simple
   D. Political quibbling

The correct answer is A. The imitation of bad habits
The author takes great pains to explain that bad English is the result of bad habits that have been allowed to grow and spread without care.

129. By characterizing language as a "natural growth," the author emphasizes its: *(Objectives 2 and 3)*

   A. Personified qualities
   B. Duplicitous nature
   C. Inconsistency
   D. Changeability

The correct answer is D. Changeability
The author believes language grows naturally, and thus can be corrupted or corrected. This is the central understanding of this piece.

130. What tone is the author striving for in this piece? *(Objective 5)*

   A. Humorous
   B. Academic
   C. Angry
   D. Disappointed

The correct answer is B. Academic
The author is discussing English, specifically its defects and methods to improve them. This is a topic of academic interest, and the author explores it with a professional, scholarly tone.

Read the following passage to answer questions 131–138.

On the domestic front, life was not easy. England was not a wealthy country and its people endured relatively poor living standards. The landed classes— many of them enriched by the confiscated wealth of former monasteries— were determined in the interests of profile to convert their arable land into pasture for sheep, so as to produce the wool that supported the country's chief economic asset, the woolen cloth trade. But the enclosing of the land only added to the misery of the poor, many of whom, evicted and displaced, left their decaying villages and gravitated to the towns where they joined the growing army of beggars and vagabonds that would become such a feature of Elizabethan life. Once, the religious houses would have dispensed charity to the destitute, but Henry VIII had dissolved them all in the 1530s, and many former monks and nuns were now themselves beggars. Nor did the civic authorities help: they passed laws in an attempt to ban the poor from towns and cities, but to little avail. It was a common sight to see men and women lying in the dusty streets, often dying in the dirt like dogs or beasts, without human compassion being shown to them. 'Certainly, wrote a Spanish observer in 1558, 'the state of England lay now most afflicted.' And although people looked to the new Queen Elizabeth to put matters right, there were so many who doubted if she could overcome the seemingly insurmountable problems she faced, or even remain queen long enough to begin tacking them. Some, both at home and abroad, were the opinion that her title to the throne rested on precarious foundations. Many regarded the daughter of Henry VII and Anne Boleyn as a bastard from the time of her birth on 7 September 1533, although, ignoring such slurs on the validity of his second marriage, Henry had declared Elizabeth his heir.

131. Why was land confiscated from the poor? *(Objective 2)*

   A. To build a new monastery
   B. To create pastures for sheep, ultimately increasing the export of wool
   C. To create housing for monks and nuns
   D. Queen Elizabeth wanted to expand her property.

The correct answer is B. To create pastures for sheep, ultimately increasing the export of wool
The landed classes are stated to have confiscated the lands of the poor, and sometimes abandoned monasteries, in order to convert their "arable land" into grazing fields for sheep

132. A vagabond is a: *(Objective 1)*

   A. Wanderer
   B. Prisoner
   C. Poor person
   D. Rich person

The correct answer is A. Wanderer
The root "vagari" of the word "vagabond" might remind you of "vague" and "vagaries" and suggest the root meaning of "wandering." You can also look at the word in context and see that only Answers A and C are likely answers, and that Answer C would ultimately be redundant.

133. Why didn't the poor have shelter with the churches? *(Objective 2)*

A. They were already filled with beggars.
B. Religious houses have never offered shelter to the poor.
C. They were also being used to raise sheep.
D. Henry VIII had dissolved them all in the 1530s.

The correct answer is D. Henry VIII had dissolved them all in the 1530s
The text states that Henry dissolved houses of worship that could have housed peasants, thus turning many of the clergy into beggars.

134. How were civic authorities unsuccessful? *(Objective 1)*

A. Poor people remained within city limits.
B. Public service funds ran out.
C. Public housing plans extended deadlines.
D. Churches did not open their doors to the poor.

The correct answer is A. Poor people remained within city limits
The text states that civic authorities attempted to ban the poor but did little to stem the tide of beggars.

135. What is a synonym for the word "precarious"? *(Objective 1)*

A. Strong
B. Illegitimate
C. Risky
D. Determined

The correct answer is C. Risky
While "illegitimate" might remind you of the questions of legitimacy hovering around Elizabeth's birth, and so seems to fit the context, originally the word "precarious" meant "depending on another person's favor" and in the twentieth century its meaning shifted to suggest physical instability. "Risky" is not a perfect synonym but is the best answer out of the group.

136. What is the author's view toward Queen Elizabeth? *(Objective 2)*

A. Doubtful
B. Vengeful
C. Resentful
D. Supportive

The correct answer is A. Doubtful
The author states that it was widely understood that the throne's position was precarious, and Elizabeth was considered unlikely to retain it.

137. How is the English culture portrayed in this passage? *(Objective 2)*

   A. Religious
   B. Elitist
   C. Racist
   D. Diverse

The correct answer is B. Elitist
The primary characteristic of English culture in this passage is its elitism and hierarchy. The poor are described as a nuisance with few rights, having their lands stripped from them and then being barred from entering villages or receiving charity.

138. What is Elizabeth's relationship to Henry? *(Objective 2)*

   A. Wife
   B. Cousin
   C. Lover
   D. Daughter

The correct answer is D. Daughter
The text states "many regarded the daughter of Henry and Anne Boleyn to be a bastard," indicating that Elizabeth is Henry's daughter.

Read the following passage to answer questions 139–143.

I have often thought of it as one of the most barbarous customs in the world, considering us as a civilized and a Christian country, that we deny the advantages of learning to women. We reproach the sex every day with folly and impertinence; while I am confident, had they the advantages of education equal to us, they would be guilty of less than ourselves. One would wonder, indeed, how it should happen that women are conversible at all; since they are only beholden to natural parts, for all their knowledge. Their youth is spent to teach them to stitch and sew or make baubles. They are taught to read, indeed, and perhaps to write their names, or so; and that is the height of a woman's education. And I would but ask any who slight the sex for their understanding, what is a man (a gentleman, I mean) good for, that is taught no more? I need not give instances, or examine the character of a gentleman, with a good estate, or a good family, and with tolerable parts; and examine what figure he makes for want of education. The soul is placed in the body like a rough diamond; and must be polished, or the luster of it will never appear. And 'tis manifest, that as the rational soul distinguishes us from brutes; so education carries on the distinction, and makes some less brutish than others. This is too evident to need any demonstration. But why then should women be denied the benefit of instruction? If knowledge and understanding had been useless additions to the sex, GOD Almighty would never have given them capacities; for he made nothing needless. Besides, I would ask such, What they can see in ignorance, that they should think it a necessary ornament to a woman?

139. What is the best synonym for "reproach" in the second sentence of this piece? *(Objective 1)*

   A. Attack
   B. Demean
   C. Move toward
   D. Ignore

The correct answer is B. Demean
"Attack" is too strong a term, and the other answers could not apply. "Reproach" and "demean" are synonymous.

140. What is the author saying with the second sentence of the first paragraph? *(Objective 3)*

   A. Education for women is a necessity, and the fact that we deny it to them is a national disgrace.
   B. If women possessed education, they would be able to give men a taste of their own medicine.
   C. Men often oppress women, and if women were educated, they likely would not do the same.
   D. Education is a privilege, one that women must earn for themselves.

The correct answer is C. Men often oppress women, and if women were educated, they likely would not do the same.
The author is espousing the virtues of women with that sentence, claiming that educated women likely would not be as petty as men are.

141. With the last sentence of paragraph two, the author is implying that: *(Objectives 3 and 14)*

   A. A man with no education is hardly impressive, even if he has other advantages.
   B. Certain qualities of upbringing handily offset the downsides of no education.
   C. Upper-class men have little need for education.
   D. Education is only one facet of many that makes a man worthy.

The correct answer is A. A man with no education is hardly impressive, even if he has other advantages.
"Examine what figure he makes for want of education" suggests that a man who lacks education still has little to offer, even if he is rich and well raised.

142. The author primarily supports his argument with: *(Objectives 3 and 14)*

    A. Citations
    B. Direct observation
    C. Common sense
    D. Examples

The correct answer is C. Common sense
The author primarily supports his argument with assertions that he insists should be obvious. It is "manifest" that education is a necessity, and it is likewise obvious that women being denied it is a travesty. He also insists, based on his own common sense, that if women were educated as men are, they likely would not be as oppressive.

143. Throughout the piece, the author makes frequent use of: *(Objectives 3 and 14)*

    A. Rhetorical questions
    B. Hyperbole
    C. Direct quotation
    D. Appeals to authority

The correct answer is A. Rhetorical questions
The piece contains many rhetorical questions throughout and makes less use of hyperbole and no appeal to authority.

144. What are the five key concepts of media literacy based upon? *(Objective 17)*

    A. All forms of media are designed to trick the viewer.
    B. All forms of media are texts and all texts are constructs.
    C. All forms of media are distracting, so students need to be vigilant.
    D. All forms of media improve learning in the classroom.

The correct answer is B. All forms of media are texts and all texts are constructs.
All forms of media are constructed texts and as such are a product of individual and group decisions (ethical, economic, social, cultural, political). Some of these decisions are conscious and some are unconscious.

TEACHER CERTIFICATION STUDY GUIDE

145. What are the three main types of appeal in a persuasive text, whether an advertisement or a persuasive essay? *(Objectives 3, 14, and 17)*

   A. Pathos, logos, gyros
   B. Bathos, logos, ethos
   C. Pathos, logos, ethos
   D. Pathos, media res, ethos

The correct answer is C. Pathos, logos, ethos
The three main persuasive appeals are pathos (emotion), logos (reason or logic), and ethos (the credibility of the author/speaker/messenger).

146. In choosing images for a campaign for mouthwash, which advertising appeal would be the most effective? *(Objective 17)*

   A. Beauty
   B. Lifestyle
   C. Independence
   D. Peer approval

The correct answer is D. Peer approval
Showing someone surrounded by friends, colleagues, or admirers would appeal to viewers' desires to be accepted. Conversely, using the same technique, images could show someone alone, without friends, and make the viewers worry that they will lose friends if they don't use the mouthwash.

147. What is a key question to ask when interpreting images and/or various forms of media for stereotypes or audience focus? *(Objective 17)*

   A. How might different individuals or groups see this text differently?
   B. Who paid for this media?
   C. What design choices did the creator of this media make?
   D. How would this work if the creator used a different media?

The correct answer is A. How might different individuals or groups see this text differently?
Although all these questions are important, Answer A relates the most to audience, stereotype, bias, and interpretation. It is necessary to understand that readers and viewers can interpret the same text differently, depending on their backgrounds, experiences, and points of view.

148. Which of the following is *not* an essential part of crafting a presentation for a particular purpose and audience? *(Objective 17)*

   A. Discover—choose a topic you and your audience care about.
   B. Gather feedback—make sure you have forms ready to distribute to get some feedback on your presentation, otherwise, how are you going to learn?
   C. Organize—start off with a hook, organize the body of what you are going to say, and end with a strong finish
   D. Edit—make sure your presentation is polished and practiced, your images are clear, your technology works.

The correct answer is B. Gather feedback—make sure you have forms ready to distribute to get some feedback on your presentation, otherwise, how are you going to learn?
Although feedback always helps us learn, it's not necessary to prepare feedback forms before a presentation. Answers A, B, and D are all important for crafting an effective presentation. Getting feedback can be part of it, but you don't necessarily need forms or need to do it right away.

149. Which of the following statements about copyright issues is true? *(Objective 17)*

   A. Copyright is a legal and ethical issue.
   B. Copyright issues are important for everyone and not just professionals.
   C. Copyright issues are useful to teach in school because attribution and citation are complicated.
   D. All of the above.

The correct answer is D. All of the above
Just as with composing written texts, there are ethical issues related to using and presenting media. It is essential that students are aware of copyright issues and proper citation, for legal as well as ethical reasons.

150. Which of the following is not a good reason to add media to a presentation? *(Objective 17)*

   A. As something to keep the audience from being bored
   B. To illustrate, explain, or represent an idea
   C. As evidence to support an idea
   D. To evoke emotions, to provide a subtext or commentary

The correct answer is A. As something to keep the audience from being bored
Your presentation should be interesting with or without media. In fact, if your ideas and presentation style are boring and you include media, your audience will focus on the media rather than your main point.

www.ingramcontent.com/pod-product-compliance
Lightning Source LLC
Chambersburg PA
CBHW080728230426

43665CB00020B/2658